Illuminations

an anthology of Welsh short prose

i'm mrawd
LLOYD
ac er côf am ein rhieni

Illuminations

an anthology of Welsh short prose

selected and translated by
Meic Stephens

Welsh Academic Press

Published in Wales by Welsh Academic Press 1998

Welsh Academic Press is an imprint of

Ashley Drake Publishing Ltd.
PO Box 733
Cardiff
CF4 6WE

First Impression – November 1998

ISBN
Hardback edition: 1 86057 010 0
Paperback edition: 1 86057 016 X

Copyright © The authors and their estates

English language translations © Meic Stephens 1998

All rights reserved. No part of this publication may be reproduced, stored in a retrieval system, or transmitted, in any form or by any means, electronic, mechanical, photocopying, recording or otherwise, without the prior permission of Welsh Academic Press.

British Library Cataloguing-in-Publication Data.
A catalogue record for this book is available from the British Library.

Typeset by WestKey Ltd, Falmouth, Cornwall.
Printed and bound in Wales by
Creative Print and Design, Ebbw Vale

Contents

Preface		vii
O. M. Edwards	The Village School	1
Eluned Morgan	Fear of the Sea	7
R. Williams Parry	A Windy Night	9
W. J. Gruffydd	The Late Lemuel Parry, Esq., J.P., O.B.E	12
T. H. Parry-Williams	On Drowning a Cat	18
J. O. Williams	The House across the Way	21
Saunders Lewis	Weobley and St. Emilion	25
Robert Beynon	The Man in the Street	28
T. Gwynn Jones	Old Dent	31
R. T. Jenkins	On Collecting Roads	34
Iorwerth C. Peate	'Their Land they shall Lose'	42
D. Gwenallt Jones	The Red Flag	46
Ffransis G. Payne	Strolling Players	50
Jac L. Williams	One Sunday Afternoon	57
E. Morgan Humphreys	Salem	61
T. J. Morgan	A Trip to the Circus	63
D. J. Williams	Thoughts on Coronation Day, 1953	68
E. Tegla Davies	From the Pulpit	72
Harri Gwynn	How to Choose and Treat a Wife	77
Ifor Williams	To the Mountain	83
Islwyn Ffowc Elis	The Imperative upon Me	88
R. Gerallt Jones	Disenchantment	92
Ifan Gruffydd	The Hiring Fair	94
Gomer M. Roberts	The Man at Chapel House	97
Kate Roberts	Question and Answer	102
Dafydd Rowlands	The Little Llandeilo Boots	105
J. G. Williams	My Last Day in Prison	108
R. Tudur Jones	A Discovery	118
Alun Llywelyn-Williams	A Land of Romance	121
Urien Wiliam	Hi-ho!	129
Glyn M. Ashton	Ancestors	133
Gwilym R. Jones	While Shaving	138

Dyfnallt Morgan	Of Time and Distance	141
R. Emyr Jones	A Methodist Deacon's Advice	146
Selyf Roberts	Of Violets and Bells	148
Eirwen Gwynn	Remembering Mrs Newbould	151
D. Tecwyn Lloyd	Good Morning, Lloyd	156
Hafina Clwyd	In Modesty and Trembling	162
Rhydwen Williams	Christmas in the Valley	166
John Gruffydd Jones	On Stammering	169
Gwilym Tudur	Butlins	172
William Owen	A Millionaire	176
Gareth Miles	A Scene from Military Life	178
R. S. Thomas	An Exile	180
Bryan Martin Davies	The Fox Under Glass	183
John Roberts Williams	A Doctor's Medicine	186
Eigra Lewis Roberts	The Little Huts	189
Prys Morgan	Three Heads	191
Gruffudd Parry	On Memory	198
Bernard Evans	Uncle John's Boots	202
Gareth Alban Davies	The Fur Coat	207
Robin Williams	An Holy Kiss	214

Notes on Authors and Texts 217

Acknowledgements 238

Preface

Like so much else, the essay (or more properly *yr ysgrif*, since it differs in some important respects from its English counterpart) was a late arrival in modern Welsh literature. It may have had forerunners in the latter part of the nineteenth century, in the primarily didactic work of certain Radical authors, but only in the 1920s, when T.H. Parry-Williams began publishing his *ysgrifau* in the magazine *Y Llenor*, was the essay recognized as a distinct literary form in Welsh.

T.H. Parry-Williams brought to his prose the same rich vernacular, the same wit and erudition, the same sceptical mind, that give his verse its unique quality, and indeed, the difference between his poems and essays is sometimes a subtle one. By the time of his death in 1975 he had published more than a hundred essays and had for long been acknowledged as a master of the genre. Such was his achievement as an essayist that he was to have many imitators, notably in the competitions set at the National Eisteddfod, and great were their endeavours in reproducing his special effects, often to the point of pastiche. It might be argued that the development of the essay since the 1940s has been, for not a few Welsh writers, an attempt to shake off T.H. Parry-Williams's influence and take the form in new directions.

That this has happened to a very considerable extent is largely attributable to the renewed vitality of writing in the Welsh language since the second world war, and in particular to the dedication of a number of accomplished practitioners such as T.J. Morgan, D. Tecwyn Lloyd, and Islwyn Ffowc Elis, who chose the essay in which to express themselves. In their work, as in that of later writers, the horizons of the essay in Welsh have been extended, quite literally so, for there has been as much memorable writing about foreign parts as there has on subjects closer to home. If nostalgia, or at least a fascination with the past, its certainties and rigours, is still the prevailing mode, by today, in the work of writers like Dafydd Rowlands, Gareth Alban Davies, and Robin Williams, the form has matured, having discarded the mannerisms which were once its hallmark and now displaying a new vigour and sophistication. No longer an exercise in belles-lettres, the essay has found room for political comment, psychological analysis, humour, metaphysical conceit, social satire, and speculation on numinous issues; it is not fiction, but it allows free play to the imagination; it is not journalism, but it is rooted in the real world. This writing has kept its literary pretensions, of course — it is often to be found at its best in *Taliesin*, the magazine of the Welsh Academy — but it has shed much of its whimsicality and precious style. It is not insignificant that some of the prose included in the present anthology was first written as journalism, as polemic, as a prison-diary, as a radio-talk, as topographical description, as a mock-obituary, as a speech for a public occasion, or as part of an autobiography. Fine writing, we must conclude, is not confined to the pages of our literary journals, and the *ysgrif* comes in many guises.

I have tried to reflect something of this diversity in my selection of the essays which appear here in English versions. But my choice has not been in any way schematic or thematic, and it can lay no claim to being fully representative of such a broad field. What I have done is to choose, from the several hundred essays I must have read since I first began learning Welsh some thirty-five-years ago, just fifty-two that have given me particular pleasure for one reason or another. I was constrained in my choice to some degree by having to select examples which were not inextricably bound to their time and place, as many were, and which would be easily intelligible to English readers with only a modicum of explanatory notes about specifically Welsh allusions. It is a matter for regret, too, that certain of the most distinguished Welsh writers of this century, among them Waldo Williams, Bobi Jones, and Gwyn Thomas, have not employed the essay form (all I could find by Bobi Jones was an essay on why he does not write essays); and that for reasons to do with the eventual length of the book, I was unable to include anything by up-and-coming writers. Furthermore, if for some readers there are rather too many clergymen and academics among the contributors, and alas, too few women, that only points to the source of so much modern Welsh writing. Again, I expect Welsh-speaking aficionados will be disappointed at not seeing their favourite authors and essays, and will take delicious umbrage that some of the finer nuances of dialect and idiom have been lost in translation; that, too, seems to me inevitable.

Nevertheless, I think the book's time-span, geographical spread, and thematic mix will enable the attentive reader to catch here something of the *Zeitgeist* of Wales during the course of the twentieth century. That is why I have called it *Illuminations:* not only because so many of these *ysgrifau* are about epiphanies but because I think they will cast a little light not only on human society as it has existed here in Wales, but also on human nature in its universal aspects. For it seems to me that *yr ysgrif* has both these preoccupations in about equal measure: it reminds us, if we need reminding, not only that Welsh is a language in which we can discuss anything under the sun, including ourselves, but that we are most ourselves when discussing the universal.

The most recent general anthology of essays in the Welsh language was published as long ago as 1975 and the form has had scant attention from our literary critics since then. It may be that as the form lost its appeal in the England of the 1960s (the pleasant shades of E.V. Lucas), yet curiously not in America where 'the personal essay' has continued in vogue, so the *ysgrif* has slowly fallen into neglect. Perhaps too great an obsession with the snows of yesteryear and the charms of the parish pump, as well as a surfeit of 'popular' writing, has had something to do with it. Nor has there been, apart from the six examples of the work of T.H. Parry-Williams which I translated and published as *The White Stone* in 1987, any attempt to interest the wider world in the Welsh essay. Although I undertook the task of translation for my own pleasure, if this new book were to prompt a re-appraisal of the essay form among Welsh critics and writers, upon whom its future depends, that would be the most satisfying outcome for which a mere translator could hope.

Meic Stephens,
Whitchurch, Cardiff,
August 1997

The Village School

O. M. Edwards

Before I started going to school there was no happier child than I anywhere in the hills and mountains of Wales. I knew where all kinds of flowers grew, I knew where scores of birds were nesting, I knew of every white stone that gleamed in brook and river. It was not without effort and some difficulty that I came by this knowledge — I can recall the moment when, on my hands and knees on the mountainside, having been left there by my father while he cut peat, I reached out to pick the stem of a daisy; I also remember how, confined to my little chair, but carrying it on my back, I would make for the fine gravel in the spring's basin. I would watch the lark rising until it was lost from sight in the sky: I gazed at the snow coming down all feathery, thinking it was bees in their new clothes that I saw; and I remember being frightened at hearing the sudden roar of the thawing wind and the terrifying crackle of the ice in the river.

On long winter evenings a neighbour or some passerby would take their turn to call at our home, to chat by the peat fire at the snug old hearth; and they would see my small, sallow, inquisitive face inviting them to spin their yarns. I knew the ghosts in their stories by name, although my name for the ghost was usually that of the story-teller. I knew, too, who had witch's powers, and I would skirt the boundaries of their fields whenever I was out looking for new flowers or birds' nests.

I began going to Sunday School[1] at an early age. I well recall the first time, one fine morning in June. The old tailor had been on his feet until nearly midnight, making my new clothes; I shouldn't say on his feet, but rather squatting on the table. The coat and trousers were ready, but it hadn't been possible to make the waistcoat in time. So a confabulation had been held to discuss the clothes, the pieces of cloth, and me. It became obvious that the old waistcoat wouldn't match the new garments; the bird-nesting season had just ended, and the waistcoat had been through many a mile of hedge. Everyone was in a quandary; none had wanted to disappoint me, for I had so looked forward to going to Sunday School, and yet it was clear that it would have to come to that in the end.

'Well, my brave little chap,' the old tailor said, 'your waistcoat isn't ready, what will you do?'

'Go to school without one,' I said without the slightest hesitation.

'The lad has hit the nail on its head', he replied, 'the weather's fine enough, so do his coat up tightly, and let him go without any waistcoat.'

And that was what was decided. The tailor went off home across the mountain, leaving his last and flat-iron behind as a pledge that he would come back on Monday morning to finish off the waistcoat.

Next morning I was up before the lark. And at long last the time came for me to set out. My coat was carefully done up, and there was no chance that the new buttons would come undone. At the Sunday School I was put to sit on a bench, in a class taught by an old man, with a few others of my own age and background. We were supposed to look at a book, but looking at that book all the time grew tiresome, and taking my eyes from it, I could see almost everything that was going on around me. The scene is vivid before me this very minute. The bustle of the school, and the sound of many voices raised in exegesis of the Bible, are in my ears now. There are the 'grown-ups' — well-built men, vigorously arguing among themselves — they have long since been gathered, or else they are now the old men of the Sunday School as once their fathers were. There are the youngsters, now well used to the vagaries of life, and there are us children, today scattered far and wide. And there are the girls — inexplicable creatures as far as I was concerned, for they couldn't climb trees, nor open a penknife, nor even throw stones except with their left hand.

My lesson that morning was the ABC, and by the time I had recited all the letters after the teacher, it seemed to me that I had never before seen anything more strange. I couldn't work out how the other children knew each letter by name; it was much easier to recognize the prints that birds leave behind them. When the time came for Sunday School to end, the letter A was stuck to the nail of one of my thumbs, and B to the other; and my task for that first week was to memorize those two letters. I knew stories that were much more fun than any A and B, but I was soon told to be quiet whenever I started talking about the flowers of the may and a wren's nest. And so the Sunday School drew to a close, and then to my delight they began singing the verse of a hymn that I knew, slowly, like the sound the wind makes. I must have seemed older than my years as I tried to join in, to the great amusement of the children who were much the same age as I:

> 'Come, old and young, O come
> To Jesus, it's high time;
> The wondrous patience of God
> Has long been waiting for us;
> The afternoon is passing, and soon it will be late,
> The door of mercy is not yet shut.'[2]

Up to now I hadn't run into any real difficulty. But on the way home, I remembered my new clothes, and bet a red-haired boy that I had more buttons than he had — an old knife-blade against a reel made into a spinning-top, that was the wager. I had counted all the buttons on my new clothes, and the one on my cap, but I was still two buttons short. 'Show us the buttons on your waistcoat,' one of the boys said. There were two buttons on my shirt, and I ventured to show them that I wasn't wearing a waistcoat, so that I couldn't count those, but afterwards not one of us was able to do my coat back up again. On reaching home I related what had happened with all honesty, but was nevertheless chastised for the sin of vanity and for betting on the Sabbath.

On a working-day, before I started going to school, I don't recall ever being idle. Whenever I wasn't being good, I was hard at it being naughty. And yet the desire to raise up was ever stronger in me than the desire to tear down. True, I put the tines of a harrow in a stook of hay belonging to someone who had once beaten me; and true, I attached smoked herring to lines that some cheeky clerk had left in the river; I could also imitate the voices of many of the local women-folk. But I preferred to be on my own, thinking up little schemes, and putting them into practice. My favourite dream was of being able to build a bridge or house. I went on quite a few excursions to look at bridges that were not too far away, and would eventually find out how they had been constructed, and why they stood up so well. I threw scores of bridges over small brooks, little fine-stone bridges that cattle could easily walk across. Sometimes I would lay a wide bridge across a stream, and raise a small house upon it that would be snug all winter through — with a carpet of smooth, dry turf on its floor. On seeing my walls, everyone would exclaim that I should make a splendid stonemason, and delve into the detail of my family-tree, to see whom it was that I resembled. When it was found that none among my ancestors had been a builder, but rather that they had all been pullers-down, people would shake their heads, and say my walls wouldn't be upstanding for long.

Nevertheless, everyone shared the belief that I should become a famous man one day, if only I were sent to school. That was the question on everyone's lips: 'Why don't you send this lad to school?' They believed in schooling, and more's the pity for them. But in the end, when I was between nine and ten years old, it was decided that to school I had to go. And so it was there, to my great chagrin and loss, that I proceeded.

The school was in Llanuwchllyn, a few miles from where I lived. It belonged to the landowner, as did almost the whole district, and his wife, a tall, dignified lady, took a great interest in educational matters locally. At the time I first went to the school it had a schoolmistress. I was taken to the schoolhouse; classes had already begun, and not a child was to be seen in the village. The schoolmistress appeared, a small woman with piercing eyes, her hands held folded in front of her. She spoke a little Welsh, the language of the common people, with an English accent; her language, quite obviously, was English — the gentlefolk's language, the language of the parson from Cardiganshire. She was able to smile only when speaking English. Her face was very sour at having to degrade herself by speaking Welsh; if it comes to that, it was sourness I always saw in her countenance, except when her thin face wore a smile to meet the generous lady who paid her wages. I didn't listen to her words, and I didn't like her features: they put me in mind of the nose of a vixen that I once saw, close up, after dark.

'My boy,' said my mother, 'this is your new teacher. Look at her, take the peak of your cap from your mouth, she is going to teach you everything. Shake hands with her.'

She offered me her hand, with a weak smile dying on her face — 'Oh, we shall,' she said, 'we shall teach him everything he needs to know; we'll teach him how to behave.'

I didn't want to learn how to behave; I wanted to know how to make a bridge and build a chapel. A great urge came over me to go home with my mother; but it was with the schoolmistress that I had to go. The school's door was opened; I heard a strange din, and I could see children tightly packed together on many benches. There were two open spaces on the floor of the school, and I could see two people on their feet, one in each open space. I understood later that they were the assistant master and the assistant mistress. The schoolmistress took me to one of them, but of what she said I can recall only the words 'new boy'. I was able to read Welsh quite well by this time, and I was put in a class with children who were beginning to read English. The reading-book was one of the S.P.C.K.'s,[3] and I still loathe those letters, on account of the cruelty I suffered in trying to learn from that book. The teacher was a pleasant young fellow, and he was very kind to me, but after the reading-lesson he went back to his other pupils. The word soon went around that someone new, and ridiculous at that, had come to school. Several of the cruel children had their eye on me — I know about them all, they were mostly loud-mouthed children from the village, and they have never made much of themselves. The teacher had quietly told me not to speak a word in Welsh; but those naughty boys did all they could to make me raise my voice, and in the end they succeeded. I lost my temper, and began to speak my mind to the treacherous busybody who had contrived to torment me. As I began to speak up in my rich Welsh, everyone laughed, and a cord was put around my neck, with a heavy wooden block attached to it. I didn't know what on earth it was, but I had seen a similar block around a dog's neck to stop it running after sheep. Perhaps it was to prevent me from running home that the block had been put around my neck? At last it was mid-day, the time to be released. The schoolmistress came in with a cane in her hand. She asked some question or other, and every one of those servile children pointed a finger at me. Something like a smile came over her face when she saw that the block was around my neck. She recited some long rhyme at me, not a word of which I could understand, and she showed me the cane, but she didn't touch me. The block was pulled off, and it was then I understood that it was hung around the neck for speaking Welsh.

That block was hung around my neck hundreds of times after that. This is how it was done: when a child was heard to have uttered a word of Welsh, the teacher had to be told, and then the block was placed around the speaker's neck; and it was to remain there until someone else was heard to be speaking Welsh, when it was passed on to the next poor child. At school's end the one who was wearing it would be caned across the palm of the hand. Each day the block, as if by its own volition, would come from all parts of the school to end up around my neck. Today I take comfort from the fact that I never tried to seek respite from the block by passing it on to someone else. I knew nothing about the principle of the thing, but my nature rebelled against this damnable way of destroying the basis of a child's character. To teach a child to spy on a smaller one who was speaking his mother-tongue, in order to transfer the punishment to him! No, the block never came off my neck, and I suffered the cane daily as school drew to a close.

Today many of those who were my fellow-pupils, both boys and girls, are dead. Some passed away after suffering and languishing at home, some died in distant lands. These were tender, kind-hearted children, to whom punishment caused more pain than the one punished. And many of them took flight before they had experience of anything save innocence and compassion for others. I have often thought, what if I had taken the block from around my neck and put it around the neck of one of these? Many's the time I have gone down on my knees to thank God for sparing me that particular bitterness in life.

Some of my former classmates are alive and flourishing. But from time to time I hear of the sad loss of one or another of them. And it is then I draw comfort from the thought that it wasn't I who was the cause of their being punished for speaking Welsh.

The young man who was an assistant master when I first went to school is now a reputable farmer, and the years have done nothing to dim the mischievous laughter in his eyes. The young woman is the wife of a farmer, and her thoughts sometimes soar above the thousands of sheep that she grazes on the Berwyn, back to the old village school.

I don't know where the headmistress is, and I don't care. I have only a faint recollection of her, for I never dared to look at her except without her knowing. It's likely that she left our mountainous parts at the first opportunity, and moved to some small school in an English village. I don't want to do her character an injustice. Perhaps, if I had known her in her own home, after school hours, she might have been a tender-hearted woman who worried a good deal about us. Maybe the fault lay in what she believed and not in her. According to the credo of many an educationist at that time, her main task had been to teach the children English. And the most effective way of achieving that, or so it was thought, was to forbid the Welsh language outright, and to prevent children from speaking anything but the little English they could pick up from books or from the sayings of someone who was more or less familiar with that language. It was assumed in country districts that a schoolmaster wasn't able to speak Welsh, and that it was insulting to him to believe that he could. I have thought many times since then that it must have been out of a strong sense of duty that schoolmasters would have put the block around children's necks. They believed, perhaps, that it was quite legitimate for them to turn a child into an informer, if only they could thereby teach him English. But as far as I was concerned, this disciplinary method was a complete failure. It made me hate books and school, and even hate knowledge itself; it made me disobey my parents for the first time ever by hiding in the woods rather than go to school; it made the years that ought to have been the happiest of my life — years when the mind opens and wonders are revealed to it — it made those years for me the bitterest of all.

Abominable old system! I give thanks that I shall see the day when I dance upon your grave. It was not the schoolmistress who was to blame, but the system. She was a victim, just as I was. I was able to speak a language, but it wasn't used as a medium to educate me. I spoke one language and my headmistress spoke another — and I learned nothing. If it hadn't been for the Welsh Sunday School, I should today have been illiterate, having to depend on someone else for the means of salvation. I learned many languages thereafter, but no one was so foolish as to try teaching me except through the medium of the language I already knew. It is in Welsh that a Welsh child must be taught to think and through Welsh that he can be taught another language. I had one morning a week of Sunday School, and six days of English schooling. My testimony is this: I am indebted for everything to the Sunday School; to the English school, prior to a Welshman's coming to teach through the medium of Welsh, I owe nothing at all.

Clych Atgof (Hughes a'i Fab, 1906)

Fear of the Sea

Eluned Morgan

None but the old, experienced traveller remembers that the next stage of the passage is the crossing of the Bay of Biscay; but I am not one to give the old Bay a bad name, for this is my home, and hateful is she who does not love the land, or sea, that bred her.[1] I had no need of a mother's hand to rock my cradle: I had the waves of the Atlantic for that. I have seen the old Bay in both its glowering and more genial moods so many times, and I am never happier than when I am in my native element.

Yet for the ordinary passenger the Bay of Biscay is a terrible bogey, and all regard it with fear and trembling.

There is one thing I have never understood — fear of the sea! For me, the divine and the infinite are to be found at sea more than in any other place. The mind and power of the great Sovereign are to be seen there on every hand; there is nothing save the little shell that is called a ship that has anything of the human form about it. On realizing how helpless we are in the midst of such tremendous powers, it is very natural that every thinking being should trust more completely and confidently in the Creator of those powers.

The wide expanse about us and the starry firmament over all proclaim the power of the One who made us. If it is He who steers through such mighty waters, why should we fear? Can He not also guide our own small lives if only we are willing to put the helm in His hand? If we were to face the storms of land and sea in that spirit, there would be no room in our hearts for fear.

We had started out from La Palice at evening, having spent several happy hours on shore enjoying the exotic scenes, and buying curiosities to take home to our dear ones.

I had had a bit of a shaking while crossing the Channel, but if we had only known, it was no more than a sea-murmur from a long way off. It was so calm in the harbour that we had flattered ourselves the tempest would have been tamed by the time we were due to set out, but it had been resolutely gathering its strength, and as the craft left the shelter of the coast the old Bay rushed to meet it like a warrior eager for the fray.

The captain shouted from the bridge: 'Clear the deck!' But my heart was brimming with rebellion: I was not willing to miss one of the Creator's most glorious spectacles. With some difficulty I managed to find the captain and pleaded with him for fully five anxious minutes, arguing by fair means and foul. I wanted to see the storm as well as feel it. 'There's only one safe way,' the kind helmsman said, 'you will have to be lashed with a strong rope to one of the masts.' I was ready to agree to anything for the sake of having my wish: and so, wrapped in sailor's oilskin, lest I be drenched to the skin, I was firmly bound to the mast while the officers and crew smiled pityingly at my madness. But the old captain understood perfectly; he was an Irishman, and the Celtic dream had not been extinguished in his heart.

The storm was increasing, and as if the wind and furious waves were not enough, thunder and lightning now came to swell the chorus; the mountainous waves washed over the frail vessel, and the lightning flashed on the boiling blue-white foam, making the sea seem a rainbow, and then came darkness, the firmament and the waters at their blackest, and in that horrible gloom the thunder could be heard as though coming from the bosom of the maddened sea, roaring and resounding until every plank of the old ship shuddered and seemed about to split, and then the forked-lightning came again, darting and weaving between the ship's rigging like fiery serpents. But the most splendid sight was to see those fiery messengers striding the waves, going from one mountain to the next and, as it were, kissing the ridges of blue-white water.

And for the life of me I could only admire the old ship as it struggled so valiantly through it all. Marvellous and terrible are His powers; yea, and marvellously terrible too the devices of men who were created in His image, though I had never before seen or felt how close the connection.

I had four hours of bliss which were to leave their mark on my whole life, and blessed are they who have had such an experience. But while my soul was feasting joyously, my poor body was rigid with cold and fatigue; and most tenderly did the old captain show his concern for me, and he had the grace to remain silent, moreover, for his warm Irish nature understood that speech was not possible after so much emotion, and that my greatest need now was for rest, which I then took in all its sweetness. I was later informed that I had slept round the clock, and when I awoke and looked out through the port-hole, the sun was shining cheerfully and the green slopes of Portugal gradually coming into view, and Oh! the world was beautiful that morning; it had never been so lovely, and I had begun to live anew.

Gwymon y Môr (Y Brodyr Owen, 1909)

A Windy Night

R. Williams Parry

I most prefer to listen to the wind within the walls of my own room. I have been out in it on the mountain; but this invisible one, which blinds men wherever they may be, also deafens them out there. Out there, when it gets up its roar, nothing else dares whisper. The course of the world is seen as if through a telescope, because the silence imposed by distance has been cast over everything. Nothing is heard of the train's chugging, as it fails to overtake its own smoke on the embankment below. It runs, moreover, on rubber rails. The trees twist upon themselves along the nearer slopes, but nothing that can be comprehended is to be heard of the moan. 'The waterfall's tumult!

It ceases to roar'[1] when the wind goes a-strolling. The wind on a mountainside is a boxer with a heavy punch, a pitiless tyrant. But along the lower slopes and down on the valley floor, there is no cottage that it doesn't turn into a musical instrument. Like Nero, there was never a worse oppressor, nor as good a fiddler.

Whether I am on land or sea, the wind is my visitor. He is the only friend whom I welcome by shutting the door in his face. And why not? He is only a homeless wanderer. And so I bid him welcome as a homeless one, while taking my comfort from his discomfort; for there was never a sweeter protester.

How hesitantly he visits a prodigal, arriving only after much perplexity. I do not recognize his first intonation, nor his second, until he complains a third time through the curtain of my half-open window. There is no point at all in trying to go on reading (for I always have a book by me), except when the wind starts up.

His orchestra is not yet at full strength; only a pipe or two and the fiddle so beloved of the sailor's wife. On a wind such as this I too can expect to see many a ship into my harbour. They come in out of the night, each bearing a cargo of memories. One arrives that was thought to have been lost for ever. Others are identified by their markings. There are few among them that are whole.

To the season of old age the consolation of reminiscence is usually attributed. But youth — so much richer in its talents than old age — excels in this respect, too. The horizon is no further off at journey's end than it was at the outset, and no one was ever so young that the wind did not beguile him — the wind that makes a lifetime of a single day, and an age out of a lifetime. The span of memory is a measure of eternity. The heyday of Arthur's knights is as but yesterday to the terrible distance of youth. How many centuries have passed since I saw that form which I have never seen since? I do not know how old I was; but I do know that I had been sent to bed the night before, prior to the arrival of some late visitors. I got up next morning to seek out someone who would help me to dress, and went into the bedroom where my mother and father usually slept. Through the half-open door, and first of all reflected in the mirror, I saw a woman — my mature years now tell me that she could not have been more than twenty — drawing a comb through the abundance of her hair. I have in mind the luxuriousness and blackness of that hair, and the brightness of the dark eyes I glimpsed in the glass that betrayed us both. The woman disappeared from the mirror, and I saw her next in the doorway which was by now wide-open. She took a step towards me, but not before I had marvelled at the whiteness of her bare arms, and the swinging of her full breasts. She lifted me on to her lap, and gave me an affectionate kiss. I broke away, as any boy would, to wipe off the wetness with the sleeve of my shirt, and to seek the refuge of my own bedroom. I never saw her again. Who was she? In what part of what continent does she dwell today, a contented, middle-aged woman? She was and then she was not in the watchfulness of morning, and though she comes back to me with the wind, she disappears, too, for ever young and beautiful. He says not a word on her account, and he does not come now. Like the poet, he does not recount everything he knows.

Who was that lecturer, and what became of him? I had gone (holding my aunt's hand) to hear him in the days when she was still a single woman. (I know that I was five years old when she married.) My mother had sent me to stay the night in the old home, and lovely was that sleepy journey, past bed-time, to an unknown chapel-vestry. I have seen that vestry a hundred times since then, and seen stars as bright on many a moonless night. But I never saw the speaker again, nor found out who he was. All I remember of his lecture is its subject — it was 'The Beehive'. He was a tall, thin, bright-eyed man, and I can see his courteous manner now as he answered questions at the end, and the gentlemanly look in his eyes. What audiences is he entertaining of an evening now? Many's the time I thought of asking my aunt about him. But I never did, and so missed the opportunity. Today she might be entreated, and questioned still more earnestly; but she will not answer. From the top of the crag at the back of her old home, on a clear day, I can see the spire of the churchyard where she lies. May the wind blowing on her from the mills of Anglesey be ever gentle.

May it be gentler than it is here at this moment, because by now its commotion has spread like a pestilence from the window through the whole house. The singers fall silent in the great noise of drum and tabor, all except the lone piper on the threshold. There is a sea-sound in the chimney and the shuddering of the sea throughout the whole house. I open my door expecting to see the tumult of the sea-shore. But there is nothing there save the post-road and, alongside it, the railway, and the wind as it rides along its curving track seems to be mocking the company's cautionary sign. Before me, and above my head, a new heaven and a new earth are being created. Though it is early yet, there are only drunks on the road tonight. They make their way, with loud voices, and straight-backed against the wind, like intoxicated soldiery leaving town for camp; or else hunch-backed and zig-zagging against it, as if retracing their steps in search of some valuables that have been mislaid. Overhead, there is a strange haste to the moon: it retreats from cloud to cloud at great speed, like one whose beauty is a tribulation to it among a crowd of people. Yet, however strenuous the attempt, when I look again, it is not a whit nearer the end of its journey. But the earth comes and goes with the moon. When it disappears, the slopes of the hill and its cottages disappear too, and there is only a gleam or two hanging in the emptiness to mark where they once had been. When it appears, the mountain re-appears in the guise of a mountain's ghost, and the houses like the ghosts of houses, because no sooner do they appear than they vanish. In the mean while, between the squalls of the wind, I hear the sound of singing coming from the direction of the largest light among those I see in front of me. Suddenly it goes out, as the Llanddwyn light goes out, but not, like it, to come on again, for in the next instant the moon lights up the dark windows of the Cwm chapel.

Y Brython (23 Rhagfyr, 1920),
Rhyddiaith R. Williams Parry
(gol. Bedwyr Lewis Jones, Gwasg Gee, 1974)

The Late Lemuel Parry, Esq., J.P., O.B.E.

W. J. Gruffydd

Only a few people in Wales have not heard about our dear, lately departed brother, Lemuel Parry, Esq., J.P., O.B.E., and the fragrance of his memory will remain among us for many years to come. This good servant was called from his labour to his reward at about a quarter-past seven o'clock on the fifth of May 1922, when the family was about to sit down to dinner, and so twelve months have passed since he was carried to his bed for the very last time, and I am grateful now for this opportunity of giving a sketch of his useful and self-sacrificing life.

The subject of this obituary was born on a Saturday evening, the fifth of May, in the year 1850, when the whole family except one was at supper, in a low, mean cottage known as the Twmp in the parish of Llanfihangel Mechdeyrn[1] in the county of Caernarfon. His father was a labourer, yet as honest as any gentleman in the district; at least, that was the testimony of those who knew them best. His mother was a niece to the daughter of a cousin to that fine old Christian gentleman Wil y Llan, as he was known, who would always drive the immortal Matthews Ewenni[2] on his preaching tours of North Wales. Of course, the story about Wil's 'having taken a drop too much' and tipping the witty old preacher into the ditch is so well-known that we need not recount it here. 'If Wil had had as much in his head as in his belly, he would have been quite a card,' remarked Matthews with his customary wit, causing everyone in that large congregation to split their sides with uncontrollable laughter. I heard Mr Lemuel Parry recounting on scores of occasions how it had been seeing the listeners being carried out like carcasses that had given him the idea of endowing the Ambulance Corps which is now the glory of his native parish.

He received his education in the Church School at Llanfihangel, and ever after harboured a perfect hatred for the Church[3], even to his grave, because at school he had had to waste his time and energy in learning the Catechism; that is what doubtless gave him his zeal for Disestablishment[4] towards the end of his life. At school he was a model of goodness and frugality and diligence for all the children. If some of the boys were naughty, it was not long before the master was given their names by Lemuel, and whenever some of the children in their carelessness left some small object such as a knife or top behind, little Lemuel would soon find it; and his frugality and concern for such possessions were held up for emulation by all the children of Wales.

When he was barely twelve years old and had just reached Standard I, he was obliged to go out into the world. He worked for a while on a nearby farm, weeding and clearing stones, and was a great help in keeping his mother and father, and his brothers, in food and clothing, but his master was so mean and miserly that one morning he complained to young Lemuel that he had not bargained for having to keep Abraham Wood's[5] entire family at his own expense. Lemuel's tender heart was so wounded by the farmer's unseemly language that he left his employ, and for a long time afterwards had nothing in particular to do. But Providence took good care of him during these years, and of his family. The district of Llanfihangel at that time was in a very poor state, its inhabitants ignorant and jealous and fond of bearing false witness against one another, and Aaron Parry, Lemuel's father, and his entire family, were obliged to move to Liverpool.

The first thing Aaron Parry did was to join the chapel in Barn Street — subsequently Golder's Row — and the minister, the immortal Dr Morgan, found a job for the father on the docks and a place for young Lemuel as a junior at the well-known premises of Messrs Parrett and Jones in Scotland Road. We are unable to follow his career at this point, but suffice it to say that he was promoted to serve behind the counter whenever Mr Parrett went to look for Mr Jones, and this was long before his promotion over the heads of the other employees to the position of manager. He always attributed this unexpected move to the fact that he regularly attended the weekly service and never missed the Fellowship and the other meetings. Another reason was that Mr Parrett and Mr Jones never saw him under the influence of strong drink, and that doubtless had made a deep impression on their minds. Throughout the time Lemuel remained in their service, though they lost many things from the shop — indeed, it was this in the end that drove them bankrupt — they never caught him taking anything. In this, too, he was to be held up for emulation by all the young lads of Wales.

After the bankruptcy of his employers, Mr Parry opened his own business in an adjacent street. By dint of thrift and careful living and blameless conduct he had now gathered unto himself quite a lot of money, and with that and money from his wife, Mr Parrett's daughter, he had enough to set up his shop on firm foundations. I once asked him (with that keen admiration which is so typical of an Anglesey lad with regard to a prosperous Liverpool tradesman) how he accounted for his worldly success. His answer deserves to be put up in a golden frame on the walls of all the cottages of Wales: 'First of all,' he said, 'by taking every opportunity of counting the pennies, or as the old proverb has it, adding a field to a field; secondly, by not spending my money on novels and the rubbish that is printed by the English press, and by keeping away from the theatre and other such disreputable places; thirdly, and above all, by striking a bargain with the Lord that if He would make me a success, I in turn would contribute substantially to His causes.' With the last in mind, his custom had been to give threepence out of every pound to the work of the denomination, but once, a few years ago, he had quite naturally thought that he had given enough, except in that year he made exceptionally heavy business losses, and never again tried to withdraw from his bargain. 'You can break a bargain with men,' he said, 'because they are not often aware of it, but God sees everything.' Let Welsh boys who wish to get on in the world bear this supremely important distinction in mind.

His wealth and standing increased thereafter from one year to the next, and in 1910 he was made Chairman of the Bi-Monthly Meeting. Soon afterwards he pulled out of his business in Liverpool and built a splendid mansion near his old home at Llanfihangel Mechdeyrn.

On the first Sunday after his return. He was chosen to be a deacon in Horeb Chapel and when the National Eisteddfod was held at Caernarfon, his generosity and bardic talent were acknowledged by his ordination as a member of the Gorsedd[6] under the name of Lerpwlfab Mechdeyrn. It is certain that he would also have received an honorary degree from the University if only he had not removed from England.

Everyone knows about the good work he did throughout the county of Caernarfon in these later years. He devoted himself to the service of religion and good causes, and his money and time were ever at the disposal of his denomination. How many of Caernarfon's young ministers did not feel the benefit of his generosity? They were all, for their part, gratefully recognisant of it and devoted to serving him. And at this point I really must protest against the denominational narrowness and jealousy of certain ministers belonging to other sects who tried to bring disgrace on Ministers of the Word by reproaching those young men that they had become dependent upon Mr Parry. Indeed, the denominational zeal of Lemuel Parry was as holy fire, and it is him above all that our denomination has to thank that so many of our youngsters have been given places in the country's schools. He wore himself out for them, openly and behind the scenes, and nothing less was to be expected from a man like Mr Parry, because for him religion was a practical matter and not some pointless, pliable sentiment.

In 1911 he was made a Justice of the Peace, and he did his best to keep Wales a sober Wales by fining drunkards to the limits of the law, and to keep it a pure Wales by the dire warnings that he always handed out to those who had been found guilty of offences against morality and chastity. Indeed, he was so keen in this respect that a young woman who had lost her virtue and good character once threw herself into the river in shame after listening to an earnest speech of his in court. But he knew full well when to show mercy from the bench; only to the lowest dregs and the prodigal poor was he at all hard, and he would always ease the punishment of the more respectable people who happened to come before him. Who does not recall the scolding he gave that policeman who had been so rash as to suggest that Sir Henry Lloyd had been found drunk, or the scorn he poured on the head of the railway company's solicitor who had dared accuse a County Councillor of travelling without a ticket?

But it was in 1914 that he was given a chance to accomplish the great work of his lifetime. At that time, when the fiendish devices of the German foe were trying to trample underfoot the homes of Gwalia[7], he demonstrated his peerless courage and intense love of country and his self-sacrifice on its behalf. He threw himself utterly into its service, and his special position as a County Councillor and Justice of the Peace and chapel deacon gave him an unusual opportunity so to do. He addressed hundreds of recruiting meetings, often in the face of much hostility. The parish and district of Llanfihangel was full of unthinking and light-headed lads who held their own lives dear, and they refused to muster under their country's flag to fight for freedom and equality. But when Mr Parry was made Chairman of the Tribunal, the selfish old men and foolish old women of the parish soon had to bid their sons farewell. Of course, he himself was not so credulous as to think that the country would be better off if everyone were to be sent to the front. His three sons were needed at home for duties that were essential for the kingdom's security, and Wales will never be grateful enough to those patriots who sacrificed themselves for their country. Indeed, the youngest of his sons, Major Trevor Parry, R.A.S.C., D.S.O., O.B.E., was unable to resist the call to arms, and joined the Army as Superintendent of Hay and Animal Foodstuffs for North Wales. I heard Mr Parry describe in many a speech, with tears in his eyes, the heart-breaking scene when Trevor left home to go to enter the fray at Wrexham. When the conscription laws rendered Mr Parry's speeches no longer necessary, he threw himself into a recruitment drive and went up and down the County encouraging young women to join the W.A.A.C. He urged parents to send their daughters, promising that their physical and moral well-being would be better looked after in the Army than at home. And everyone who has been in the Army knows how true that was.

But immense though his patriotic energies were, he did not forget the County's business interests. He had realized early on the extreme importance to the kingdom of the businessman, and he was offered a safe seat in Parliament and a place in the Government as the Navy's Inspector of Food. But Lemuel Parry was not a man to accept such honours when duty called closer to home. He had noticed that the country's sugar supply was in the hands of completely unsuitable people, and the account of what he did with sugar is worth repeating for the benefit of the people of Wales. He purchased all the sugar in the country for a penny-farthing a pound, and for a fortnight he refused to sell it to the Government. In the end, the Chancellor of the Exchequer had to arbitrate between the two parties, and the Government eventually bought all the sugar from Mr Parry at a shilling the pound. Britain could never give adequate thanks to the Chancellor for his wisdom and judgement in this matter, nor to Mr Parry for his patriotism and self-sacrifice in selling at a price much lower than the market. As a small acknowledgement of the service he had rendered, he was appointed Superintendent of Sugar Supplies for the duration of the war, and the people of Wales ought to know that he received not a penny in official payment while he was in that post.

After the victory of our forces in the War, and when the peace was declared that was to put an end to all war, Mr Parry devoted himself anew to helping those poor boys who had fought on our behalf. His self-denying determination to prevent work being given to 'conchies' will long be remembered, and many an ex-soldier has today, through the good offices of Mr Parry, a job for which none but 'conchies' applied. To him more than to anyone is praise due for putting the chapels out of bounds to 'conchies' and their like. We heard of a minister (belonging to our denomination, we are ashamed to admit) who had been in prison, as a student, for refusing to join the Army, and he had been brazen enough to go preaching at Horeb. To the eternal honour of Christianity in the vicinity, and likewise the healthy influence and wealth of Mr Parry, only five people came to hear him.

When the Government decided to award five thousand O.B.E.s to the County of Caernarfon, no one was surprised that Mr Parry was given this rare and special honour by his country. Just before his death he had been sounded out with a view to his becoming a peer of the realm in recognition of his services to the sugar industry and his contribution to military recruitment, but on hearing talk that a committee was about to look into these honours, he refused them outright being too proud and too much of a conscientious Nonconformist to allow the State to interfere like this in his private affairs.

As has already been stated, he departed this life full of years and elevated in the admiration of his own nation. Llanfihangel has never seen a funeral as princely as the one that this good man was accorded. But let us not be sorely afflicted; he has gone to his just reward.

Y Llenor (2, 1923),
Y Tro Olaf (Y Clwb Llyfrau Cymreig, 1939)

On Drowning a Cat

T. H. Parry-Williams

I was helping a friend drown a cat one gloomy evening in November — or rather I was keeping him company in order to lend him a bit of moral courage and provide him with support — and everything and everywhere was exceedingly dismal. We were more fortunate than the Red Cobbler of Rhuddlan[1], because the cat, which was in pretty poor shape, had died in the sack as we went along, if that were a matter of any consequence. But coming back across the field from the river's bank, my companion remarked that he would sooner be hanged than ever again drown a cat, or at any rate a cat he knew like the one that had just gone to its doom, a cat which had shared his hearth, one of the family. I didn't feel any pang of grief that evening, but then there was no close connection between me and that cat, and so there wasn't a sudden emptiness in my life as there was in his, although I too could not but feel a certain sense of loss at seeing a creature that was likeable enough, as I knew from casual acquaintance, meet its end, while still fairly young, in sackcloth and waters. By dint of careful enquiry, I came to understand that it wasn't his fondness for that cat as much as an association with something that had occurred earlier in his life, of which drowning a cat had been part, that caused the distress to be so intense in his heart. The association, the connection — that, in fact, was what mattered; and it's astonishing to think how everything of significance and every eventful period and special time in life, however brief it may be, is tied to and connected with something that has gone before or is presumed to be yet to come. That is what causes the particular events or circumstances to imprint themselves so deeply on the spirit. Unless there is such a connection, the thing is too new and too unfamiliar, and we do not experience it fully because there is about it no aura of our own making.

I know a sensible, level-headed man who is fascinated by the patter of cheapjacks at the small sixpenny shows to be found here and there in fair and circus. But he can't bring himself to enjoy these things without being able to conjure up some circumstance that occurred in his boyhood when he first heard the hubbub of the stall-holders and the voices proclaiming the wonders of those little shows when he went to a fairground holding his brother's hand. He can't enjoy a play thoroughly without being able to recall and re-live the first time he went to a theatre and heard a man who was playing a curate say 'damn', to his considerable amazement at the time. It is the ability to recall all that vividly and clearly (but not through conscious effort) which creates the proper atmosphere for him to become absorbed in a play's performance on stage. A shower from the past has to fall on him first.

The important things or the actual existence of the present are thus a kind of two-way mirror reflecting what has been or is to come; and whichever way we turn it, we see backwards or forwards, and the reflection of one of the two directions is cast on everything that matters in our view for the moment. We are bound on both sides, and obliged, as we proceed, to re-live everything, or live it in advance, in some measure. I once heard a married man say that it was his first sweetheart he wed when he married his present wife; and how many while walking in the funeral cortege of someone else's beloved have buried some dear one who is still alive?

Only now and again in life do we live, and having lived about half-a-dozen experiences we are ready to depart. The great things are done only once, except that we re-live many of them and live others in advance. There are some people who, early on in life, have done with everything except dying, and from then on are waiting just for that. That is the final happening, and it comes just once, although it may be lived in advance, perhaps, many times over.

Yes, there are about half-a-dozen events, more or less, in the course of life, and in between hardly anything of real importance. When the greatest things occur, we are conscious of nothing else, for we can feel only one transporting happiness or one fierce grief at a time. It is they that fill the place, while they last. As for some of them, we know before their coming that they are to come, so we live them in advance, and after they have been we live them over again. We know, too, that there is not much difference between grief and ecstasy at their zenith: it is the zenith of being conscious of them that matters most.

After it has gone through the last pass and has finished with experience and emotion, I wonder whether there is in what remains of the body's machinery some old craving to bestir itself and re-live some of the great things that have occurred in its past? A grave-digger once told me he fancied he had seen sure signs of this when his spade, in digging a new grave, brought up a skull from the earth. It had been placed in the unearthly yellow-whiteness of its old decrepitude on fresh soil piled at the grave's edge, and he had brought himself, with an effort, to come face to face with it. But he thought he could see signs of movement in the skull. After the blacksmith had been summoned and it had been examined with spiritualist excitement, it was discovered to contain a mole's nest and the agitation to be nothing more than the purblind wriggling of the mole's young. Thus we are always disappointed on the threshold of discovery. 'Worm of the earth — shall that be admitted into Heaven?'[2]

The hope of a similar discovery was once nurtured in me too, in Havana. In that city there is a cemetery splendid in its size and outlook, a magnificent place for the body to rest for ever in sunny country between tropical woods. But in a secluded corner behind high double-gates in that cemetery there is a dreadful pile of bones and skulls, and these appeared to me as if they had tried to come back to the sunshine and fresh air to re-live some of the old experiences. Yet it was a calm and terribly hopeless look that they had when I peered at the heap through a crack in the gate. I heard later — although I have no guarantee of the story's veracity — that they had been brought up from their resting-places because their graves had been rented, and when their relatives stopped paying, the cemetery authorities had had no choice but to take responsibility for raising the dead. So it was little wonder that I found them looking so dejected, bare bones all jumbled together up there on that execrable tip, under the rapacious eyes of the vultures that were hovering continually above the spot.

No, though the bones be disturbed and the skulls unearthed, there is no returning. When life is finished, there is no more re-living or reviving here. And the great things are experienced just once. Once only are 'the dregs of the cup of trembling' drunk; once only are 'the mountain of myrrh and the hill of frankincense' climbed; once only is a cat drowned.

Once. There is no second time.

Ysgrifau (Cwmni Cymraeg Foyle, 1943),
Casgliad o Ysgrifau (Gwasg Gomer, 1984)

The House across the Way

J. O. Williams

It stands there now, as it has always done, straight in front of me.

Here I am, back once more today on the hearth where I grew up, having spent many long years away from my old home. I feel as if everything is strange to me. But as I look now through the windows of the front living-room, my eyes alight upon the stony face of the house opposite, just as they used to do before I knew that the great world is wider than this room's limits and the wall of the house across the way.

How many hundreds of times have I gazed at it? Since it was on its bare stones that my eyes fell when first I looked out through the living-room window, that wall slowly became part of my life. That house over there was never my home, and few are the times I've been within its walls, but I am sure that no one is better acquainted with its facade than I am.

There are several other houses in the same row — some better, some not as good, some more and others less interesting in appearance; but I am not familiar with them. An old friend of mine used to live in one of those houses. I went inside it hundreds of times. But my friend's house was strange to me in comparison with the one standing immediately opposite the four windows of my own home.

There's nothing extraordinary about the way it looks, nor any great skill in its masonry, nor great excellence or oddity of any kind. No ivy creeps across its facade to break up the chill and rough edge of stone upon stone. It is bare from its foundations to its eaves under the slate roof. Yet I gaze at its stones today as if at an old acquaintance.

There it is! I recall how I used to compare the small, brownish, oval stone there just above the door to a knot in wood, when first I came to know about such things. That turned out to be bitter knowledge, as the scar on my thumb bears witness to this day. I had not imagined at that time how much strength there was in my right hand until the knife's blade sank into the soft flesh of my left. A knot in the wood, and the knife slipping. I remember it well. And I have been able to make out that knot ever since in the stone yonder. I can see it still, and feel the blade of my father's knife in my thumb this very moment.

I used to liken the yellow stone under the eaves over there to the face of old Gruffydd Wiliam in chapel. Every time I looked at it under the ledge of the pulpit the stone would come to mind, and I imagined seeing a sparrow perching on its gable. He too now appears before my eyes in the stone in front of me. I recall once more some of his words and mannerisms. I remember the great merriment I felt then at seeing the eave-stone in the deacons' pew.

When I heard in school for the first time about canals running up and down the land, I saw them one rainy day on the wall opposite in the cement pointing between the stones. I sailed many a small boat on those cement canals, and standing here I would steer them with my eyes around the corners of the stones and hide them in the coves of some of the roughest and most angular ones.

As I became lost in those imaginary adventures, the stones would grow into carved rocks, the strips of cement become wide rivers, and the recesses caves in which to hide treasures gathered from the islands of the house's stones.

Today, looking at them, I see only the bare stones of a house-wall, with their remembrance of the delight of yesteryear. The old charms have faded under the wear and tear of the years, and lost their romance in the cares of this world.

Those stones have been scorched by sun and battered by storms for forty years or more, but their shape and colour remain unchanged. The material is hard granite — grey, blue-green, yellow, greyish red, and one or two are the colour of cream — each stone in its own appointed place. The same gap is in the grey-blue stone above the living-room window that was there originally. The colour, shape, and setting of the big angular stone at the side of the window in the bedroom above the kitchen are still the same, as is the small round yellowish-white stone placed within a narrow cement strip of it.

One of them has a nasty scar running across its surface, where someone's gimlet once made a hole in order to cut it into smaller pieces. Who, I wonder? Where is he now? There is the obscure monument to him. It's too ordinary for anyone to notice — a mark of the strength in some quarryman's arm, a half-day of whose dear life is to be seen in that unremarkable groove.

How many times have I been driven by a sudden squall of rain from my childish play into this living-room, to do nothing but stand and peer out sullenly through the window? Tired of watching it rain, I would look through the downpour at the facade of the house across the way. And I wasn't long in recognizing from those stones the signs of rain setting in or rain that would soon be over. If there was no hope of it letting up, each stone would frown back at me. Otherwise, the small yellowish-white stone lit up first, and then the light spread like a smile over all the stones. The rain would stop, and I would be free once more to go out into the road. Yes, I recognized the signs in those stones almost before I knew the letters of the alphabet.

Standing at this window today is a sort of journey into that carefree and comfortable past. There have been lots of changes in the world since then. Some have been inside the house across the way, yet nothing shows on the exterior of its wall. Indeed, it would have been rather strange if it had altered, with only rain and a soft wind beating on its hard granite.

Over there between the parlour window and the front-door there are two dark-red spots between the stones. Two old rusty nails, that's what they are. They were knocked in — how long ago was that, I wonder? — almost thirty-five years ago, very likely — by old Huw Tomos. I can hear the noise of his hammering this very minute. Huw Tomos was the first occupant I remember in the house across the way. His hobby was the garden and the tender things that grew there — rosebushes, ferns, and flowers. I happened to be in poor health at that time, but starting to mend and upstairs in the bedroom. I used to lie for six weeks at a time without seeing anything except the paper on the bedroom's walls. It was pleasant to look out of the window that afternoon — a fine Saturday afternoon — and see the roses growing in the small front-garden of the house across the way, after counting all those printed red and blue flowers, hundreds upon hundreds of them, and all exactly alike. Huw Tomos was pottering about in the garden and trying to put two nails into the wall of the house. Having knocked them in, he tied a piece of string from one side to the other, over the rosebush. I recall how I tapped the window-pane, and how he turned to look up at me, playfully making a fist and shaking his head. In a while I saw him cutting three lovely roses and a few leaves, then crossing the road, and giving them to my mother. Soon the three blooms were in a water-jug on the small table in the bedroom. Thirty-five years! Every time I smell the scent of yellow roses, that sunny Saturday afternoon lives again in my mind. Now there are only two rusty nails left, like a sweet scar on the wall, and no one to recognize them except me.

I also recall that there were five perfect roses on that bush when the news came that Huw Tomos had been killed in the quarry. On the evening of the next day, when his body was brought home for burial, I was sitting on the sofa just here.

I stared in amazement at the blind windows, and my eyes wandered unfamiliarly over the wall of the house. The five roses trembled uncomfortably in the breeze, as if the grief torturing the widow inside had touched them too. I remember my father and someone else going over to the house and slowly opening the door, and then quietly closing it again after them. I heard the door opening and the mysterious whispering of men in the road outside, and the clatter of short steps made by the feet of some among them. I could see nothing but the blackness of the night through the window, yet I saw enough when the weak lamp from the kitchen cast a gleam through the doorway across the road. The sound of loud weeping came from inside, and I fled to the back of our house, weeping quietly to myself.

Next day, as I was getting up, I expected to see something different about the wall of the house across the way. No: nothing. Each and every stone stood in its place, every groove and grout and bump just the same. They were watching, every one of them, cold and silent, as men bore that tenant to the house that would be his everlasting home. They heard the mourning voices of the widow and her children without in any way changing. And it is their unaltered appearance today which has brought back for me every change that has taken place elsewhere.

Ann Tomos wasn't long across the way after burying her husband. The close family was scattered to the four winds. I don't know where any one of them is now.

Do they, I wonder, remember what kind of voices they had when they were little children? I do. I can hear them this minute as I look at the seven stones of the arch above the door: their shrill, vivacious laughter as they kick a ball about and throw pebbles at it. I can see the smallest one learning to walk with the help of the dented stone on the right-hand side of the door. Is he, I wonder, walking still?

I see the house again, empty. Four windows like so many big, open, surprised eyes, in the midst of all those unmoved stones. But there were others who came to seek shelter and warmth there: two young people setting out on life together. I can see their furniture being brought in through the doorway. I can hear the sound of coming and going, the happy settling in and the cheerful banter as they start to encounter life's problems. Across the way then ceased from being the house of Huw Tomos and became that of Elis Jones.

Hardly five years were he and his small family there. I saw Elis Jones leaning on the corner of the garden wall with his face as yellow as wax, slowly walking a few yards up the road, responding solemnly and quietly to a greeting from this neighbour and that. It's twenty-seven years since that time. Yet another family then moved in.

Before long I myself was about to be off, and beginning to feel that the world outside was rather more important than that wall across the way.

But here I am, back again, and taking my time to gaze through the window of the old living-room at the same old stones opposite.

Today another family is living there, I see, whom I don't yet know. There are different panes in the windows now, different curtains . . .

Hey! What do I see at the window over there? Someone looking this way. A boy! . . . A small boy peering out from across the way at the front of my own house!

Y Llenor (9, 1930),
Storiau a 'Sgrifau (Gwasg y Brython, 1933)

Weobley and St. Emilion

Saunders Lewis

I was in England this summer. Not in London or Liverpool or Birmingham, but in the real England, the England that Mr R.T. Jenkins[1] talks about, the country that 'makes the heart of many an Englishman beat faster', namely in one of 'the old, golden towns' of Herefordshire, a town that has not been spoiled and turned into a Broadway by publicity and Americans, but remains quietly off the beaten track, one of the gems of English civilization. Weobley is an ancient township. It used to return two members to the parliament of England. Today its three streets are a refuge for painters attracted there by the black-and-white houses with their thatched roofs. And there is a hotel there. Not only is this the oldest house in the village, but in itself it is the very embodiment of all that is genial and amiable in the life of England. Simple, pure food is served there, local meat, vegetables from the garden, fresh fruit and cream, and cider made from the Herefordshire apples. In the lounge is heard the gentle talk of the district's farmers, here is the fine courtesy of an English country-inn, the pleasant chatter of the woman of the house, the ready service of her daughter who ran in from the tennis-court to lay the table. We slept under beams that had been polished by the centuries.

A few weeks later I was in the south of France. St. Emilion, too, is a small, out-of-the-way town, though its name is respected throughout Christendom. It has Romanesque churches, the ruins of monasteries, steep narrow streets, and dark-red roofs, while all around the town are wide acres of vineyards basking in the sun. There is in St. Emilion one of the most celebrated hotels in France, but one which has already been spoiled by fame. We stayed at another, less ostentatious hotel. In that establishment, one August evening, we partook of a classic dinner. We received, too, a warm welcome and had pleasant conversation; we were given the choice of the house's vineyard and the excellence of the kitchen's art. The magnificence of France's civilization was revealed to us there.

In my opinion, to speak frankly, St. Emilion is superior to Weobley. The soil of southern France is more generous than that of Hereford, so naturally there is a profusion and variety of food to be had in the French town which is not to be found in the English. Also, I had rather drink the fruit of Gascon vines than of Hereford's apple-trees. It is more of an education and cultural experience for me to take dinner at the Restaurant Germaine in St. Emilion than at the Red Lion in Weobley. Nevertheless — and this is the important point — these two places, these two splendid establishments, although so far away from each other, belong to the same tradition and the same civilization. For me they each represent best the humanism of the West. In both places a man's body and soul are shown every due respect, every guest is waited upon with simple courtesy, in both places served food and drink which are fully as much a tribute to his intellect and culture as they are to his body, and in both establishments the prices asked are not only reasonable, but proof of the gentlemanly spirit. And what lends character to both is that they are local. The Red Lion dinner can be tried only at Weobley; in St. Emilion, yes, only at the Restaurant Germaine can one partake of Madame Germaine's dinner. In neither place was there a broth made from boiling a cube in tap-water, nor fruit from Californian tins, nor Danish butter, nor Canadian cheese. And I thank heaven that there are still establishments even in England, and thousands of them in France and Italy, where the 'self service breakfast' of Mr Philip Snowden and the Manchester economists has been banished as something barbarous.

But there is one difference between Weobley and St. Emilion that struck me quite forcibly. Both towns are old, though St. Emilion is the older by centuries. And yet the older of the two is very much the younger. St. Emilion's eyes are on the future, it is looking forward. 'Yes,' the mistress of the house told me, 'we have three vineyards, but we don't sell the wine from the best vineyard. You see, we have three children, and my husband is keeping the wine from the best vineyard in the years when the vintage was good (that is, 1920, 1923, 1924, 1926, 1928, 1929) so that the children can have it after they are married.' In Weobley it was a very different story. There it was despair, with the children leaving for London or the industrial towns. I felt that the heart of France was beating robustly, but that some cancer was gnawing at the entrails of England. Looking back and telling old stories was what gave the Weobley mothers pleasure; the heads of St. Emilion's households were keeping the best vintages for their children to enjoy after they had gone.

By gaining an empire the English have lost England. The very character and temperament of Weobley belong to the old England, the England of the poet Chaucer, the England of which St. Emilion in France was once a part, belonging as it did to the same order and the same tradition as France. England was once part of Europe, and that goes to explain dear little townships like Weobley. But with Sir Francis Drake and Sir Walter Raleigh and their followers, the English betrayed their own country. They gained the world, and lost England. They did a bad turn to their country's genius. Today Drake and Raleigh are heroes in England's schools; their tale is told to English children and they are held up as models of the Englishman in whom there is no deceit, and attempts are even made to cast Welsh children in the same mould. But the heirs and disciples of those heroes are Melchett and Beaverbrook and Sir William Morris who maintain today that it is business which should regulate a country's government. It was men of this tradition who made England's empire, who brought India to its present sorry plight, who stole South Africa, who stretched their rapacious fingers into China and Egypt — and who gave us the grimness of the industrial areas of South Wales and the North of England, and then crowned their exploits by making two million unemployed.

And it is men of this tradition who insist today on persevering in their mischief, and in turning the empire into one large business with its head office in London. We are told, too, that it is in the present Labour Government's mind to steal a march on Beaverbrook and his cohorts by trying to bargain with the British territories at the Empire Conference that is soon to be held. It was the same government not so long ago which impatiently rejected a memorandum from M. Briand, the French Foreign Minister, which was in favour of a Union of European Countries. England's policy, whichever party may be in power, still remains in that tradition.

This policy is a danger to the peace of Europe and exceedingly damaging to at least one small country in Britain, namely Wales. The Welsh Nationalist Party[2] can be expected to resist all the tendencies of this policy. But the point now is that England, too, has been injured and mistreated by the tradition of her government. By means of her one-sided, unbalanced development, and by neglecting and violating her geographical position, England for a while in the last century accumulated exceptional wealth and power. But her life has been the poorer for it. Sir William Morris declares it is high time that 'business ruled in politics'. England's disaster is that business has ruled her for three centuries. It was business — that is to say, the capitalists — which made the empire, and it is a few capitalists who are now the sole beneficiaries of that empire — the same capitalists who are arguing for the empire's economic union. That policy at least is bound to fail. Economic union cannot be created where there is neither natural unity nor geographical connection. Having failed in that, perhaps England will then be prepared to lend an ear to an alternative policy, and will attempt economic and political union within the continent to which she rightly belongs.

Y Ddraig Goch (Hydref, 1930),
Canlyn Arthur (Gwasg Aberystwyth, 1938)

The Man in the Street

Robert Beynon

He is an ordinary man and his wife is ordinary too. There was nothing exceptional about his father, nor his father-in-law either. The book of days has very little to say about his birth and will not mention his death unless there is an inquest upon it.

It is not to insult him, nor to set him below all others, to call him ordinary. There are ordinary men in plenty who are not in the street, and it's only fair to recognize that not every prominent or well-known man is greater. It is not impossible for the man who lives in the street to be greater than he who owns the street. More prominence is given to many men, not because they are greater but because there is more under their feet. They have the advantage of an official position or influential job and so appear greater than they are, and greater than he, for the reason that they have something to stand upon that is higher than street level. On ordinary ground, they too would be ordinary. Ordinary men are to be seen in extraordinary places, but this one is an ordinary man in an ordinary place: a man in a street with hundreds of his kind all about him. In a mansion he would not be called ordinary, not because there he would seem greater than he is but on account of his greater standing. But as it is, he is in the street, with nothing between the soles of his feet and the common earth.

He is one of thousands, and if he were to be asked, he would probably reply that his name is legion. And since he is one of many he does not receive the attention he deserves. He is like a tree hidden from sight in a large forest. There is much talk of the man in the moon. As far as I know, he too is an ordinary man, and in the street he wouldn't attract much notice because people are more numerous there than they are on the moon. If he likes being in the world's eye, he had better stay in the heavens, lest in falling among the multitude that so resembles him, he be lost from view.

With that exception, the man in the street has achieved nothing that sets him apart. He knows as much as his brothers, but doesn't know more. He has as much talent as most, but not enough to be among the select. He has eyes, but he is not a seer; he can speak, but he is not a prophet. Something of what great men have is also in him, but not in sufficient measure to make him one of them.

For these reasons, he is never seen in the higher echelons. He is always at the eisteddfod, but never an adjudicator; that is, he is not paid for his criticism, since there is no remuneration for assessing the worth of adjudicators; there is pleasure enough to be had from such work. He is usually to be seen in the cheaper seats; he goes on to the stage only in a choir. It is he who sings bass and tenor, his wife and daughter soprano and alto; it is he and his family who do everything except conduct. He is also to be found in chapel and in church, but not in the pulpit. There is no funeral without him, and if you want to catch a glimpse of him, see who is helping to bear the coffin.

Yet although he is not to the fore, the world cannot do without him. Without him there is no comfort in either cottage or mansion; his hand is behind everything. His name is not carved on the foundation stone, but it was he who fashioned it. Someone else must be found to conceive a plan, but the hands of the ordinary man are needed to bring the work to completion.

It has been said that there is nothing exceptional about him. But let it be remembered that no one else would be considered exceptional if it were not for him. He is the mean standard. To be great is to be greater than he is. An obligation quite often neglected by great men is to give this man thanks for not being greater than he is and thus for not jeopardizing their own position. The nightingale, I fear, is unconcerned about her debt to other birds for not singing better and so not detracting from praise of herself and family. The man in the street should be a great consolation to those above him. There is no pleasure in anyone's being set on high unless there are others to look up to him. It is pointless being a politician when there is nobody to applaud him, and there is no enjoyment in being an idol in a world where there are none to worship. The shepherd who has no flock is exceedingly lonely.

The man we are talking about presents an opportunity for anyone with position or rank; he is the orator's audience and the general's army. He is not a member of parliament, and he has nothing to do with law except in so far as he keeps or breaks it; and yet he has a vote, and occasionally he will assume great importance to those who are generally considered to be greater than he.

If it is truly said that he is the mean standard, and that to be great is to be raised higher than the pavement on which he stands, the best way to elevate the world would be to raise him up first. When he is promoted, the leaders too will have to move up or else lose their place and go back to living in the street. When he is better taught, it will not do for his teachers to slumber, lest one day they find themselves his pupils.

He is more of a man these days than ever before. He knows just as much as his father, and to him there now belongs a wider measure of independence in both spirit and mind. He is not prepared to believe everything; he knows enough to understand that no one knows everything. He has begun to ask questions and to seek answers; the street has been illuminated and he now sees supposedly greater men as less than they were when it was night. He becomes more interesting with every year that passes because he is growing. He has been given visions and he is dreaming dreams. It is this that makes him restless; in the excitement of his new enlightenment he forgets that the world is old. He tends to doubt everything that was in the world before him and to believe everything that is new; and he has no respect for infallibility except when he is 'the man in the street'. It is interesting to hear him weigh things up; no one is too great nor too important to come in for criticism from him. He is a champion at pulling ikons down; the only work he does better is to put up others in their place, and before them he prostrates himself utterly. He is full of the virtues and weaknesses of a man who is still growing. He cannot be ignored, for when he is aroused, he is dangerous. Scorned by many, he often forgets that his worst enemy is the man who stands on his shoulders in order to be seen.

This 'man in the street' is an important, interesting fellow. Though the world does not always recognize his worth, there could be no world without him. His heart is not far from being in the right place; he knows what it is to give his scant pennies for the building of a college, and to endeavour to provide a better chance for his children. He is a man, though not famous, who will often be found among the heroes of the hidden places.

It has been said more than once that he is not to be seen among the high and mighty. The level ground is where he dwells, and he enjoys neither reputation nor praise. Nevertheless, we have taken care at least once to accord him an honourable place in the company of the nation's great. At Westminster Abbey in London — the burial place of the famous — the tomb of the unknown soldier is to be seen. He is 'the man in the street', and he was never found in a more dignified spot. Whatever else is said about him, when the call comes he can die as well as the next man.

Dydd Calan (Foyle, 1921)

Old Dent

T. Gwynn Jones

Old Dent, that's what we all called him, always, because none of us had ever seen him wearing a hat that didn't have a peculiar dent in it. I used to have difficulty understanding how he was able to make exactly the same kind of dent in every hat he wore. But I came to understand later. He never bought a new hat, I'm sure of it, all the eight years I lived in the district.

He was the son of a well-to-do farmer, and the family lived in one of the most fertile valleys of North Wales. His father belonged to that class of Welsh farmer in the last century who had, as it were, retained the characteristics of the eighteenth century to the fullest extent — a big, well-built man, of gentlemanly appearance, a slow talker, graceful in his movements, a good deal more gentlemanly in his manner, voice and way of speaking than the half-bred squireen who owned the farm on which he lived.

His son, Old Dent, was a very different man. He wasn't very old when first I knew him, yet in some respects he seemed older than his father. A man of middling height, thinnish, as if he were made of only skin and bone, and hard as steel from top to toe. A narrow face that seemed wizened, like an apple, with small creases across it. A thin, light-grey beard that was always kept short. Two kind blue eyes that sometimes gleamed strangely when he smiled. He chewed tobacco that had turned his strong teeth yellow. When he smiled, one side of his lower lip would curl more than the other, and one of his eyes would close, as though he were winking at you. For that reason you might have thought he was a bit of a wag and that sharp words might be spoken. But even if they were in his head they were never uttered by those lop-sided lips.

He walked with something of a stoop, the nearest you ever saw to the bearing of a man with a scythe in his hands, striding along as though he were about to use it as a weapon, and when he walked quickly — come to think of it, I never saw him going slowly — he would swing his arms from side to side, very like a man cutting hay. In fact, Old Dent had been born a scythesman. Watching him brought to mind a scythe which had been turned into a man. 'He's a keen one all right, is Old Dent,' everyone would say, and then they'd recall how once, while in the hay, he strode forward with such zeal that the scythe's blade sliced between the sole of his boot and his toes. I don't think that could have been literally true. But it was true enough in another sense. Old Dent's function in life was 'to be hard at it', and his favourite words were 'pressing on', 'getting on with it', and 'sticking at it'.

He had received almost no schooling, although his sister had. From childhood, it seems, he had been taught to 'press on'. It was said that he was able to handle a plough at the age of eight and was following the team by the time he was twelve. His only concern was at not being able 'to get on with it'. Whenever the weather was wet, he'd complain that he couldn't 'get on with it'. While others were just getting up of a morning, Old Dent was already 'getting on with it', and when everyone else had finished for the day, he was still 'at it'. Once he injured his hand while making hay, yet he 'kept at it' all day, though afterwards he had to take things easy for a while under the doctor's orders. He nearly broke his heart at not being able 'to get on with it'.

He was incapable of buying and selling. He was never seen at fair or market. His father was the one for that. But if Old Dent did happen to go to a fair, his father would call it 'a waste of time', and besides, there was always plenty of work to keep Old Dent at home, 'getting on with it'.

He went to chapel on Sundays, but between services he would be 'getting on with it' all the same. He would also attend on week-nights, always in a mad rush and unable to finish his work and set off in time. And he was to be seen hurrying along the road, making for the chapel, to listen to his father and others talking about the next world and the evils of this one. How much satisfaction or benefit he drew from it all is not known, but Old Dent was never heard to breathe a word about any world other than this, and how he had 'to press on' in it.

His parents died and his sister married. The greater part of the property which Old Dent had accumulated by dint of his 'getting on with it', went on the upkeep of the sister and her family. As for Old Dent, he was obliged to go out to work for a wage. It was a small wage, too, about ten shillings a week and his food. Yet this was the first wage that Old Dent had ever earned — no, the first he had ever been paid. Why didn't he become a farmer himself? the neighbours used to ask among themselves. How could he? He knew nothing about buying and selling. 'Getting on with it' was his only function in life, and the fruits of his labour went on keeping others.

Old Dent made no complaint, as far as is known. He became 'a common farm-hand', as the saying goes, 'getting on with it' year in year out, for ten shillings a week and his keep. For all anyone knew, 'getting on with it' gave him as much pleasure as before. And his new master wasn't a whit kinder to him than his old master, his father. What on earth was Old Dent good for except 'getting on with it', and what did it matter for whom he worked?

I lost touch with him because I in my turn had to start 'getting on with it' in my own way. Years went by. One day, I happened to be in the district. They were burying Old Dent that very day. I was given the rest of the story, and took off my hat — a soft hat with a dent in it — as I stood at his grave, poor old man.

His brother-in-law had died, leaving a widow and three or four children with no provision made for them. And Old Dent had kept them for as long as he was able, by 'getting on with it' to his dying day.

Innocent, honest, hard-working, generous, inarticulate. That was his life. A sacrifice to narrow, merciless notions about this world and the next. Yet I don't suppose it ever occurred to him that there was anything wrong with them. And sadder still, nor did it occur to his father. Nor to his class. Nor to anyone.

Cymeriadau (Hughes a'i Fab, 1933)

On Collecting Roads

R. T. Jenkins

I had bought a new toy, for three shillings; that's how it began. The other day a friend of mine took me in his motor-car to Shrewsbury. It's a journey that I very often go on, and now I'm so familiar with it that I'm able to make fairly firm arrangements. The length of the journey is four pipefuls: light up at the outset, light up again in Betws-y-coed, light up a third time at Corwen, and for the last time on coming into Gobowen. But there's a difference between one friend and another, and one of them is such a lightning driver that the aforementioned timetable is often upset. Mind you, he's a capable and perfectly careful driver — he always slows down to forty miles an hour when he sees the 30 sign. But in his car I'm in Bethesda before filling my pipe, in Capel Curig before lighting it up, and somewhere around Corwen before finishing it. And so with him, it's a two-pipe journey, filling up again at Chirk. It was this friend who was at the steering-wheel on the day in question.

Well, having got the pipe to draw quite well, near Betws-y-coed, I began looking about me. In the glove compartment, as I tried to stuff my tobacco-pouch and matches into the usual muddle of spectacles, an old glove, a tangle of fishing-line, the A.A. Handbook, and half-a-dozen maps, I saw a brandnew book, its paper wrapping still keeping its dust-jacket clean. I pulled it out — *Road Atlas, 3 miles to 1 inch*. I opened it and my shout of joy very nearly frightened my friend into turning off up the road to Trefriw. 'Here it is — the very thing I've been wanting for years!' Maps on a scale big enough to show the smallest roads; but maps that were almost colourless; apart from an innocuous grey denoting the uplands, there was only the red of first-class roads. It's true the lettering was painfully small, but I didn't want to read the maps, I wanted to mark them — to note the roads that I had walked or had been transported along. The ordinary maps don't allow for this; they are too gaudy, all red and green and blue and yellow — it would be impossible to make ink that could permeate such a rainbow. But now, here was an opportunity for the sweet (and if you like, childish) pleasure of making a record of all the curving bends of my career. That afternoon I scoured Shrewsbury for a copy of that book, but in vain. I had to return to Bangor and order it specially, but *it came*. And with it I bought a bottle of blue ink (royal blue, it said on the label) that pierced even the red of First Class Roads. From now on I shall be filling in my idle half-hours happily in blue. Already I've finished doing Wales and only England remains to be done.

I shall, nevertheless, hardly have as much to do on England as I had on Wales. Only around Oxford shall I have to be really meticulous: a long and splendid series of Summer Schools has given me experience of almost every road round and about that city; yes, even many a country road and one or two grassy lanes. Come to mention it, I can't help smiling when I call to mind that evening an old friend took me for a ride out through Abingdon and Steventon. I believe his intention was to turn right after reaching the Portway, and go through the two Hendreds to Wantage. But somehow or other he crossed the Portway without realizing it, and went straight on for quite a way; and only then did he take the first turning on the right. The road was somewhat rustic, but reasonable enough, for a mile or two; but then we found ourselves on open ground, and the road turned into a dead-straight strip across the surface of green pastureland. It didn't occur to either of us that we had in fact stumbled upon one of Britain's oldest roads, the Ridgeway, a branch of the prehistoric Icknield Way, which connected the eastern coast with the western in the dawn of Man's life on our island. It wasn't, however, by an Appeal to History[1] that my friend's problem could be answered — back, or forwards? He gritted his teeth, and persevered, advancing over the sward slowly, as if at a funeral, while all the time I kept getting out to open gates. From time to time, the driver could be heard to let fly a prayerful oath whenever some sudden jolt threatened his back-axle; or else I heard him, like a rider with his favourite horse, coaxing his motor in a low, tender voice: '*Come* on, little Cowley, come *on*!' Eventually, we hit the main road over the Downs, from Hungerford to Wantage, and downhill we came all three, the Cowley, its owner, and me, very gratefully into Wantage and Oxford.

That wasn't the first time I had been on that main road — I have two ministers of the Gospel as witnesses that I once *walked* with them from Wantage to Hungerford and beyond. Indeed, a sort of triangle — with its corners roughly near Oxford and Worcester and Weymouth — is the only part of England inside which I shall probably have to colour all the red roads blue. Outside that triangle, some poor researcher will one day see only a few stray blue lines on an empty background, as he turns over the pages of the atlas. Some of my readers will know only too well how much appeal *roads* have for my imagination; and with the low-cost assistance of the motor-bus I've been fortunate enough to go up and down most of the great historic roads of England — the whole length of some of them: the Holyhead, of course, old and new, the Dover, the Portsmouth, the Bath, the Milford Haven, the Worcester; others only in part, such as that section of the Great North Road which runs between Newark and London, and the Exeter road as far as Salisbury. It's not thus, to be sure, one comes to *know* the places situated on these famous routes. Yet there's a certain charm in the quick, tantalizing glimpses one gets say at Stamford or Cirencester or Sherborne, and in the sudden panoramas looking out from Hindhead or Birdlip or Shaftesbury, which open out under your feet, as it were. And there is an even greater charm for me in the awareness of the main road itself, running over hill and dale, on and on, like Fate, to its inevitable conclusion. I am not being fanciful when I say that more than once, at some quiet, lonely spot in Wales, I have had a thrill come over me while looking at a milestone and seeing there a rubric such as LONDON 200 MILES.

But let's get back to Wales, since I have used most of the bottle of blue ink on her. I should like to be able to claim that there are certain roads that I have *walked*, but alas, it's not true. It's sad to realize, as I look at the maps, that my walking days are over. I am overwhelmed with longing whenever I see the long lines, like the spokes of a wheel, shooting out from Brecon[2] in every direction — all of them blue, because at that stage of my life I took great delight in the strength of my legs and walked everywhere. That, I admit, was no virtue; I didn't know then as much as I do now about the places through which I strode; I wasn't aware of their historic secrets in the way that a lifetime's experience has brought them within my grasp. Probably, moreover, in the relief of my feet's rhythm, my eyes were as good as closed for miles at a time, and my mind busy with other things that were far enough removed from Wales. I was a fast walker, and even today I am incapable of dawdling, either striding along or else standing still. The vigour and restlessness of youth demanded their expression. Yet it has been sweet, with the pen in my hand, to recall those far-distant Saturdays, and the long tramps — from Brecon to Builth (on the bottom road *and* the top), from Brecon to the Hay, from Brecon over the Beacons to Merthyr Tydfil, from Brecon to Llandovery, and from Brecon over to Abergavenny. The *main road* each time, mark you; this wasn't merely wandering about according to whim, and the road, I'm afraid, was only a strip of track on which to *walk*, like a railway for a locomotive. Well, this walking has been over and done with for many a year now. Cardiff didn't give it much of a chance — on the one hand, there was school on Saturday mornings, and on the other, the tedium of having to put miles of bricks-and-mortar behind me before starting out on the journey proper. By the time I came to Bangor, the old tramp in me had died. The other day, while colouring in blue the road from Bangor to Betws-y-coed, on the basis of my motoring experience of it, I suddenly remembered that I had once *walked* every step of it. But I also realized, with an awkward smile, that that had been in my Brecon days.

About three times in my life, and this was more than a half-century ago, I have had just a little experience of travelling in that splendid old manner, by horse. I shall always believe this to be the finest mode of transport; faster and less encumbered than walking, but slow enough to get to know the country with that intimacy found, for instance, in the writings of Wesley or Pennant or Cobbett. Just a little experience, I said, for I wasn't on the horse's back but sitting behind it. I had an uncle who was a draper — not just an uncle but a great friend, in so far as the difference in our age allowed; a man whose health was poor and who died, alas, in his prime. His doctor had given him sound advice, to buy a pony and trap and take up peripatetic tailoring; to go about the countryside in summer-time measuring customers and taking orders, and sending them to Manchester or some such place; in this way he would enjoy the fresh air without losing any money. It had been my privilege to accompany him. I don't know to this day on what principle he planned the trips, that is to say, how he knew in advance that there was a customer in, say, Aberaeron or Porthmadog; but anyway, the itinerary was always beautifully zig-zag, and I never knew (even if he did) where we should be going next. I had a map that was four inches to the mile, and I fed my youthful imagination to the full — not without disappointment here and there when my uncle quite definitely refused to go somewhere which had taken my fancy. One of the most curious effects the map had on me was to raise 'far-reaching desires' to see places shown in bold type; big, exceedingly important places, or so I thought. *After* seeing them, I realized sadly that they weren't any bigger than Bala. yet even today I haven't really rid myself of the idea that places like LLANFYLLIN are centres of 'the great life of the world'.

I remember one of these perambulations in particular. We had gone up over Bwlch-y-groes to Llanymawddwy and Dinas and Machynlleth, and then on to Aberystwyth and Aberaeron. I have been in Aberaeron several times since then but this was the only occasion I was to cross the harbour in that packet which used to ply from one side to the other. Then, up the lovely vale of Aeron to Tal-y-sarn, I suppose, and to Llangeitho[3], on a Saturday afternoon. I spent there one of the most miserable Sundays of my life. My uncle was delighted to be there, in the second most important Caersalem of Welsh Methodism, the *second*, of course, because he was a Bala[4] man. I didn't know, on the other hand, that in years far distant I should be meddling in the history of Methodism, and I wasn't at all interested in the place. We were given lodgings at chapel house, together with the preacher for the following day, a grandiloquent, affected, unsociable old fellow, and an exceptionally dry-as-dust preacher. Between the means of grace he read Charles's Dictionary earnestly to himself, with only an occasional 'really?' or 'well, well!' for my uncle whenever he tried to break the ice. Go out for a stroll? — no, please remember that we were in Llangeitho, and that 'the Sabbath in Wales' was in full force at that time; you might as well have been foolhardy enough to light a cigarette at a prayer-meeting. I was to hate the place for years thereafter. But my uncle was highly content, especially when asked to start the evening service. Today I can recognize and appreciate the gentlemanly qualities of Llangeitho's saints in inviting a complete stranger, who was neither preacher nor deacon, to lead the service — the kindness which led them to comprehend (without so much as a hint from my uncle) that it would be a golden memory he would cherish for the rest of his life — the courtesy that was content, since they were all in their Sunday black, to see of a Sunday morning a stranger in a Norfolk jacket and knee-breeches ascending to that historic and sacred pulpit. Yes, there was something fine in our forefathers, laugh about their foibles as much as we will. How difficult it is for young and old to understand one another! And shouldn't I myself show some patience in trying to explain the last century and its ideals to those young people in my classes, when I recall how stupid I was at their age?

Monday morning came, and I was quite late getting up. But for some reason or other (business, perhaps) we had to wait there until after lunch. After a visit to the church, I insisted on cutting the traces and going for a walk on my own, and on that warm morning (when everyone else was in the hay), I went to the church of Llanbadarn Odwyn, which stands on a steep hillock about a mile from Llangeitho. Everything in the church was wonderfully untidy. Near the door there was a chest, with no lock to it; inside, all jumbled up, there were old books, and a bundle of old surplices, and a Communion plate, and a cup with the words *Poculum Eclesie de Llanbadarn Odwyn 1574* inscribed on it, in desperate need of polish — I wonder why more respect and concern can't be shown? Forty years, I'm sure, have wrought a big difference at Llanbadarn Odwyn, as in every other Llan, in this particular respect. And it was the same in Llanddewibrefi[5], that place of great renown, which we visited as part of our itinerary. I recall how the extent and architecture of the church caught my imagination — but I also remember the hundreds of dead bees that covered the crucifix, testimony to neglect by sexton and vicar. Alas, reform 'does not come alone'; when I visited Llanddewibrefi a little while ago, the 'house's zeal' had gone so far as to put a lock on the door, lest wayfarers call there to spoil things! It's a pity so many of our churches, and chapels too, are locked; only a few of our chapels have escaped the whims of 'restoration', and are therefore worth bothering to go inside for the person who is just passing through — Maesyronnen[6] or Heol Awst, Capel Cildwrn or Salem in Cefncymerau, to mention but a few of them. Not often, on the other hand, do you get an old church without *something* to see inside.

I'm not absolutely sure now how I escaped from Llangeitho — I *know* we saw Lampeter College that summer, and I *know* that we somehow found ourselves in Ffair-rhos — come to think of it, I am inclined to believe it was *before* going to Llangeitho that we saw Lampeter and Llanddewibrefi. However, it was Ffair-rhos for us — Ysbyty Ystwyth and Cwm Ystwyth, and so along the old mountain-road to Rhaeadr — I remember they were working on the Cwm Elan reservoir at the time. A miserable, rainy, misty day; a poor, narrow road, dangerous for a small pony. Llanidloes next; its townspeople will be glad to hear it made a pleasant impression on me — probably because its Severnside comforts were more to my taste than the austerity of Elenid from which we had come. From then on we tasted the sweetness of Montgomeryshire at every turn. The factory where my uncle used to buy his flannels was in Newtown, and we had to make an unfragrant pilgrimage through that place. I then had a chance to climb to the top of Montgomery castle, and see Welshpool, too, before going on to spend the second Sunday — a sunny, summery Sunday — in Llanfair Caereinion, without going to chapel more than once! From there we went through Meifod and Llanfyllin, and then home across the Berwyn.

How, I wonder, did my uncle, who was such a staunch Methodist, not remember Ann Griffiths[7] when we came to the signpost for Pontrobert just before reaching Meifod? Perhaps he *did* remember, but had hardened his heart thinking it was high time for him to turn homewards after three weeks teaching me geography. Or perhaps it was concern for the pony. For ever since that trip I have understood full well what lies behind the frequent references in tour-books of the eighteenth century — numerous, yet cold and impersonal — to 'the horse'. That pony was an infuriating creature. Not that he kicked or bit. But for one thing, when he halted, he *halted*, and it was hard work getting him to start again. When we came in sight of a gate across the road, I was obliged (in my capacity as footman) to leap down from the trap before we came anywhere near the gate, run as fast as my legs would carry me to open it, close it behind me, run after the trap, and set my foot once again on its step, all this without slowing down the pony's progress — if I had not done so, we should have been there for ages. Another thing, it was a very puny creature. Perhaps some of you, in your motorized innocence, think of a horse as a strong, muscular beast; bless your hearts — its health is as delicate as the high-born young ladies' in Victorian novels. This one was extremely fussy about its food, and caused its owner daily anxiety. You will know of the unsleeping suspicion that lurks in the hearts of motorists towards garage-hands; well, convert that into horsy terms and then you will understand precisely how things were between my uncle and our country's ostlers. I don't want to insinuate that there aren't sufficient godly men to be found in stable and garage alike; but to be sure, it never dawned on my uncle that an ostler could be a saint. He stood by the manger for a long while to make sure that the feed was all right; one might almost think that it was the habit of ostlers to pick grains of oat *out of* the mix, once the customer had turned his back. And yet, despite this compulsion, the pony's health was very shaky. Some days it snuffled and sneezed, on others it was suffering from internal complaints, and I have a faint recollection that my uncle had to spend the better part of one whole night in nursing it — at Pen-y-bont-fawr, if I remember aright. So it wasn't surprising that we found it sweet to turn homewards; and that the pony felt the same way, too, for after we had half-dragged it to the top of the Berwyn, it miraculously came back to life, and from Melin y Clettwr to Bala it galloped like a horse in a fire-brigade.

Nevertheless, very little of the blue ink would be needed to record my movements on foot or by trap. It is the motor-car has made work for me. I am a member of a great number of Committees, which meet in many different places. And many of my fellow-committeemen have motor-vehicles. I don't know whether generosity is a characteristic of motorists as such; but certainly the ones I know are generous in the extreme, and kind — teachers and headmasters, lecturers and professors, School Inspectors, Druids and members of the Gorsedd, as well as ministers of the Gospel. So much so that I'm in danger by now of forgetting where I have been, and who took me there. The colouring of this Atlas in blue will be, I hope, an aid to my powers of memory and to my sense of obligation.

But, says someone, why were you so foolish as to go rushing around the country like this? And why insist on playing about with a bottle of ink, just like a child, when you surely have better things to do at your age? Well, I could, if I wished, put my hand on my heart and testify in all seriousness that a man cannot profess the History of Wales without at least trying to get to *know* his Wales, as thoroughly as that is possible. But I shall climb down from this sublime platform to meet my opponent on his own low terms. What's wrong, my friend, with this blue manifestation of my innocent achievements? Did I not observe in your house, the other day, your golf trophies, your eisteddfodic chairs — yes, the head or plumage of some innocent creature which you had shot (so you said), or the oar which helped your College boat to win the race? So why can't I, too, show off a little?

I confess that making records of things entices a man to go on to something else, namely *collecting* records, and I have been guilty of that, too. If I am ever in a position to pass up or down a section of road that I have never before been on, I tend to jump on a bus going in that direction. When I went with others to proclaim the Eisteddfod[8] at Mountain Ash, rather too confidently I noticed a bus going from Aberdare over to the Rhondda Valley. The temptation was too much for me: off I went through Maerdy and Blaenllechau and Pontygwaith to Ystradyfodwg[9], and then back again. I didn't regret it (despite the derisive laughter among my stalwart friends in Aberdare), because the extensive view from the tops above Cwmdar and Cwmaman, and from Penrhys across the Rhondda, is truly rewarding. But I'll give you another example, that does me a lot less credit. If you go from Llangollen to Chirk, you will have to pass an old junction with the road from Wrexham. But if you set out direct from Llangollen to Wrexham, you will take another road, through Rhiwabon. The segment of untrodden road, between the turning and Rhiwabon, was for years a thorn in my side. But one day I was coming home from Shrewsbury with a family who are close friends of mine, but so much younger that I knew (cowardly and sly as I am) that they wouldn't like to refuse an old man a favour. On reaching the junction I smothered my conscience: 'Come on, my children, let's go through Rhiwabon, please!' Without so much as a murmur, the vehicle was turned around. But I couldn't help blushing and feeling just a little ashamed and repentant as we came into Rhiwabon at seeing the lady (for it was she who was at the wheel) struggling to take the nasty corners near the station. I learned a lesson, and I shan't be so impudent again. That's what collecting *for the sake of collecting* does to you. Yet, at its very worst, dear reader, is not my collecting habit just as respectable as your hobby? If you can collect First Editions (completely worthless things, if I may say so), or else old jugs, why can't I collect roads?

Y Llenor (19, 1940),
Casglu Ffyrdd (Hughes a'i Fab, 1956)

'Their Land they shall Lose'[1]

Iorwerth C. Peate

The last week of June 1940 was a sad one for me, a week of seeing a part of the Welshness of Wales being torn up by its roots and the destruction of a gentle society deep in the heart of the countryside. I am speaking of Epynt and Mynydd Bwlch-y-groes, a district now lost to Wales, at least for the time being. It runs from the vicinity of Llywel and Pont Senni in the south to beyond Pentre Dolau Honddu and the southern side of Llangamarch in the north.

Epynt and Mynydd Bwlch-y-groes are uplands of special significance. They are mostly Old Red Sandstone — or rather wholly so, except for the northern and western slopes. This rich, red soil extends from the south-east to the highest ridge of the uplands. One of the consequences of this geological pattern is the exceptional fertility of the land. Although the uplands reach a height of 1,500 feet, they are worked in places right to their tops. And because of the nature of the soil, and its fertility, whoever goes up to the far ends of the valleys has the feeling that he is on the rich lands of Herefordshire. I was there in June, the sun hot and the breeze gentle: the first time the hawthorn cast a white mantle over everything, the second time the elder-flower did the same. Not until I had crossed over to Tir Abad and Cefn-brith and left the Old Red Sandstone did I feel myself to be on upland as I knew it, and there the whinberries were purple and the lapwing loud.

Apart from the many valleys — Nant Gwydderig, Nant Fawen, Cilieni, Nant Bran, Yscir Fawr and Yscir Fechan, Honddu, Craig Ddu, Dyfnant, Dulas, and Y Glyn, with their farms and cultivated land clustering at their heads — the uplands are used for grazing, supporting tens of thousands of sheep and several thousand ponies, that splendid breed known as the Epynt. Now most of the sheeps' grazing has disappeared, or many square miles of it, and in the same way the market for ponies has been badly affected.

I had come to Epynt in order to visit all the houses that had been vacated, to measure and photograph them, wherever that was necessary. In this way a record could be made of one particular aspect of the culture that had once existed on Epynt, although the military had knocked down the walls and made the district uninhabitable. It was a sad task: my final visit was in the last week of June, and since the firing was to begin in the first week of July, everyone was expected to be gone by the Saturday night. Most had remained in their old homes until the last possible day, and I had arrived in the middle of the evacuation. I nevertheless went up one valley and found house after house all locked up, the windows bare and the panes staring blindly at me, a frightened cat that had been left behind fleeing through a gap in the barn-door, the occasional calf or heifer, which they would have to come back to collect, running trustingly towards me, glad to see a live being in this deathly, incomprehensible silence. I could only think of John Steinbeck's marvellous novel, *The Grapes of Wrath*, where there's a description of another emigration that in its essentials was not unlike this one. I met the Hirllwyn family with their load of furniture coming on a cart through the mountain-gate. At Waun Lwyd the lorry was at the back of the house, busily loading up. I went around the side to the front of the house. There I found an old woman of eighty-two. I shall never forget the scene: she had set an old chair at the far end of the yard and was sitting there like a graven image, staring intently at the upland with tears streaming down her cheeks. She had been born there, and her father and grandfather before her. She was leaving today and now she was spending her last few moments to take it all in, with one rich gaze at the ancient mountain, or perhaps recalling all the days of her life in the old smallholding. I don't know which; but there she was, and I could see only her grief and foreboding. I felt as if I had stumbled upon a sacrament and I tried to get away quietly. But she saw me.

Without moving a hand or her head or an eye, she shouted at me: 'Where have you come from?' 'From Cardiff,' I replied. When she saw I was a Welshman — or at least, that's how it seemed to me — the surliness disappeared, and the tears multiplied. 'My dear boy,' she said, 'go back there as quickly as you can. The world has come to an end here.' And although I knew that German bombs were falling on Glamorgan at the time, I also knew that she was right: it *was* the end of her world.

One day in the Cilieni valley I called at the door of a farmhouse to ask permission to take a picture. The woman of the house came to the door, a woman of about thirty. I told her in Welsh what I was about. She hesitated for a moment, then said with a smile, 'Of course you may.' Then she went on, 'I thought at first you were one of those devils from London, and I would have set the dogs on you if I hadn't remembered that none of those buggers would ever speak Welsh.' Rough language, but not rough enough to express the bitterness of her feelings. As I was about to leave she asked for my advice, wanting my opinion about what she could take with her from the house. 'I was born and bred here,' she said, 'and my father before me. Do you think I could take the front door with me, to remember the old place by?' Sentiment, call it what you will, but it was 'the end of the world' for her too. And an end to a Welsh-speaking community. For although I had travelled about four hundred miles back and forth, up and down and all around that district, I had scarcely heard any English. I had come across only one or two people who didn't understand Welsh, but several who knew next to no English. By dispersing the people of Epynt, one of the last sizeable strongholds of Welsh-speaking culture in Breconshire — the culture of John Penry[2] — had been shattered. And although it may be possible to repopulate the area when men return to their senses from the present madness, it's not the people of Epynt who will be there, with the indigenous language on their lips, but rather people 'from away'. And it will take centuries for them to put down roots in the soil like the rooted community that was murdered there in 1940. It can only be hoped — and ought to be ensured — that Welsh will be their language, too.

Nowadays a man can draw some comfort from the fact that at least buildings of any architectural significance are not usually destroyed. But there's no comfort in knowing how a culture and community can be torn apart, and these are much more important than houses. The Welsh language and its culture, as we all know, are on trial today. When the Government grabs a piece of land in England and turns its farmers out of their homes, at least those unfortunates have a whole country in which to find new homes where the English language is spoken and where there is still an English-speaking community. The taking over of forty thousand acres in England is a misfortune, to be sure, but it's not a disaster because it doesn't endanger England's language and culture in any way.

But in Wales it's an unmitigated disaster. For under the present system of education and the present economic regime not only is the survival of the Welsh language and culture uncertain, they are staring defeat in the face. So in uprooting sixty Welsh-speaking families from their native ground at one stroke, a part of Wales has been killed off, and as things stand at present, it cannot be recreated. It would be different if we had a system under which Welsh was accorded dignity and honour and respect as the country's first language: to have lost Epynt would then be a misfortune and the unfortunate people could move to some other part of our country in the certainty that they would find a home there. But as things are, it's a disaster — in Anglesey, in Meirionydd, in Ceredigion, in Pembrokeshire, and in Breconshire: in every one of these areas a mortal blow has been delivered to an extensive part of the Welshness of Wales. In the Vale of Glamorgan our social system had already brought about the metamorphosis, and the aeroplanes arrived in a district which had already lost its Welsh. The same process will soon be happening in the Welsh-speaking districts, and because of this disaster I thought it worth putting on record the sad experience of a Welshman who visited the country of John Penry and William Williams[3] during the last remaining days before a hell was let loose there that time can never cure.

Y Llenor (20, 1941),
Ymhob Pen (Gwasg Aberystwyth, 1948)

The Red Flag

D. Gwenallt Jones

The chapel I attended was in an industrial village. I used to go every Sunday to the morning service; in the afternoon, to the Sunday School[1]; to the five o'clock service at which the young people were taught how to pray in public; to the evening service; to singing practice; once a week to the prayer meeting and the Fellowship; the dawn-service on Christmas morning; a whole week of prayer meetings in the first week of January; I sat examinations in Scriptural knowledge; and in summer went on Sunday School trips to the seaside.

I would take my father his mid-day snap in the steelworks. I remember the greyish-yellow gleam that lit up the interior of the works, and the hot air that surged in waves up my nostrils to make me breathless and parch my throat. I was allowed to go up on to the platform by the furnace where the men in their vests, their cheeks reddened by the glow and their eyes protected with blue goggles, were throwing scrap into the furnace's maw with long shovels. One of them used to put the goggles over my eyes, and through them I could see the metal boiling in white heat on the floor of the furnace. I would watch the tapping process, the molten metal being poured into the ladle in the pit, and from there into moulds; and after it had solidified, the crane would lift it in the form of steel ingots which were then piled at the side of the tramway. I was frightened whenever I saw the crane swinging the ingots from a hook high over the heads of the workmen in the pit below.

There was a strike in 1910. We would go with our fathers to scour old disused levels for coal, and dig the tips for lumps that we used to carry home in sack and wheelbarrow. Every Saturday we went to the tinplate works to gather coke, and underneath it in the bottom of the sack, quite illegally, we would hide grease for lighting the fire. We saw policemen guarding the coal-pit and protecting the blacklegs as they went in and out, and patrolling the streets to prevent workers from assembling. For us youngsters the strike was great fun, but it left its mark on our minds and memory, and in the years that were to follow it made us search for an explanation of why we were rebelling.

Keir Hardie[2] provided the explanation in his speeches and in his Socialist newspaper, *The Labour Leader*. The economic system was a capitalist system, and it was based on competition; its purpose was to amass wealth for a few and keep the workers as slaves, and under it unemployment and war were inevitable. The Christian churches accepted it all meekly, and even justified it. We were shocked and disappointed. The capitalists were like Scribes, and the chapel-goers were the Pharisees, but Christ's sympathy, we believed, was with the common people in their sweat and toil, their poverty and distress. His Gospel was the Gospel of Love. The true Christians were to be found outside the Church, in the Labour Party, and in the movements working for social reform. I saw the difference between my father as worker and as a man praying on his knees, the wide gulf between chapel and steelworks.

The literature we enjoyed reading in those days was Russian literature — the works of Tolstoy and Dostoevsky. Tolstoy had attacked the theology and dogma of the Church in Russia, particularly its other-worldliness, and had built on the foundations of the Sermon on the Mount a social gospel and political philosophy that might be called Christian anarchism. From him we learned our pacifism. In Dostoevsky's novels we recognized the same kind of problems as were to be found in South Wales: the clash between political oppression and Christianity, between freedom and justice, between nihilistic and atheistic tendencies and Man's cruel thirst for eternity, between the capitalist system and Messianic rebellion. His novel *The Brothers Karamazov* made a deep impression on our spirits, especially the soldier's poem about the Grand Inquisitor. Our sympathies were with both Christ and the Grand Inquisitor. Why wasn't it possible to have the bread of heaven *and* bread on earth? It was the pseudo-Christian churches that were the stumbling-block and the boulder barring the way. They spoke of 'the freedom of God's children' — and they let the children starve.

We read in Russian novels about atheism and atheists, and we also endeavoured to read the books of unbelievers and agnostics, writers such as Ingersoll, Bradlaugh, McCabe, Tom Paine, Blatchford, and others; and we read *The Free Thinker*. They all attacked the Book of Genesis, the creation of the world out of the void, a serpent talking, Man's damnation depending on a bite from an apple, the making of a woman out of a spare rib, and they wondered who Cain's wife might have been. If Moses was author of the Five Books, how was he able to describe his own death and claim that none but God knew his grave? If the Bible had been written out of divine inspiration, how were there contained in it such immoral stories as the one about Noah drunk and naked, or the one about David coveting another man's wife, or the other about all the concubines of Solomon? It is not the Church that is described in the Song of Solomon but one of the sage's paramours. How could a man like Christ be born of a woman who had not known a man? The whole thing was so unreasonable, as were the miracles. Historians of the time make no mention of Christ whatsoever. He was a figment of the disciples' imagination. A man's religion is formed by the land of his birth. Anyone born in Turkey is a Muhammadan, in India a Muslim or Hindu. In parts of India one of the gods they worship has three heads, while Christians worship the Three Heads that are in the one God. From our reading of such authors as Frazer and Grant Allen we learned that pagans had rituals in their religions that resembled baptism and the Last Supper. There was no historical basis for the Bible. It was mythology. No, the Grand Inquisitor was right, not the Count, because he too was a myth. There was no such thing as sin, only hunger.

When Communist ideas began to come into the Labour Party, Keir Hardie didn't agree with them, because for him Socialism meant a conflict of interests, not the class struggle, and he believed it was by constitutional means, through Parliament, that a Socialist State could be established, and not by bloody revolution. The Communists started an evening class in our village, not far from the chapel, under a teacher who had been a student at the Central Labour College, a Marxist institution. I could see that the Communists had the most accurate interpretation of history — the clash between economic interests was the only true history, and it was they who had the logical analysis of the capitalist system, namely the struggle between two classes, and they who had the clearest, most effective medicine; and they were atheists. From Lenin we took our critique of Tolstoy's ideas. Tolstoy was a count trying to be a peasant, and his point of view belonged to the rural, old-fashioned villages, completely different from that of the industrial proletariat. His Christian pacifism had grown out of the anti-Marxist earth. Under the capitalist system not only was war capitalist, but peace, too. It wasn't pacifism that could transform society, nor the Sermon on the Mount either, but dialectical materialism. We responded readily to every influence and theory that came our way, because our sentiments and passion ran much deeper than our reason and understanding. For us the bloody revolution of the Communists was unacceptable, and yet we asked ourselves whether society could be transformed by pacifism.

Preachers eloquent in their pulpits, and middle-class intellectuals, used to attack Communism on account of its atheism and materialism. But what if they had been obliged to work at the furnace or in the rolling-mills, or squat as colliers did in the soaking-wet darkness of the coal-face? We hated the sight of all clerics, whether priest or minister, and complained to our fathers for contributing to the upkeep of these 'parasites' out of their scant wages. 'Christ,' said Robert Smillie of clergymen, 'Christ rode into Jerusalem on a donkey's back, but ever since then the donkeys have been riding on Christ's back.' Marxism for us was a gospel far superior to Methodism. It *was* a gospel; and we were prepared to live by it, to sacrifice for it, yes, and die for it; but we wouldn't have raised a little finger on behalf of Calvinism. Capitalism was for us something in our own lives. We had seen with our own eyes the poverty, the hunger and near-hunger, the filth of hovels, mothers growing old before their time, the cruelty of soldiers and policemen during strikes, doctors putting 'tuberculosis' on the death certificate rather than 'silicosis' so that compensation wouldn't have to be paid to the dead man's family, and the corpses being brought home after accidents. My own father's body came home years afterwards: he had been burned to death by the molten metal, and there was no proper explanation. At his funeral, during the sermon when the minister said it was the will of God, I silently poured out all the hauliers' curses on his sermon and his God, and when they sang the hymn 'Bydd myrdd o ryfeddodau'[3] at the graveside, I sang 'The Red Flag' in my heart. If I could have lifted the coffin from out of the grave, I would have used it to smash the blasphemous capitalist system that set more store on production than on life, on profit than on a man. How could mercy be shown to capitalists, how could they be forgiven? There wasn't any mercy in their bowels for the workers. Mercy, forgiveness, pity — these were women's virtues, anyway. Nothing could change the system except the glorious flesh and blood of the proletariat. I remember, in a London prison one night, hearing the cells shake with the triumph of 'The Red Flag' and 'The Internationale', for news had just reached us of the revolution in Russia: Russia, the land of Tolstoy, Dostoevsky, Lenin.

Credaf (gol. J.E. Meredith, Gwasg Aberystwyth, 1943)

Strolling Players

Ffransis G. Payne

We were talking about the theatre. 'When I was a lad,' said the old man, 'I saw a performance given in a tent by a company of strolling players. I have never seen better acting since. Those people could break your heart with just one little gesture . . .' I ventured to agree with him — too heartily, perhaps. For he was very annoyed: 'Agree, indeed! What do you know about them? Such people had disappeared long before you were born.' But my friend was mistaken. Yes, I too had seen the strolling players, and I too had felt a pang in the heart.

I should never have done so had not ours been a small country town. You know the kind of place: like Brecon or Builth or Kington. Quiet little places, aren't they? Yet life there is varied and complex. It would be easier to sum up life in London, England, than in Llundain Fach[1] in the vale of Aeron. For in a town like ours you live on a boundary, indeed, on many boundaries. Not only between small town and countryside, but on the boundary between small town and town, and between town and city, too. For in a small country town there are elements of all these. Some are ageless, like the apple-trees in your garden, or the west wind bringing the scent of bracken into the narrow streets. Others are more recent intrusions, like the branch railway from towns to the east, while others such as the Civic Spirit are spiritual vanities from much further afield.

Many people will turn their backs on such a place as soon as they are able, making for the environment they have already tasted from whatever has penetrated the town or lingers there. Isn't it a splendid place that can suggest to its inhabitants the rich variety of other worlds and lives? And to the small town is granted one of the rarest things: time does not hurry *there*. Some strange power of extension is to be found here, which causes the course of time to overlap before your very eyes. Here remain the old customs of a previous age that have come down from the city and through the town, and so to the small town. The ways of the modern world come too. Though they come late, come they will in turn like the fine clothes of the proud man to his kinsman of lowlier estate. The years dawdle in the small town, for although the Civic Spirit holds the front-door ajar, all the stubborn sullenness of the old country life presses against the back-door.

Sooner or later there would come to our town what neither city nor large town wanted any more. Especially people. Things, on the other hand, were not so easily cast off. The city is fond of old tables and old chairs and old books, perhaps because they help a man to ignore the brevity of life. But the city soon tires of old people and old amusements. We knew that well enough in our town. The eleven o'clock and the six o'clock train contributed gradually to the number of rejects in our midst. From time to time a company of players would come to perform in the public hall. They were always getting on in years, and their powers of improvisation nearly extinguished. The plays were old-fashioned and crude. They had all the appearance of people with some curse upon them, who had gathered outside a city that no longer wanted them, and who were bound together to decline on a meaner stage, where their feeble gifts might shine more brightly, while keeping up the appearance of talent and enjoyment of life. The companies would invariably announce that they intended staying 'for one week only'. But they all stayed for a month. Where else could they go? Beyond the town the countryside lay among its quiet hills, sullenly indulging its own native talents. It would take a month for them to hear of another place that was willing to take them, let alone scrape together enough to pay their debts before moving on.

Sometimes, too, there came individuals with the dust of the roads on their boots — Punch and Judy men, professors of magic and illusion, fire-eaters, one-man bands — all the old-fashioned, discarded playthings of the big cities. And one day a troupe of strolling players came, with a portable theatre made of wood and canvas.

These people were of a different quality from all the others. I don't know where they came from to our town. Not from a city and certainly not from a large town, for such places had not seen their like for a generation or more. Cities in those days were fewer in number and smaller. It was announced that they would be staying with us for a month, but it was generally known that they had provisions to last a twelvemonth. At first, there was a different play each night, 'preceded by a hilarious farce', as the publicity leaflets put it. Even after the month had stretched into several months there were never less than three different shows each week. It's true they put on some rubbish at first. Perhaps they were trying to compete with the company that played the public hall. But although they started with bombast and fustian, they came eventually to high spirits and heart break, taking the long road from East Lynne and

Uncle Tom's Cabin to the Forest of Arden and that fatal field by Dover.

It was a hard road for them. In time it became clear that our small town could not go on supporting a playhouse. The town's traditions were against it, too. We made our own entertainments, while at the same time grateful for occasional help from outside. And so the players began to decline, step by step, through the various grades of lodgings which the town provided: from the velvet parlours of respectable houses down to the bare severity of the establishment kept by Jones Clean Beds. This was a pilgrimage that was only too familiar to the new arrivals. The thin, city accent that boasted in the hearing of regulars at the Oxford Arms was eventually to be heard cadging a drink in the Bridge Tavern. Many an old pilgrim crawled in the direction of Jones's house! I can still see the pensive faces of some of them, ranged in my mind's eye like divines in a framed picture. But the players were a bunch on their own: it's easier to hear their voices and laughter than it is to see them.

I came to know some of them quite well. We used to keep a draper's shop, and this often proved convenient for the wardrobe-man from the playhouse. Fashions changed sooner or later, even in our town, and there would always be some old stock available for a church bazaar and other such occasions. To this material some of the productions owed some small part of their splendour. I have seen Lady Macbeth listening to the dread knocking at the castle's door while clad in something unsaleable from the shop. And I saw, more than once, gleaming beyond the footlights, a piece of white cardboard (usually from a blouse-box) that was meant to be the shirt-front of a gentleman in evening dress.

Before long some of the players found their way from the shop into our house, because my sister thought she might learn some fancy dance-steps from them. From that moment on the house became a theatre. There was high-stepping in the kitchen and, amidst the whirl of lead-weighted skirts, low curtseying in the parlour.

But they taught us more than dancing. They demonstrated for us an inexplicable courage and indomitable high spirits, though their stomachs were as empty as their pockets. Nothing seemed to come amiss with them, neither experience nor food. Well, that may be a bit of an exaggeration, for as their season in our town wore on, they grew poorer and poorer. Their playhouse became so tattered that nothing could be done for it. The canvas roof resembled a strainer for collecting rain and pouring it on to the few heads beneath. The tent stood in a field near an old barn in which, it was said, the child Sarah Siddons[2] had first gone on stage. The seating in the tent was made of planks that rose in steps towards the rear. The admission was twopence to the gallery, up the steps, and that was the most comfortable place of all. There you could put your feet between the people who sat on the lower bench in front of you. Your feet would be dry and your legs warm. Down in the sixpenny seats you would have been trampling the mud like swine. Some heat was given out by braziers placed here and there in the aisles between the benches. The invisible smoke from the burning coke nearly chokes me as I bring it to mind. Finally, the stage was lit by carbide gas.

It was not only the stage that was lit by the gas-machine. Light was cast on many a mishap and blunder by its erratic working. As the months went by it became the custom to find your way to your seat by the dim light of the braziers alone. When the time came for 'the hilarious farce' to begin, the director would come on stage with a lighted candle in his hand. 'Ladies and gentlemen,' he would say, 'I regret to inform you that a completely unforeseeable accident has befallen the lighting equipment. Nevertheless, our gifted engineer is busily at work, and I hope he will enlighten us soon. In the mean while, by your leave, I shall recite those immortal lines . . .' We didn't mind this addition to the programme in the least. We understood one another perfectly. The elocutionist knew that everyone was aware that 'the gifted engineer' had just collected enough money at the door to enable him to run down to Meredith's shop for carbide.

The players could not have put on any tragedy that would have made you feel sorrier than did their own woeful plight. How could I not help thinking, at a moment of high terror in the play, of where Lady Macbeth's costume had come from? There was something amiss in their attempts to convey fear and misery and terror. You felt they were acting. Perhaps they were too familiar with grief, and couldn't break through the perpetual forbearance that was their daily defence. It takes a very happy and contented man to portray all the agony of creatures such as Lear or Othello. Only such a man is able to immerse himself in all the horrors of the imagination. But there was no such man or woman or child in this company. They were Falstaff's children, every one. On stage or off they kept up a cheerful front, spinning yarns and pretending and scraping and starving — and laughing all the while.

Falstaff is among the greatest — and saddest — creations of the world's imagination. But in the flesh, the world doesn't want anything to do with him. For he is the enemy of the Civic Spirit. As I have suggested, that spirit would sometimes sweep through our town as abruptly as the wind from the east, rattling the inn-signs and stirring up litter from the gutter and driving it about the town. Poor players, ensnared at the bottom of the sieve on Jones's lousy mattresses. Their virtue was sapped and people had had enough of them. They were chucked out through the back-door like so many tea-leaves.

There was nothing left for them then but to traipse to a row of empty cottages on the outskirts of town known as the College. There could not have been a more appropriate place for them to huddle together. On one side there was a visible reminder of the fifteenth century where Hergest Court still stood, with its orchard all around. On the other was an Elizabethan building, the old grammar school. And as it happens, there had been a connection between the cottages and these two a long time ago. Thus the shadow of the dead ages to which the players' talents belonged fell across their last lodging. By some instinct, perhaps, they had done everything according to pattern.

Mr Jones's beds were not unoccupied for long. Two strangers came to their historic sheets one night, unnoticed. But their luggage attracted everyone's attention. Station waggons brought a number of long, coffin-shaped boxes up the street and placed them at the door of the Odd Fellows' Hall. At the time the Order was moribund among us. It used to flourish or decline with the fortunes of the foundry, the nail-factory and the tannery. Only a few members paraded to church now beneath their banners and pennants on festival days, and their hall was unused, except for the indigenous needs of our little town.

In each of these boxes there was a murderer, or rather the waxen image of one. Charles Peace, Steinie Morrison, Dr Crippen, William Corder, and all the rest — they were carried in cold procession up the steps and placed in a careful row against the back-wall. At the far end of the room a small stage was erected, like a doll's house, and in front of it were placed the chairs of the vanished Odd Fellows. Then a notice was nailed to the door: 'Waxworks and Puppets. Admission one penny, seats threepence.'

Puppets are in fashion again now, but in those days the word meant some old entertainment that your grandmother talked about. They were an amusement so old that they are were once again completely new, and they received a warm welcome from the townsfolk. As was usual, the two men who worked the puppets stayed well beyond their schedule. But it was the first time ever that anyone had prospered by doing so, exchanging the austerity of Jones's beds for the comfy parlour of a respectable landlady. Every evening as the players came into town, walking down to their damp theatre in the field, a long queue of people would be waiting at the door of the Odd Fellows' Hall. Ours was a rainy town. Let that be our excuse for having anything to do with Charles Peace and his accomplices in their warm room, and succumbing to the magic of 'the puppetry of idols' as denounced long ago by the Reverend Joseph Jenkins[3] of Wrexham.

That reverend gentleman has nothing to do with this story. More than a century and a half has gone by since he thundered against 'the enjoyment of sin, laughter at ungodliness' which he saw in these performances. Yet, from a long way off, I must endorse his famous sermon with a faint amen. For I, too, found something evil in the antics of the little wooden men, but something fiendish that the preacher didn't notice. It's possible that I saw some of the plays that had tempted his flock, since some of them are traditional, like the History of Faustus and the Adventures of Tim Bobbin, and the old, cruel, and violent tale on which Punch and Judy is based. Child's play, you say, that's what Punch and Judy is, and yet isn't the very fabric of the story rather odd? A man beats his wife to death, throws his child into a ditch and kills it, then cheats the gallows and hangs a policemen in his stead. A man with a face of a special kind which is an ancient symbol of carnal lust.

We didn't know much about such things in those days, but sensed there was something evil mixed up in it all. Down in the field the players would be helping people to have fun and entertaining them. You would say of their most dire tragedy that it was 'good'. But here, in the presence of the little wooden images, there was only apprehension. There was no deep feeling, nor any genuine fun. There was something rather unpleasant in those puppets as they pranced through the most hilarious farce. Their laughter squeaked out of their stubborn inanimation with a noise as malevolent as a man's words coming out of a parrot's beak. It was inhuman. A painful travesty of the human condition. Laughter was here turned into jeering. A wire was pulled and a wooden lever raised to pour scorn on humankind.

But if the comedies were offensive, then the tragedies were almost unbearable. A disaster was a complete disaster, a villain a villain through and through. Here was conveyed, to perfection, the cruelty and evil and misfortune that the players in their tent had never been able to portray, though they constantly had experience of it. It may be that only the inhuman little puppets could sustain the chill of unmitigated evil. In them there was nothing of the breath that warms all clay and heals all villainy. Their power lay in the Frankenstein gait and baneful rigidity of the mask. Weren't the melodramas funny down there in the field? But up here Sweeney Todd would chill the marrow of your bones with his whispered longing: 'Oh that the whole world was one smooth, white throat — and I to cut it!'

Perhaps the waxworks at the back of the hall had something to do with the ambiance. There were about a score of them, all in a row, and each one taking up as much room as a man. But, as they stood there motionless, the air about them also grew stiff. There was always a tense silence at your back, a silence that invaded space and filled it. Your mind sensed it and would pause, just as your body grew instinctively aware of some material obstacle in the darkness, and stand stockstill. Forty unblinking eyes would be staring at you and at the pitiless scenes up on the little stage. I wonder whether the showmen had any feeling for them as they manipulated their dolls and tried to please the dead masters of their craft. I wonder whether they were endeavouring to earn a spark of recognition from the hard, knowing eyes in front of them: 'Is this how you put her under the floor-boards, Dr Crippen? . . . Is this how the poison was mixed, Mr Seddon?'

Did they know that the killers were still committing murder in their pale and bloodless immortality? For these phantoms were slowly smothering the players with the weight of unprofitable days. We were all assisting them to do just that. They took from me enough pennies to put on the closed eyes of all the players. That is how we repaid the debt for hours of fun and laughter, and for the enduring magic of their immortal lines. It's a pity that youth and understanding don't come at the same time. In those days I felt sorry that people should grow old and fail to earn their living in a damp tent. Often I would meet one or two of them at the supper-table. They were sure to call at the shop on their way back from the field. There would be some message about empty boxes or unwanted clothes for the theatre. My mother was the kindest woman in the world. She laughed with them, she helped them, and when the door was shut after them, she would sit in a kind of puzzled reverie. For a while she would be like a wren with cuckoos in the nest. And then, like cuckoos, they disappeared. I do not know where, nor how, nor when. They seemed to evaporate silently from the town: 'Like the mist from the stream's grasp, they quietly took their leave.'[4].

They left their playhouse for the wind and rain to finish off the performance. That is how we knew they had gone. One evening it wasn't lit up any more. The braziers weren't shining through the dark eye of the door. The place lay cold and silent and empty like a skull in the mud. Nobody came on to apologize for the unexpected mishap and recite immortal lines. The shreds of canvas fluttered overhead in the rain-filled wind like wordless tongues.

Chwaryddion Crwydrol (Clwb Llyfrau Cymreig, 1943),
Cwysau (Gwasg Gomer, 1980)

One Sunday Afternoon

Jac L. Williams

The early May sunshine was 'calling mountainwards'[1] and I couldn't resist the invitation. After an early lunch I cut some sandwiches, put them in my pocket, and took a walking-stick in hand. I caught the first tram that would take me to the outskirts of the city, sitting near the exit so that I could alight the more easily. I began observing the other passengers as they got on or off. I tried to imagine where each one was going. I should have liked to think that a more or less tidily dressed child or two was going to Sunday School,[2] just as I used to as a boy. I saw some with swimming costumes under their arms, which suggested that they were on their way to the baths or the lake in the park. I recalled how firmly my own mother would refuse to let me go bathing in the sea before the end of May. I stared for a long while at a young mother with a small child fidgeting on her lap as if to show the world how great his enjoyment was. It was obvious that they were all pleasure-bent, and the bags of sandwiches made it clear that they intended staying out all afternoon. I couldn't blame them. Perhaps many of them had spent the whole week indoors, in an office or factory by day and many an evening in the stuffy air of a cinema. We used to condemn townsfolk for coming to lie half-naked of a Sunday afternoon in the district where I was brought up, but nowadays I can sympathize with them and forgive this transgression. I know about their captivity during the week, the lazy sleepiness of their minds and bodies, and the urge for some kind of freedom on Sunday afternoons. I decided that they too, in their own way, were going 'to worship God in a park'.

We arrived at the park's gates. The passengers all alighted except for two. I was still sitting near the door, and the other man was in the opposite corner at the front of the tram. There was a limp, heart-breaking look about him, and his clothes hung on him almost as if on a frame. Although I was some distance away, I could see the creases in the yellow skin of his unhealthy-looking face. I noticed a shock of hair under his cap and the scurf on the collar of his coat and his waistcoat. Through the unloveliness I could make out the shadow of a smile about to break around his mouth with its dirty, gapped teeth. There was a large bag hanging around his neck and down between his outstretched legs, with the words 'News of the World' on it in half-obliterated letters. I gathered that he had once seen better times, and that something had gone missing from his life.

The journey came to an end and I alighted without thinking any more about him. I was going somewhere. I didn't know where. It didn't matter, as long as I was getting out of the city. I walked for a while along the main road. There was no end to the houses and I had to walk faster. A bus stopped close by. I boarded it and asked for a ride worth half-a-crown. The windows were open and the warm breeze played in my hair, giving the impression that I was moving faster than I really was. I sat on my own, uttering not a single word to anyone. I was happy to be going somewhere.

Having travelled like this for about forty minutes, first through genteel suburbia, and then through a good stretch of countryside that still had something of its old splendour, we came at last to a small village. I took a liking to it because of its ordinariness. There were only about a dozen houses, but there was a church, a chapel, a school, a shop, and two pubs, the Black Lion and the Red Lion, facing each other. I asked the time of the bus back, and alighted.

The village had its square, and a narrower road intersecting with the main road. I noticed that there was a somewhat rougher road leading out of it over the brow of the hill that stood behind the village. It didn't appear to be much more than a cart-track leading to a farm, but I could see that it wound over the brow and perhaps down the other side. So I took it.

There were hazel-trees growing tall in the two hedges on either side. I pulled out my pocket knife and cut a small branch, about the thickness of my thumb, to make a whistle. This was one of the first crafts ever taught me by my father. I came to a gap in the hedge with two posts across it, and nettles under the lower one, to keep stray animals from the barley-shoots that were beginning to come up through the soil. I climbed on to the top one and balanced with my heels on the bottom one. I started on the whistle. I cut a twig off the branch and whittled it until only a short stump was left. I put the knife's blade on the bark about two inches from the end. I gave the stump a full twist. I inspected it. The two ends of the incision had met perfectly. I put the knife into the slit a second time, and gave another twist, to make sure the bark would be loose after it had left the twig. I wet the two front inches thoroughly. I put that part on my knee and tapped it hard and regularly, every whit of it, with the handle of my knife. I then gripped it and gave it a twist. The bark came off smoothly and swiftly. I put it in my pocket and fashioned the twig. I put the bark back and tried it. It gave a sound like a whistle all right. I knew that making a whistle is like swimming or riding a bicycle. Once learned it's never forgotten. I was very content with my world.

I jumped down. Crouched on the earth, I looked across the field with my eyes at the same level as the shoots. Looking across them like that, I caught a glimpse of the lovely light-green that would be seen there in a few weeks' time. I was put in mind of how another farmer's boy had once been persuaded on the way home from school that our barley was not as sparse or slow-growing as he had maintained out of pride in his own field. In those days every field was as if owned by us children. I went on my way happy. Although I wasn't treading old paths, I was reliving old experiences.

There wasn't so much hedge now, and hardly any growth to it. I could see the wide, flat valley, and a river meandering through it. The shoots didn't fully hide the redness of the soil and there was a freshness to everything, a sort of greenness that's to be seen only in early summer. I saw youth without blemish in those shoots, and in the leaves of the alder, and I heard it in the song of birds. I felt it in the breeze. There was an echo of it in my own heart, too.

I climbed until, coming to a farm, I stood for a few minutes leaning on the gate. Near by was a barn-door. The top half of it was open and the lower part closed. I could see an old-fashioned threshing machine just inside, and a large black cat with a white front lying upon it. She was obviously tired, or had eaten her fill of leftovers from the family's Sunday lunch, and was resting there before going back to catching mice. I admired her. She must have been a splendid mouser. There was a dung-heap in the corner of the yard, and a dozen hens of various kinds and colours upon it, some lying quietly, some settling, and others scratching hard at the manure. I noticed the diligence of the hens and chicks in the dry straw on the lower side of the heap. I liked the yard's quiet harmony. It struck me that the world has a lot to learn from a farmyard on a Sunday afternoon, and then I went on my way. Even a dung-heap's smell had seemed sweet to me.

The road was beginning to go downhill now, and some way off I saw a small chapel sheltering under the hill. I decided to go as far as that chapel before settling down with my sandwiches.

As I drew near I could make out the sound of singing. I recognized the hymn — it was a favourite of one of the staunchest members of the Sunday School in which I grew up, *'Wele'r dydd yn gwawrio draw'*.[3] I have fond memories of that teacher. My conscience was pricking me somewhat. Had I not mocked him often for choosing the same old hymn Sunday after Sunday? Had we not many a time thrown paper pellets at him while he was down on his knees, with eyes shut, praying? They were starting the last verse of the hymn. I waited quietly until they had finished.

The silence of the countryside was all about me, with only the twink of a bird in the hedge. On I went to the chapel-gate on tip-toes. I wanted to go inside. The door was open, but I could see a small, wood-and-stained-glass partition obscuring the door from inside and the interior from the road. Again on tip-toe, I went up to the door. Someone was praying aloud. I approached the partition as quietly as a mouse. The best I could do without being seen was to get an unclear view through the small yellow panes. I could see there were no pews, only long seats with single-planked backs to them, and about a dozen people sitting on them here and there. Nor was there any pulpit or deacons' pew — only a table in the corner at the front end, with a Bible on it. In the other corner there was a small organ but nobody sitting at it. In their midst there was a fireplace, and standing in front of it, the man praying was in full spate. I could see from his bearing that he was getting on in years. My impression was confirmed by the meekness of his voice. There was something very saintly about it. He talked about the great things in life, of God's love and the frailties of men. He touched upon the little things too, the sparrow. He talked about the lilies of the fields. He gave thanks for the privilege of coming to God's House of a Sunday afternoon. I felt that I too, surreptitiously and wholly unintentionally, was sharing in that great privilege. I understood better than ever before why some who love me wish me 'to hold to the things that matter'.

The prayer came to an end. Someone in middle-age, in a voice rather coarser than that of the man who had been praying, announced that the service on the next Sabbath would be at a half-past-two, and he gave out a hymn to be sung before departing:

> How beautiful the gathering
> In God's wondrous temple,
> To worship together sweetly
> His seemly, holy name;
> We come to his gracious altar
> For every pleasant gift,
> To hear the voice of mercy
> Sounding Oh, so sweet.[4]

The little congregation rose to its feet and began singing. I wanted to join in the chorus, but some kind of apprehensive shyness, perhaps a feeling of unworthiness, held me back. To the sound of the hymn I went out and back along the road.

As I passed by the park gates, I remembered my fellow-passenger on the bus. I could see some resemblance between us two, and I fell to wondering whether he too had been given a wistful glimpse of something lost.

Yr Efrydydd (1944),
Trioedd (Christopher Davies, 1973)

Salem

E. Morgan Humphreys

A few weeks ago there were some interesting articles in *Yr Herald Cymraeg*[1] about the painting known as 'Salem', and someone asked me whether I knew anything about it. Most of us have seen that picture at some time or another — the simple country chapel with its window in the background opening on the countryside; the old woman in her tall hat and Paisley shawl, making for her seat; a bearded, middle-aged man, pressing his forehead on his hands, and another in the same posture near the farthest wall; a small boy with bowed head in another pew, and a few more neighbours here and there in the others. As it happens, I know the chapel, and I knew some of the people in the picture, which was painted about forty years ago by an artist know as Curnow Vosper. Salem is a Baptist chapel in Cefncymerau, above Llanbedr and Gwynfryn in Ardudwy, and the figures in the painting are the people of those hills.

The old lady in her Paisley shawl is Siân Owen of Tŷ'n y Fawnog, and later of Ffordd Groes, at Llanfair, near Harlech. The old man with his hand at his ear is Owen Siôn of Carleg Coch, and Laura Williams of Tŷ'n y Buarth is sitting at his side. The boy is Evan Edward Lloyd of Tŷ'n yr Aegerth and the bearded man is William Siôn of Carleg Coch, with Mrs Mary Rowlands, later of Dolgellau, sitting near by. The man sitting under the clock is Robert Williams of Cae'r Meddyg. I remember him well. Robert Williams was a farmer and carpenter, living in a cottage within sight of Y Moelfre and Y Rhiniog on one side, and in view of the sea and all the splendour of Arfon's mountains, from Snowdon as far as Bardsey, on the other. From the gate leading towards Cae'r Meddyg you can see the length of Dyffryn Artro, a long, wooded valley, with its little rocky fields and slopes purple with heather in season, rising on all sides, and the rocks of Cwm Bychan blocking the view in the far distance. The arm of a hill hides Cwm Nantcol with its winding river and green meadows. I know of no more beautiful scene on a summer's evening — the rays of a setting sun streaming across wood and escarpment, over fields and rocks, the slow, pearly smoke of a farmhouse and an unseen cottage rising now and then from the valley like a light mist, and some sweet and magic silence, a gentle stillness, over all.

And it is Cae'r Meddyg and that scene, and the people of the stone cottages and the sunny slopes, that come to mind whenever I see the painting of Salem. I know a little about their life — as it used to be, at any rate — about their kindness, and hospitality, their daily labour and their regular attendance at chapel on Sundays. I remember well many a meal in the snug, cheerful kitchens of Cae'r Meddyg, Glyn Artro, Allt Goch, and Penbryn in the days gone by — many years ago now — the furniture and crockery gleaming, the scent of a wood-fire, and bread in the oven sweet to the nostrils, the talk about what was going on in the locality, and the atmosphere so neighbourly and kind. I used the word 'neighbours' deliberately when referring at the beginning to the people in the chapel at Cefncymerau, for that was the great thing about their way of life — they were people of the same background, the same language, the same interests, living together in their own neighbourhood, and it is that, when all is said and done, which amounts to something priceless in the life of a nation. Look at the face of Siân Owen in the painting; you will see there sadness and calm, strength and gentleness, and these were characteristic of the hill-people. Their lives were often hard and they were no more perfect than we are, but they were part of a community and a tradition, and that put mettle in their characters. And hard though their labour was, from those slopes and within the old chapel's walls a few caught a glimpse of Jerusalem's towers in the clouds of the setting sun, and saw the sea of glass shining between them and the far horizon.

Lleufer (4, Gwanwyn, 1948)

A Trip to the Circus

T. J. Morgan

Although I was taken to the circus only once as a child, and once to a menagerie, when some time ago we saw a circus advertized as coming to the town of P—,[1] we had the feeling that the War had deprived our children of the great amusements we had regularly enjoyed in our own childhoods, and that we therefore had a duty to take them there, to make up for the loss in some part. And so it was arranged that we should go. According to the advertisement, there were to be jesters, an acrobat riding bareback on a prancing horse, a dog that could dance, doves like Branwen's[2] starlings (although that wasn't how the poster put it), a female juggler with a Chinese name, and so on; and to crown it all, there was going to be the most ferocious lioness in the whole world, and alone in its topless cage, the bravest of men and the most courageous of women would be suspended from ropes, performing acrobatic wonders within just a hair's breadth of those terrible jaws.

It would be an exaggeration to say that the place was packed out — and there I go, despite myself, starting to libel and make fun of the pitiful gaucherie claiming to be a miracle of entertainment, dexterity, and daring. And rather than proceed with my jeering, it would be more seemly if I rose to the heights of trivial moralising. So my first observation is this, that advertisements are now completely different from the things they advertise, and what's more, that the dissimilarity between the two is taken for granted, and that this is equally true of infallible drugs and grand concerts and letters of recommendation alike. These letters worry me, and the responsibility for assessing and evaluating them is quite beyond my inexperienced understanding. Since every letter is commendatory, it must be that appointment committees have some faculty which enables them to rule out a certain amount of praise from each letter, and allows them to reach a decision on the basis of what's left. If you read a praise-poem by Iolo Goch[3] and then one by Guto'r Glyn and then another by Tudur Aled, it's very difficult to say which one of the three noblemen praised by these poets is the bravest, the most generous, and the wisest; it seems to me that an appointment committee's work is just such a task. But if the candidate and his referees only knew about this principle of cancelling out part of what each letter has to say about the candidate, they could arrange for it to contain an extra meed of praise to make up for the reduction, so that a sizeable share still remained. And if every one of the candidates and their referees were to do this, those appointing would in turn have to see to it that there was a higher proportion of testimonial and character reference to be ignored in each case. These musings of mine are not entirely imaginary. And to come back to the circus and the poster: how can it be deduced from the advertisements whether a performance is going to be excellent or poor, since the claims for the poor are just as misleading as for the excellent? And I should be silly if I expected circus posters to say plainly and without boasting that the performance would be 'not bad, at best', and that I ought not to expect much from the acrobats.

A fair indication of this performance's quality was that the four clowns' main trick was for three of them to take a long draught of water from a bottle and squirt it from their mouths at a fourth. Now the chucking of a basinful of custard and blancmange over someone is very funny; there's an innate, instinctive element of humour in splashing about in a mucky sort of way; but this squirting was too like spitting, and somehow or other, spitting is ugly and odious. Nor was the feat of riding a horse without a saddle and standing on its back while it ambled around much more dangerous than standing on the arms of a sofa and letting someone rock it a little. Amidst all this non-artistry there were two examples of undoubted skill. The first was a man throwing knives at a girl who stood against a sort of door, until each of the knives was stuck into the outline of her body's map, even in both sides of the isthmus at her neck. I don't remember the name of this Llew Llaw Gyffes,[4] but he was a foreigner — from Mexico, probably, or perhaps Nicaragua; from one or other of those knife-throwing countries that lie between the Americas. He was extremely clever (and his map was quite daring, too, to be fair to her), but our perception of his skill was twice as great just because he was a foreigner — brown-skinned and uttering not a word. It's difficult to avoid the tendency to believe that foreigners, of necessity, are cleverer than we are; the belief, for example, that every Negro is a terrific boxer, or that every Jew is a masterly pianist, or to give a less obvious example, the conviction among supporters of the Welsh rugby team that the French backs, especially the two wings, are by nature faster than their counterparts on the Welsh side. It would be easy to refer to other examples of the innocent but firm belief that the foreigner is faster, cleverer, craftier, tougher, and more thorough. A small part of the explanation is that we are a bit fearful of foreigners, and that the fear tends to turn into reverence, and another part is the belief that it's proof of wisdom and prudence to run down your own country; but the most important thing is that we form a judgement about another nation, or the black or yellow race, from seeing only their champions. It's only the best who become famous and we let the exceptions represent the quality of the whole because we haven't seen the average and those without skill among their compatriots.

The girl from China was even more of a wonder and I doubt whether I ever saw her equal. Her particular act was to spin two plates on the tip of two small sticks without interruption, and to go on doing this — difficult enough if this were all she did — while at the same time bending her head and body backwards and forwards, as if there were no bones in her back, until her lips were touching a glass of water (back and forth, and upside-down, with the plates spinning on the sticks all the while); then she picked up the glass with her teeth, straightened up again without spilling a drop, and drank the water. Indeed, I feel my syntactical constructions having to weave and bend under the strain of describing, through the medium of the written word and without the help of diagrams or pictures, the complexity of the two feats going on at the same time, as if with one hand I were composing a *cywydd*[5] with the most intricate alliteration in every line, and with the other a sonnet with double-rhymes throughout.

It's not easy to say exactly what a performance like that is worth. There was no beauty in it. Let no one ask me to define beauty, yet everyone will agree, I think, that we don't consider this kind of thing 'beautiful', if we go by natural and sensible standards. And it was not 'good' for anything; there was no 'goodness' in it, save for the profit that the girl herself and her employer might have got out of it. And it would be completely senseless and irrelevant to ask how much 'Truth' was in it. It might be said, of course, that it had a certain amount of abstract 'Good', the goodness that comes from making entertainment, but the purpose of these queries is to ask what precisely there was in the performance itself that was capable of giving enjoyment. I and my sensible, unphilosophical readers are content to keep our feet on the earth and say simply that what gave enjoyment was seeing something difficult being done, and for the purposes of philosophy, I should say that the essence of enjoyment is indeed 'the Difficult'.

And my conclusion is that we must provide more room in our critical values for the standard of the Difficult. Of course, the Difficult or the element of excellence is dignified enough for our critics to talk about it; there's no need for much original, wordy extrapolation if all there is to say about a performance, is that it succeeds in accomplishing something extraordinarily difficult. But say whatever you will, 'excellence' is an important part of all art. The *cynghanedd*[6] is difficult. When Goronwy Owen[7] felt that Milton's rhymeless metre was unsatisfactory because it didn't have sufficient 'rules', what he meant was that the metre, according to Goronwy, didn't have enough difficulties. And if you look through the Grammars of the old master-poets, you will see that one of the merits of art, in their view, was that it was meant to be very difficult. And should critics of a later time be less ready to compete with one another in originality and profundity, they too will use the word 'difficult' or 'excellence' more often. The first thing to be said about the pictures of the old masters is that they are difficult; and what's come over us, tell me this, that we can talk about 'the art of the camera'? And if I may, in my ignorance, dare speak about music, there are large parts of the most splendid music which entertain because they are examples of 'excellence'; that is to say, they were intended to be an opportunity for demonstrating the composer's skill and the performer's dexterity. And I don't mean the flashiness of Liszt; I am thinking of the way in which the melody is developed in the first movement of Beethoven's Concerto for Violin: it's pure complexity, for its own sake and for the listener's entertainment. And what value can there be to some of the most typical things in a Handel aria, such as making the voice hold out for a long, long while without drawing breath, except that it's terribly difficult?

I shall have to leave the matter there for the time being. However incompetent and clueless I myself may be, I am always more than ready to acknowledge skill and I can only admire sheer cleverness. I have to come down now from those heights and back to the circus. There isn't much to record about the most ferocious lioness in the world. Her cage was dragged to the centre of the ring; the sheets were removed; she looked sleepily at the audience; she opened her mouth to yawn and then went back to sleep, the very epitome of a sultry Sunday afternoon. If she had been at home with us, I know full well where she would have been sitting. Near the cage stood a man with a spear in his hand; he was there to convey the impression that it was necessary to keep the lioness under control, lest she grow too ferocious, and to re-assure the anxious that, should she become too wild, he and the spear were there to tame her. His real job was to poke at her every now and again in order to keep her awake, to show that she was still alive, lest anyone think her completely dead. It's a very strange feeling to be melted with pity for the most ferocious lioness in the world, but I was really sorry for this one, because it was obvious her only desire was for perfect peace in which to lounge and grow old without interruption. And talk about being suspended from ropes over the cage! It would have been as good, or as bad, if a kitten had been in the lioness's place. The feat was only the shadow of a feat, because the danger, or what should have been difficult about it, was considerably less than it appeared.

The only other things worth mentioning were the dancing dog, which pranced on its hind legs to the beat of the orchestra, and the doves flying backwards and forwards to their master's commands, and which never failed to come to roost in their appointed order, filling a small cart pulled by the dog, just like a pony-and-trap taking a family for a jaunt. I don't want to deny that these performances were remarkable and seemed wonderful. Every child was enchanted by the scene and by the obedience of the doves. But I wasn't able to put aside the little knowledge I possess of such things as Pavlov's experiments with his dogs, and I tended to explain the wonderful away. Besides, I knew that it was often by means of cruel stratagems that dogs are taught to go through routines that are considered to be intelligent and human, and I suspected that this little dancer, the ugliest mongrel you ever saw, had suffered quite a bit in his schooldays. But even assuming that it wasn't by cruelty and threat that he was trained, and that it was by being drawn on by kindness and by being indulged with sweetmeats that he was taught mechanically to obey the rhythm of the dance, the little creature's stupid look plainly showed that it was some compulsion which he didn't understand, some conscription in his training, which kept him on his hind legs and made him give a little skip to the drum's beat; and I have to say that I felt great pity for him. And when he stood between the shafts of the little cart, he looked so wretchedly stupid, as if he wasn't enjoying the work or the unfamiliar surroundings, that the charm of the pretty scene vanished from my eyes under the cloud of misery which I saw in the poor beast.

But if the cruelty of his training could be forgiven, and the dismal look I could see on that dog, even then the little I know of psychology and Pavlov was spoiling the wonder of it all, for such things as the dog's dancing and the discipline of the doves seem wonderful because we believe their behaviour to depend on their own wills and understanding. But when it's understood that the apparent intelligence is only a trick played with the creature's instincts and glands, then it all seems much less of a miracle. It might be concluded from what I am saying that scientific knowledge, in making a man suspicious, limits the scope of his enjoyment. But that is not the case, and it would be fairer to say that 'understanding' can take the place of 'wonder' as a means of entertainment, if only we remember that 'understanding' is in itself also a way of enjoying.

Cynefin (Llyfrau'r Castell, 1948)

Thoughts on Coronation Day, 1953

D. J. Williams

When I tell you at the outset that I can remember three crowned heads in succession (I don't mean side by side) adorning the throne of the Isle of Britain, you will realize immediately that I am now getting on in years. And as it isn't likely, in the natural course of things, that I shall ever see another coronation day, at least not on this side of the grave, you will perhaps allow me to put down here some of the thoughts that ran through my head during the three coronations that I most clearly remember. The others have gone into the mist, and it's best to leave them there.

These three coronations all took place on a fine summer's day, and the great sun itself seemed for a while to be humbled in the presence of a greater splendour, that of the Great British Empire on the bounds of which the sun was never supposed to set in those days. There was, however, one small fragment of it that was beyond the light's piercing rays.

It may seem to you a rather strange coincidence that the appointed day of the first coronation that I recall, namely the crowning of

Edward VII in 1902, fell if you please on my birthday, the twenty-sixth of June in that year. Such remarkable things do happen sometimes in the long course of history. If the crowning had been fixed a day earlier, or a day later, you see, it would almost certainly have fallen on someone else's birthday. But that was no doubt how it was meant to be.

The people of my native heath were simple, unfussy folk who took no more notice of even a saint's birthday than of the lowliest of their own children's. Nobody had a 'birth day' in those parts. It was at their own pace, not according to numbers, that the people of that district grew old. And had it not been connected, in the way I've indicated, with his royal highness, I don't know that this extra birthday of mine wouldn't have slipped as smoothly by as the sixteen that had gone before, without my being aware of it.

But I must press on: the king was taken ill, seriously ill, and his appendix had to be removed without delay — a new medical operation that was very risky in those days. Up to then, it seems the ordinary chap didn't know that he was carrying this prickly appendage about with him in his own flesh from day to day. Between you and me, it was said at the time that this ailment, for a while thereafter, became almost as fashionable as the sudden lameness that afflicted so many ladies of the court after Old Mother Victoria had had an attack of the gout. Anyway, the coronation had to be postponed, and sad to say, I lost all interest in it after that.

By the time of the second coronation to make any impression on me, namely that of George V at the end of May 1936, my relationship with the king of Great Britain had become even closer. It's true that I had disagreed with him over a certain matter in quite an inflammatory way at about this time, and that the case of 'Rex versus Me' had caused quite a bit of talk.

But by the great day of his crowning that short-lived ill-feeling had long been buried: the great sun of British freedom and blessings was once more at its zenith, blinding the whole world with its glittering brightness, and little Gwalia[1], too, as is her wont, was on the tips of her toes, giving one wild hooray, and bedecked with flags and ribbons.

I was by then a guest in one of the most renowned of his majesty's palaces, and I had no breeze from the outside world to waft over me. A very nice man was George VI, according to those who knew him, and I thought so too, deserving every word of the kind things that were said about him during the fortnight leading up to his funeral.

And now that I come to speak about those days, I also found many of his liveried servants to be very solicitous, diligent men. They wouldn't allow me, for instance, even to close or open a door for myself, lest I over-exerted myself. I paid not a penny for those holidays, and according to some old ceremony they had in that place, I was obliged to leave it as naked as I had come into the world, without being able to offer as much as a small tip to any of those kind-hearted men by way of showing my goodwill on leaving.

There were a good number of us in that royal palace at the time of the coronation — tried, experienced men one and all; and as you might expect in such an assembly of the elect, there was a fair representation from among the Chosen Race itself — the camel-nosed Pinkas who, it was said, on one great night of his life, had broken the bank at Monte Carlo; young Liepman with the head of a genius on him, not unlike that of Prosser Rhys[2], by the way, his books already translated into half-a-dozen languages; and Tannenbaum, the tailor, the chief jester of that court. There were also two other tailors, exceedingly pleasant fellows, with whom I had the privilege of squatting for a short while, learning the craft at the feet of some Gamaliel of a needle man.

Although the guests were numerous, each had a small room to himself, specially designed for meditation and contemplation. And in that solemn silence beyond 'the sound of the pain that's in the world', I spent, content in my own mind, that second coronation day that I remember so well. There was a small number of other Europeans, besides those from Wales, who had chosen to enjoy the day in the same manner. The rest of society went to foregather in the sacred place of the Chapel, where it had been arranged for them to join the choir invisible in the great chorus and prayer that God would save our Gracious King, and send him happy and victorious everywhere.

But now I come nearer home, to the coronation day of Elizabeth II, yes, and an ascension day too, as a symbol of the modern British religion that first issued forth so fairly in the Virgin Elizabeth, and her father, the Defender of the Faith, before her. This is the Second Ascension in our lifetime. And surely this too was a day to remember for ever and ever for everyone who lived through it — the millions who saw, heard, and experienced the eight-hour triumph of that crowning, and procession, and the giving of praise around the blessed throne. Maybe, some said, this was the day foreseen by Tennyson so wonderfully well as 'the great, far-off, divine event to which the whole creation. . . .'

By means of the latest technological media, both aural and visual, this day can now be carried in its entirety down the furthest paths of time, making the shows of Pharaoh, Caesar, Charlemagne, and Tamburlaine the Great seem but the echo of games played by children on the sands.

But where was I, you may be asking, on this notable day? Well, I'll tell you. For the first two hours and a half, until the crowning ceremony itself was over, and it really was a beautiful ceremony, I was glued to the wireless set — since it was, after all, a day for the queen. Then I drew a breath and had a bite of lunch, in order to keep my strength up for the afternoon.

To be honest now, I wasn't very clear in my own mind about this business of crowning people. Gwynfor[3] and Dominion Status, and common sense, as far as I could understand them, told me that I could join in the celebration. But the most stubborn part of my instinctive nature, based on the fact that this queen, like every monarch on the English throne before her, was the very symbol of another nation's right to authority over the whole life of my own nation, was definitely against it. You see, I've never been able to reconcile anything in this old head of mine.

While I was in this quandary, I suddenly remembered a quarrel that had once taken place between me and a dear old sharp-tongued friend, after I had called him a baby. 'A baby! Yes, a baby, you said,' my friend retorted, 'Yes, but there's hope that a baby will one day grow up into a man, but a donkey will never be a horse!' It was the friend, without a shadow of a doubt, who had the better of that argument. But it was the donkey in me, with his unchanging stripe, which was to win on this particular day.

I later saw in *Y Faner*[4] that Saunders Lewis had been rather severely rebuking certain other 'sour-nosed' donkeys on account of their failure to join in the celebrations, together with the Negroes, large and small, the Italians, and the Irish on Cardiff's dockside that special day. By the way, history does not record, so far, that the Irishman, at home or abroad, is over-zealous about the English monarchy. Perhaps now, having won his freedom, he can with typical courtesy, at this chance opportunity, sing 'God Save the Queen', more or less in tune. He never could previously.

But the problem was, how were these 'sour-nosed' Pharisaical donkeys to make themselves Pharisees enough to rejoice worthily with those Tory Sadducees and Quisling Herodites (if you will pardon the anachronism) and those mongrel Publicans who all their lives had objected to every national ideal and idea that was applicable to their own nation?

It is easily agreed that the romance and singing and playing of concertinas that those colourful Corinthians went in for on the Cardiff dockside, when seen from afar on a day like this, were something much more likeable and attractive than the fickle amusements of the townsfolk and villagers of Wales who take their sustenance from the London newspapers and radio. But were not these kind people made more soft-headed than ever in their understanding and awareness of Wales by the hullabaloo of the coronation?

On turning to the New Testament for light on a subject as complex as acknowledging and ordaining the terrestrial head of Christian society, it appears that the Apostle Paul, if some of his sayings are to be taken literally and in their entirety, sometimes contradicts himself dangerously, and that he is as inconsistent as anyone — a not inconsiderable solace, surely, for another inconsistent man like me. Because he says, for example, with his usual certitude, at the opening of the twelfth chapter of Romans: 'And be not conformed to this world', and so on. And yet, here he is, in the first verse of the following chapter, laying it down just as firmly: 'Let every soul be subject unto the higher powers' et cetera. And there, in two verses, we have the double-cutting edge of the sword which separates Nonconformity from Church Authority, the one from the other — the still small voice, and the voice of the council.

From what I understood at the time (I heard differently later on), there were two houses in Great Britain which didn't put out flags on the day of the last coronation — and this for the same reason. Buckingham Palace was one. There was no need to wave a flag there, said the commentator from the rooftops. And our house was the other. There was no need for it there, either.

Y Ddraig Goch (25, 1953),
Y Gaseg Ddu (Gwasg Gomer, 1970)

From the Pulpit

E. Tegla Davies

I wonder how these people facing me in their seats see me, and how I see them? They are what they are for me because I am what I am for them.

There was the time I left home for three days of preaching. Two days before I set out a child of mine had been taken ill with pneumonia. My heart was downcast as I left home, and the child in his agony was before my eyes throughout every service I took. Yet I didn't dare breathe a word about it in public, for the first principle laid down about the art of preaching is that the preacher should on no account reveal his personal feelings to the congregation. It was not for a father worrying about his child that they had asked, but for a preacher with no feelings save solicitude for their souls. On that particular occasion it was the father who carried the day, and that's why the preacher was a failure. Proof of this is that I haven't to this day been asked to go back there. A congregation can be very heartless to anyone who gives it other than what it has asked for. When, I wonder, will people see that there's no such thing as a preacher or minister who is not also a man?

But do they all see me in the same way? What am I in the eyes of this organist just in front of me? One Sunday evening, years ago now, I was more nervous than usual, so much so that I was afraid of losing the thread of my sermon, but it would have been woe to me had I shown it. While the announcements and collection were being made, I had been going over my sermon, having completely forgotten the music that was being played on the organ in front of me. When they put the plates on the table I got up to give out a hymn, without realizing that the organist was still at it. He didn't speak to me for a month afterwards. For him the man in the pulpit was no more than someone killing time while he searched for suitable tunes, and practised them with his fingers tapping on the bottom of the seat.

But am I the same in the eyes of all? What am I, I wonder, to John Edwards, who is there below me in the deacons' pew asleep most of the time? I know what I am for Mr Williams, seated on the other side of him. Mr Williams is a good listener, zealous with his amens, and loud in his praise of the sermon at the end. But for John Edwards am I only a chance to doze off for a while in a place more comfortable than any he would find at home? And I won't have much of his company on the way home either, because it's Mr Williams who does all the talking. One Sunday morning, however, Mr Williams wasn't in chapel, and it was only John Edwards and myself who walked home together. He was quiet, as usual. But little by little I dragged it out of him that his wife was in poor health. Despite himself, he also admitted having been on his feet all night, tending to a sick animal. And I had been about to chastise him for sleeping through the service. The Gospel had been so important to John Edwards that he had come to chapel not having had a wink of sleep the night before. I felt rather uncomfortable. For him I am nothing less than the mouthpiece for the Gospel of Salvation for his sinful soul. I wonder whether I am really qualified for that role.

One evening Mr Williams called by for a chat. He's a gracious, kind man. It's nothing for him to send me a sack of potatoes and other comforts every now and then. After a while he began talking about his family, saying that his grandfather had been a Justice of the Peace and that the minister in his day had done his best to exert his influence in this respect, and that his father had also been a Justice of the Peace and the minister of the day had been kind in just the same way, and what a pity it would be if the family tradition were to die out. I suggested as subtly as I could that I didn't have much talent for making J.Ps. That was all right; he wasn't thinking of any such thing; but on the following Sunday I thought the amens were not quite so warm, and there were to be no more potatoes from him. How can I possibly meet the needs of all these people? For John Edwards I am one who proclaims the Eternal Gospel, and for Mr Williams a gadget for turning out J.Ps.

And what about Mrs Edmunds over there? She presides over the Women's Guild and is their leader in all things. A sedate, very grand woman, whose opinion on the sermon is always the same — a very *nice* sermon, the most damning comment on a sermon that even the devil could think up. One Sunday evening, while I was preaching, a sentence escaped my lips that I had not prepared. I immediately doubted the wisdom of it, but out it came like a shot. Mrs Williams's satisfied smile disappeared; she suddenly looked out of the window, then she turned her head away, and she didn't come at the close to say that the sermon had been *very nice*. It was obvious that I had caused her pain. I should have to call on her the following week, and I did so at the earliest opportunity. She received me coldly. She must have taken umbrage at that stray sentence, but how to begin to apologize? We talked about the weather, yesterday, today, and tomorrow. And I could see that, since I was a *nice* preacher, she took me to be a weather-forecaster, too. The conversation was a bit strained, and I got up to take my leave. She rose, too, and stood there between me and the door. Then she grew pale, and her lips were trembling, and 'That sentence,' she snapped. I was about to explain when she collapsed into a heap in a chair and began weeping profusely as if her soul were being torn apart. Then she made a solemn confession, about a weak moment, transgression, and I saw that the grand and sedate manner had been only a veil covering an open wound. After closing the door, we went down on our knees, and a sinner was given the privilege of leading another sinner to the Throne. Ever since then Mrs Edmunds has been for me not a sedate, affected woman but a woman like any other, with an aching soul in need of a doctor's balm. She has never thanked me again for a *nice* sermon, but I've noticed that the balm has done its work.

There's another very grand one over there, Mrs Francis, between whom and Mrs Edmunds there's quite a bit of jealousy. She would be so glad to know about Mrs Edmunds's secret. I wonder whether she, too, has ever been hurt, and does it sometimes trouble her? And then there's Siân Jones, always complaining about her corns, and expecting a half-crown from me every time I call. She's an old sinner right enough, as everyone knows except her. In her own sight she's a spotless soul living in a world full of sinners.

A congregation of good appearance, rich and poor, scholars and ignorant folk, gentle people and ruffians. What description could be applied to every one of them? I know that Siân Jones is a sinner. After that experience with Mrs Edmunds, I know that's what she is too, although there's light on her face now. Would I be very out of order if I dared to say that the word for each and every one of them is indeed 'sinner'? They see me as anything but a sinner, that's why I haven't seen the sinner in them before now. How can I convince them that is what I am too, but one who, through many a lapse, has found the way to the Cross and that this is my only qualification for standing before them like this from Sunday to Sunday — not to preach sermons that are *nice* or clever or old-fashioned or modern, but to call sinners like myself to repentance?

Yes, but what about these young people in front of me who look so unconcerned about what's going on? How, I wonder, do they see me? They are all so polite when in my company. Are today's young people so very different from those of times gone by? There were a few lads with coarse tongues in my day, and lasses with quite loose morals, and all of us used to take more interest in them for that. The young people are regular in their attendance at the Young People's Meeting, and when I make my way there I hear the fun and the pounding of the piano, but a silence falls as I open the door. I wonder what they think I am? Do they think I know anything about their world, and perhaps more than they themselves know, since the young sinners of my day long ago were not so sophisticated as they? They are quite keen in discussion, and Fred the Gables rather defiant with his doubting, thinking he frightens me. I wonder whether he thinks I was reared inside a clock-case? Does he know that, long before I was his age, I had doubted every doctrine under the sun, and thought how stupid the old deacons were to believe anything of the kind? Poor Fred called on me one afternoon to ask for a reference and after asking him a few questions, I could see that all his doubting was so much fog and wind to hide the paucity of his thinking. I gave him a reference, and he was a great believer as I showed him out.

I shouldn't have thought Ann Jones of Bryn y Foel, of all people, would have fallen from grace. It hadn't occurred to me that such passion existed in her world, she was so innocent. I went to visit her. She took fright at seeing me, but during our conversation I could see that I hadn't really got to know Ann Jones, that she had her own very strong personality that had been awakened by the trouble in which she now found herself. I also saw that she couldn't help playing with fire. After we had both taken off our masks, I hope that she saw, too, that she had mistaken me, and I could sympathize with her completely, because I too had once been a hot-head plucked from the brands of the fire. Ann Jones will be very different from now on, less of an angel, but more hopeful on that account. It's a pity I hadn't thought that sooner, instead of taking her to be a dolly.

Slowly I have come to realize that there's no such thing as Young People and their Problems, only Ann Jones of Bryn y Foel; Fred the Gables; Olwen from Y Ddôl; Richard the Mill; Huw of Glanrafon; Harriet from Y Fron, and all the rest of them — each in his or her own world; and that there's a different key to each door, and that it's my task to find those keys. The greatest difficulty is getting them to see me as I am, as someone who was once a young man struggling against the same tempests as they are now. It doesn't matter much about their doubts. Those arise from their being tossed about by the winds, since they haven't learned to steer yet; and a word of sympathy from one who they know understands them, because he was once young like them, serves as ointment on the wound. But how am I to convince them that I know all this? They are not interested in the Problems of Young People, but Huw takes an interest in Mary, and Richard in Olwen, and Gruffydd in his disappointment. How am I to lead that personal interest along the paths of justice without their knowing that I am interfering? If they were to suspect that, I should have spoiled everything.

And then the children, what am I in their sight? It's easy to say what they are for me — little angels. They speak to me respectfully, taking off their caps and bowing. How can they possibly be guilty of our old tricks? Could Rhys over there ever put a live toad down the back of Agnes the Graig, as we once did at school in days gone by? It's true that Agnes didn't tell on us, because she fainted and in the commotion that followed the schoolmaster forgot all about the prank. Surely these pleasant little children couldn't be guilty of a thing like that. But how do they see me, I wonder? The answer comes quite easily. One evening I was speaking at the Children's Service about Bishop Morgan[1]; and I had a picture of him hung up at the front; he was dressed in the clerical garments of the period, all frills and pleats. At the end I asked whether there were any questions. Dafydd the Pandy is always very ready with his questions, and he put up his hand. 'Well, Dafydd,' I said, 'what's your question?' 'Is he a man or a preacher?' he asked. Nobody smiled. It was clear that the question for them was completely reasonable, and that as far as they were concerned I wasn't a man — like their fathers and grandfathers and uncles — but a preacher. And this is how I seem to them. I see a sign, when they think I'm not watching, that that one over there is trying to stick a pin into his neighbour, but do they know that I could show them tricks they have never even imagined, because in my younger days we had to rely much more on our own resources than children do today? And if they knew, would I lose respect and influence? Yes, that's my difficulty, to get to know these children as children, to get behind the angelic mask they all wear — children in their naughty and their good moods, their innocent and cruel tricks, their mindless pranks and sincere sympathy. To know them as children, and to be able to enter their world, there lies my only hope of leading them to the One who once walked upon 'the fair land of Judea', who could treat children as themselves because he was so like them, and thus was so wonderfully able to make them so like Him.

Yes, it's difficult for all these people in front of me to see me as myself and not as a preacher. If they did, would they be more ready to accept the Gospel I preach?

Ah well, the announcements are nearly at an end, and now I have to give out the next hymn.

Ar Ddisberod (Gwasg y Brython, 1954)

How to Choose and Treat a Wife

Harri Gwynn

Every now and again you come across a farmer who is also a bachelor. It may be that you feel he has a fine old life, especially if you are a youngish man. You may even find something rather charming about his unshaven, soapless bliss. You simply envy the freedom that allows him to change his shirt only on All Saints' Day and May Day, and it seems to you terrific to be able to go bed without taking off your shoes. After all, you only have to put them back on again next day, don't you? You can see how reasonable it is for a man not to be hindered and shackled by a woman's irrationality. A bachelor is rational enough not to have to clean the grate until the ashes reach the door. It is then he fetches a wheelbarrow and makes a good job of it, instead of messing about with a shovelful a day.

The same goes for the dishes. Washing up is only working for the sake of work, just as long as there's a dog or cat at hand, and if they happen to be a bit particular, there's always a lot more sense in letting dirty dishes mount up into a pile. You are then able to put a rainy day to some good use.

So too with this business about washing. It's obvious that Providence didn't intend a man to wash, or it would have given him an instinct so to do, like a cat has. As you can see from the reaction of any small boy who hasn't been ruined by what's called civilization, washing is contrary to nature. After all, cats, cows and such like have fur or hair to keep them warm. As a man grows older he too must have his fur, and a country bachelor is allowed just that, and he never catches cold, as townsfolk do who are forever in and out of a bath-tub. As a consequence, an old bachelor farmer is never said to have died: he just goes back into the earth, feet first.

That may be the lighter side of a bachelor farmer's life. But please don't be misled by the supposed glamour of living like that. There are also some dire disadvantages to that way of life, especially for a farmer.

The first is that you will always be an object of special interest to unmarried women. Ask someone who has been through a war and he'll tell you that waiting to be hit by a bullet is far worse than actually being hit. It's possible that a cock-pheasant would say the same, if asked. And a bachelor is a cock-pheasant all his life, with no particular season when it's against the law to go out after him. And there exists no poacher as cunning as an old maid or widow. So before deciding to remain a bachelor, consider ye the cock pheasant.

The second thing to bear in mind, and this is very particular to a farm, is that there are certain chores that are best done by a woman. Don't be short-sighted and say that children are more of a nuisance than anything else. I know that's the attitude of toffs and important people, including the authors of books about bringing up children, but it's an unnatural point of view. Without children, you won't have anyone to teach you how to do things when you are getting on in years. Without children, who will there be to make arrangements for your funeral? And anyway, the wills of childless people always cause trouble and tend to turn people off religion, especially if all the worldly goods have been left to the chapel. For your own sake, and society's benefit, and the success of religion, you ought to have children. This means that you must also take a wife, if you want to be respectable.

Although there's no shortage of women in this country, it's not easy to come by a wife. It's not the same as choosing a cow, though one or two have gone about it in that way, but that's only how the toffs do it: they have an annual show up in London where their young women, like handsome heifers, come out into a ring for all to see. But after an ordinary chap like you finds a wife, only to discover that she's not without blemish, it's not easy to pass her on to someone else, as happens with a defective cow. I know that this again goes on among toffs and theatrical people, but it isn't approved of in the ordinary chap. Society expects him to accept his fate in this respect, as in so many other ways.

The problem is less complicated in some other countries where a man is allowed to wed as many wives as he wishes, and if any of them doesn't come up to scratch, she's given her cards. Thus it was in the days of David and Solomon, but this arrangement has died out just about everywhere now, and it came to an end in this country quite a while ago. Trouble with the income tax probably had something to do with the change. Whatever the reason, it wouldn't have been a very convenient way of doing things on a farm, because the out-buildings are needed for housing cattle and other beasts.

How to go about it then, bearing in mind that it's not just any kind of woman will make a farmer's wife? She's rather like a minister's wife, part of the job. A doctor or bank manager or the man who sweeps the streets can afford some baby-doll of a wife to adorn the house like Christmas trimmings, but a farmer's wife is a real, special woman. For that reason, the standard must be set much higher when looking for a wife for a farmer.

The most straightforward way of going about it is to put an advertisement in the newspaper. You might try something like this: 'Wanted by All Saints' Day, on comfortable farm with twenty head of cattle, a good-looking, attested wife with good pedigree. Terms negotiable.' You'd be sure to get quite a good response to something like that, but it's a dangerous way of going about it because of the possibility that several women might turn up at the farm all at the same time. When something like that happens, with a crowd of females all after the same chap, it's easy for him to be torn asunder with one woman tugging at his right leg, another at his left, and so on. You won't find it at all consoling afterwards that they will be screeching and weeping over the pile of bits and pieces that are all that's left of you. Unless you always keep eight or nine ferocious dogs about the place, I don't recommend advertising as a means of acquiring a wife.

A more usual method is to put the matter in the hands of an auctioneer. He moves around the country quite a lot, and so gets a chance to see more than most of us. He also has a fair idea of everybody's financial affairs, and should he be able to find you a rich wife, he knows that it would probably be to his spiritual advantage later on. The snag with this method is that there's a danger he will persuade you to take on a number of piglets and a pile of old furniture as well as the woman, and thus add to your problem instead of reducing it as he's supposed to do. That said, it's a method to be borne in mind if ever the worst comes to the worst.

There remains the lucky-dip method. This means that you will have to turn out as often as you can to go on the Sunday School outing, to tea-parties, to auctions, eisteddfodau, the cinema, and the Band of Hope. It's in this way that you might hit upon someone who is prepared to take notice of you. But don't expect any woman to do that too openly at first. There's something wrong with a lass who tries to get her claws into you at the first wink. The prospects are better with a woman who gives you a box on the ear, especially if it's an unjustifiable cuff. A righteous clout is what you get from winking at another man's wife and you shouldn't derive any encouragement from receiving one of those, particularly if her husband is a lot bigger than you.

As I have already suggested, you can't expect a favourable response immediately from a girl who really fancies you. It's quite possible that she will roll with laughter at you, or go out of her way to be unpleasant. This shouldn't surprise you, since you are a farmer, and so in a favourable position to realize that women all over the world go through this rigmarole. The important thing is that she should make any sort of response, from sticking out her tongue to hurling an axe or smoothing-iron at you; mind you, the interpretation of reactions like that is not the same *after* you are married. On eliciting some not unfavourable response, persevere by making nice suggestions to her, such as going to the pictures, or taking tea in a café, or a trip round the gas-works. Attractive stratagems like this are becoming necessary nowadays. The time has passed when you could have grabbed the little scalliwag by the hair and dragged her into your cave. It's women who are responsible for the fact that Man doesn't live in caves any more, and now you know the reason why.

What will tell you clearly that you are coming along nicely is when you receive an invitation to have supper in her home. When that happens it means she is starting to tire of pretending to be running ahead of you and that she wants her mother to cast an eye over you and give her the 'he's better than nothing' look. From the moment that happens, it's the 'Dead March' for your hopes of escape and the 'Hallelujah Chorus' between the girl and her mother.

I had better not go to the trouble of trying to instruct you on how to get married. You won't have any say in the matter. The best thing to do is to slope off somewhere with your prospective father-in-law and sit at his feet as if he were Gamaliel. You two will be great consolation for each other in your tribulation.

As a farmer it's probable that you will have to be married at some time between early-milking and late, unless you happen to have a neighbour kind enough to look after the place for a few days. If he does you that favour, make sure you acknowledge it by offering him a cartful of manure or promising to look after his wife should he ever have to go into hospital or prison for a stretch — the precise offer you make will depend on what kind of wife he has. If you don't have such a helpful neighbour, you can always pretend to be on your honeymoon by taking your wife for a spin around the farmyard on a tractor, or going to spend your first night as man and wife in the hay-barn. After that you will have to settle down to married life, without my going into any further detail on that score.

You are now in a position to judge whether you have got a wife or a millstone. You won't have had much of a chance to consider this up to now. You have been too busy running about the place like a cockerel. The first point to consider is what she's like as a housewife. If you come into the house after early-milking and find her still lounging in bed, and in waking her, you get a smack across your face for not bringing her a cup of tea, don't be impatient and decide there's no hope for her. It may be that she only intends putting you to the test and that she would be quite content with coffee instead of tea. Wait until dinner-time, for many things can be forgiven a woman who knows how to cook. If you find her making soup with goose-grease or the stuff used for polishing shoes, try to be patient with her for a few months more and point out to her carefully that you appreciate the experimental spirit and realize there's a lot of nourishment in goose-grease, except that you have a finnicky stomach that won't take everything you put into it. If it's out of a lack of knowledge, rather than a wish to become a widow, that she serves the nightmarish dishes that are put before you, there's hope that the little dear will slowly respond to this policy of patience on your part, and that you will have, in the fullness of time, a dinner worth sitting down to, and one you can sit down after.

And given that your dearest is a dab hand at preparing food — and that she will let you eat some of it after it's been cooked — there remain a few other points to watch out for. For instance, what is she like as regards hygiene? If she insists on sending the dish-cloth and mop to the laundry, you have acquired a tidy wife, and it would be churlish of you to suggest sardonically that she should also send herself to the laundry on a Friday evening, so that she too is spared having to work. That is not the way to get the best out of a wife, particularly if you have a churning-pond into which you can throw her.

Preparing food and keeping the place clean are the two most important things in a housewife — during the day, at least. But much more than that is expected of a farmer's wife. To be quite honest, there is not much of a shine to any farm unless the wife runs the whole caboodle, and particularly the cash. A man is by nature peaceable and perfectly content if he can think he's a bit of a lad. The price of cattle and things like that would be ridiculously low if it were not for the fact that men are afraid of being told off by the wife when they get home. It's no exaggeration to say that more than one cow would have been sold for a pipeful of baccy if it had not been for that factor. Barter is one of a man's chief pleasures from his youth onwards. He derives a lot more pleasure from swapping a pig for a double-barrelled gun and a few cartridges than he ever gets from the money.

It takes a woman to understand the value of money, and that's quite natural, when you consider that it's money lies at the root of all evil and that Eve also had something to answer for on this score. So rest content with having responsibility for things of secondary importance, such as looking after animals and working the land, leaving the real farming, that is making it pay, to your wife. Responsibility for all mistakes will lie with you, of course, but you ought to be grateful that you are responsible for something, since you're such a silly old fellow.

Y Fuwch a'i Chynffon (Hughes a'i Fab, 1954)

To the Mountain

Ifor Williams

I don't know whether you have ever noticed the way a shepherd walks. I mean a mountain shepherd, not a farmer from the valley floor, nor his labourers either, but an old shepherd from the hills as he walks along the road behind a flock of sheep. He always walks with short, quick steps, in a sort of trot which is typical of his occupation, and he can keep at it all day long. The reason, of course, is that all his life he's had to walk for miles on the steep slopes, and no man rushes up them. Small steps are best for climbing. On the side of a mountain the long-legged man has no advantage over the short-legged.

I too was brought up in a district where there were more inclines than flat places, and for various reasons that I needn't go into now, my stride is short. I never had the privilege of raising sheep, but I know quite a bit about walking the mountains of my native patch. Not that I'm a climber of rocks, mind you. For that kind of work your arms and legs have to be long, in order to reach each gripping-place, and to climb step by step, and I wasn't cut out to be stretched like that. But in days gone by I was capable of spending the whole day on the high mountains, revelling in the light cool breeze on the upper slopes and, on reaching the summit, enjoying the splendour of the view on every side, by land and sea, and particularly the terrific wildness of Snowdonia; that was the main thing as far as I was concerned — the wildness. There's an incomparable beauty to be seen sometimes on a clear day, apart from jagged rocks and bare valleys. You can see fertile vales, green woods and fields in the distance, streams, rivers, and lakes shining glassily in the hollows. Here and there you catch a glimpse of the Menai Straits, and Anglesey, 'the imperious isle', surrounded by its deep blue waters. Nevertheless, what most remains in my memory are the vast lonely places that stretch in every direction, the mountain terrain itself, the waste wilderness, the wild wasteland. That's what strikes a man most. And for that impression, it's best to climb on your own. Climbing to the top of Snowdon with a crowd of other people holds no appeal for me. A jolly crowd is somehow out of place on the summit of a mountain. A man should not be alone, it's said. True enough, for much of life, but not true for me on a mountain-top.

There are two aspects to the experience, quite different the one from the other. On the crest of a mountain you can be raised up as well as cast down — exhilaration and dejection. First comes elevation. A moment ago there was a pinnacle of rock that was higher than you. Now it's under your feet and there's not another pinnacle higher up challenging you to reach it. You have conquered the mountain. The mountain has to look up at you and you have the sweet thrill of looking down at its summit. Such fleeting hubris!

The key then moves into the minor. You begin to become aware of the eternal majesty of the mountain, a feeling of your own insignificance like that of a tiny fly, short-lived and feeble, there but for an instant and soon to fall away. It's the mountain that's let you borrow its altitude for a moment, the mountain that's high, not you. You belong on the flat down below. It's there you live and down you will have to go with your head bowed. And the mountain remains with its head still held high in the heavens.

I feel like this whenever I read the Sermon on the Mount. It was to people like us that the sermon was delivered, by One who was seated on the mountain as on a throne. It's splendid to ponder the perfection that was given to us as a standard. Woe to us when we are concerned only with ourselves and see the abysmal distance between us and its attainment. And yet it's good for us to stand there for a moment in the presence of the Sublime. Whenever we are cast down into the depths, as we oft-times are, wave upon wave of uneasiness sweeps over us as we lift up our eyes unto the hills. And then we yearn to climb back, and linger for a while, perhaps to settle there. But it's about something else that I want to give a short talk tonight.

Looking back, I very vividly recall the time I climbed Carnedd Llywelyn[1] at night. It was like this, if you have the patience to listen. I had heard that the shepherds usually rounded up their sheep for shearing mountain by mountain, in a sequence that was a tradition going back generations and that it would be worth my seeing the Braich Roundup — that was the name for the great drive that gathered all the sheep on Carnedd Llywelyn in a single night. The appointed time came. I received word that the shepherds would be setting out at midnight on Sunday night, and so off I went to Cilfodan, the farm belonging to Richard Griffith, an uncle of mine, near Carneddi, Bethesda. I arrived there in good time and had a great welcome from my Aunt Elin. A meal, and then a wait for the clock to strike twelve. A shepherd or two turned up at the house, each with his crook and his dog. My uncle was busily preparing to set out and his dog had been ready for quite a while. I borrowed a crook. The clock struck twelve and off we went in a small silent procession, leaving the houses and streets behind for the mountain and its darkness, until we found the head of the path leading past Garth. We walked in Indian file, one behind the other. Richard Griffith was a large, fat, corpulent man and we walked behind him, feeling rather like Goronwy Owen[2] following in the footsteps of the Big Parson in similar circumstances, 'like a boat in a ship's wake'. Every now and again other shepherds joined us, taking their place silently in the file, each with his dog, each with his crook. The procession grew steadily.

After my eyes had become accustomed to the dark, I was able to maintain my place in the procession quite easily, by following the column of darkness that was blacker than night and moving steadily in front of me, namely my Uncle Cilfodan. If there was room for him, there was room for me — and to spare. By now we were on the open mountain, with Gurn Wiga on our left, and we were making for the edge of Drosgl. Turning my head, I saw that many shepherds and dogs had joined us. Nobody spoke and no one greeted the newcomers — we just kept on walking. Then we spotted a fiery signal on the mountain far off to the left in the direction of Llanllechid, and one of the company said, 'It's the Bryn Eithin lads letting us know they're on their way.' In due course we came upon two men squatting above our path, having come across Waun Cws Mai to meet us. 'You go with the Bryn Eithin boy,' my Uncle said, 'he's going farther than anyone else, to the nape of the mountain right behind Carnedd Llywelyn. I'm turning off now to the spot where I'm supposed to be.' And off he went. I looked back: the file behind me had disappeared, every shepherd and dog had turned off, one by one, to take up his appointed position by the break of day. Each one knew precisely where to go and when to go. And by daybreak there would be a girdle of men and dogs around the great mountain — on the Arllechwedd Uchaf side. At first light, as soon as the sheep with fleeces could be distinguished from the bald sheep — the ones already sheared — everybody was to walk straight on, driving the unshorn sheep towards the folds or pens on the bank of Afon Wen, at the bottom of the Braich.

But my task was to follow the son of Bryn Eithin, and to ply him with questions. Who had arranged for him to take up position at that particular spot allotted to him? He didn't know: only this, that the Bryn Eithin shepherd was expected to be there at daybreak, on the morning of the Braich Roundup, simply because that was the old, old custom.

More climbing, clambering our way up Foel Grach, and onto the ridge that was right behind Carnedd Llywelyn. Evans went on, and I turned to the right and went straight to the top of the Carnedd. And there I waited for daylight.

Came the dawn, without anything unusual about it that morning, and I went down to the peak known as Yr Elan that juts out from the Carnedd. From there another ridge led down to the bottom, and I had a good view on both sides as I slowly made my descent. And what a view! On either side far below me, I could make out the slopes alive with small sheep leaping ahead of the dogs, first sideways and then downwards, in the direction of the pens. I could see men, one here, there another, in a loose circle on the mountainside, urging the dogs on. The smaller droves of sheep joined together in larger and larger numbers as the net closed around them. By the time I had reached the last outcrop on the Braich, all these groups had come together in a huge crowd of woolly sheep. In all my life I have never seen, either before or since, so many sheep in one place. How many were there? I don't know. Three to four thousand, one of the shepherds said. Around them there darted scores of dogs that never let up — they were like rapacious wolves! Every now and then a strong young beast would break away from the drove and make a dart for the mountain and its freedom. Half a dozen dogs rushed across after it, snapping playfully at its ears to teach it a lesson. These dogs were very excited and as though rejoicing at having a bit of fun with the frisky lambs.

Then something strange happened, taking everyone by surprise. Instead of deciding to escape one by one, the whole gathering of sheep took it into their heads that they would all go back together — as if the same idea had taken hold of every one of them at the same time, that it was far better to be at home on the mountain than to be playthings for sheep-dogs down below. And they started back up the slope that I had just come down, and nothing and nobody could stop them. The shepherds ran with their arms outstretched and shouting as only shepherds know how. The dogs sped around them like mad things, but all in vain. The sheep wanted to go up, and up they went in spite of dogs and men. They encircled a shepherd or two and turned him into an island in their midst. I had run and shouted as much as I could manage, until eventually I was capable of neither, and had to lie down to recover my wind, gaping all the while at the sheep's victory.

But now an old shepherd took matters in hand. Too many sheep in one drove, he said, the drove too big by far. The huge throng had to be broken down into smaller droves, and be kept apart. Men and dogs ran up and cleverly pushed their way into the midst of the sheep, and by dint of tremendous effort they succeeded in doing just that: the smaller droves were brought back towards the dip and were kept strictly apart. The trouble was over.

They began dipping and shearing, diligently and busily, on the bank of the Afon Wen. There was hard, monotonous work for scores of men lasting many an hour, and to tell you the truth, I wasn't at all keen to remain there watching the busy shears. I was conscious that I'd eaten my last sandwich hours before on the summit of Yr Elan, so I made for home as fast as my tired feet could carry me.

When was this? More than fifty years ago. It left an indelible impression on my mind. The scene remains as vivid in my memory as though it were only a few months ago.

The poet-preacher J.T. Jôb[3] once went to take up a ministry at Fishguard, in Pembrokeshire, and he composed a poem of farewell to Carneddi in Arfon. He had been fond of fishing the Ffryddlas, the Llafar, and the Gaseg, the rivers which flow through the waste places that we had walked that night. Cwm Pen Llafar is the great cavern between Carnedd Llywelyn and Carnedd Dafydd. It's worth seeing. Mountains three thousand feet high close it in on three sides, and one side is wide open for the Llafar to flow out. Jôb was fond of his rod and enjoyed fishing in the Cwm. But he went there on his own and so had the true experience of the mountain and its lonely places; and this is what he wrote:

> 'Farewell to Cwm Pen Llafar
> And its lonely, peaceful ground,
> Where a man may meet but an ewe's low bleat,
> And God, and the water's sound.'

I Ddifyrru'r Amser (Llyfrfa'r Methodistiaid Calfinaidd, 1959)

The Imperative Upon Me

Islwyn Ffowc Elis

I can't help being a Welshman. I could have chosen not to think in a Welsh way. But I should still have been a Welshman, because my forebears were Welsh-speaking Welsh people, and because it was the land and weather of Wales that shaped the way of life into which I was born.

It's my parents more than anyone else that I have to thank for the fact that I write in Welsh. Although English was my mother's first language, it was decided from the start that we children should have Welsh as our native tongue. And in the years of my youth, at a school that was almost wholly English-speaking, whenever I tended to think in English and even began writing a little in it, the Welsh language would always draw me back to it, because that was the language of my home and most of the books there, the language of my chapel, my people, and my community.

And all this for me is a destiny from which I can't escape — the imperative that's upon me day and night to be what I am, a Welsh-speaking Welshman. This, perhaps, because Wales herself is under a destiny. It's incomprehensible to me how Wales has survived. There's no sense in the fact that a number of tribes so mixed in blood and so ambivalent in their outlook should have gone on being a nation over fifteen long centuries, despite relentless attack from without and constant schism within.

It's not her language which is the reason. That could have disappeared long ago, as it did in the land of the Gododdin[1] and in Cornwall, and as languages have disappeared in other countries. Neither is it her system of laws. Those ceased to exist in the memories of old men more than five hundred years ago. Nor are her mountains the reason. Those were as much a hindrance to her unity as they were a safeguard of her separate identity.

It seems to me that there's something of a cat-with-nine-lives about the Welsh nation which resembles, to say the least, a destiny. It's true that every cat has to die sooner or later, yet that doesn't detract from the wonder that it saves its skin in the teeth of so many dangers and manages to live for so long.

There's something peculiar, say what you will, about being a few hundred thousand people on a narrow strip of upland who have retained their language and their sense of belonging to none but themselves from the fall of the Roman Empire to the decline of the British Empire. And not in the impassable solitudes of Turkestan or in the forest depths of Africa, but here, in view of Europe, a mere two hundred miles from London, under the nose of a mighty nation that was for two centuries mistress of the world and whose language swept continents.

And not only that. But to lose her leaders one by one, and her patrons by the hundred, and her people by the thousand. To lose her Cadwallon[2] and her Rhodri and her Gruffudd and her Llywelyn; to lose her noblemen to the London court and then her gentry to the language and manners of that court; to lose her sons and daughters as mercenaries and conscripts in English wars for century after century, to lose her common people to America yesterday, and the children of her miners and quarrymen to England today. To lose, lose, lose — and still to go on living.

I don't see any sense in a thing like that. The continuity could be explained if Wales had had borders and a government like such small places as Monaco, Andorra, San Marino, Luxemburg, and Liechtenstein. It would be explicable if she had a parliament and a sea on all sides like the Isle of Man. But vulnerable as she has been, and still is, to the ravages of nearby England, which penetrate all aspects of her life, there's no sense in the fact that she has gone on living.

There's no sense in it, but there must be meaning somewhere. There must be in this frail nation some genius for survival, for avoiding what it cannot confront, some tough compliance that bends without breaking, some deceptive greenness that bursts into bud in a display of culture after long bouts in the darkness, flaming out as revivals after paganism and exploding as nationalism after centuries of not thinking as a nation.

Yes, her language does have something to do with her survival, after all. But a language as complex as Welsh doesn't go on living unless it's the symbol of some deeper will.

I've been talking about Wales rather than about myself and my own emotions and writing. The reason for that is a simple one. If it were not for Wales, there would be no meaning or purpose to my life. That she and her language have survived up to now is of special significance for me. Why was I born in Wales if not to stay here? Why born a Welshman if not to serve Wales? And why was the Welsh language given to me if not to use it fully for all purposes and to the utmost of its powers and mine?

I'm not saying that the world outside and its peoples and its languages are of no importance to me, as fools might rush in to aver.

The splendours of the countries of Europe thrill me, and their history and art never fail to enthral me. The English language comes easily to me, and its literature, too, is a treasure-house that I shouldn't want to be without. But all these delights only serve to make me an even more ardent Welshman. The alps and shores of the Continent make me prouder of the beauty of Wales; the freedom of Switzerland, the Netherlands, and Belgium make me ashamed of my own nation's servility; and the architecture and art of all these countries make me sad at the poverty of my own.

With every day that passes I become prayerfully anxious about the safety of the world from megaton bombs, worried at the oppression of my black-skinned brothers, vexed that millions of my fellow-men are rotting in detention camps. But I can't help these people more by serving Wales less. Indeed, it's because I belong to a small nation which has long been oppressed that I'm able to feel so sincerely for the other unfortunates on earth. And I believe that Wales will be more alive, more free, more responsible — if I can help to make her so — more able and readier to help rid the world of its misery, and to work for its safety, than she could ever be in her present helpless condition.

So it's only as a Welshman that I can serve humankind. The world will not come one jot nearer to the Kingdom of Heaven as I turn away from it. There are, here in Wales, twisted things to set straight, darkness to throw light upon, bitterness to make sweet, prejudices to be done away with. And I can cast my poor mite into the treasure-house of literature just as well in Welsh as in any other language — better, since it is the language in which my thought is woven.

Yet the fact that Wales has so far continued to be Welsh, and is in some measure still Welsh in speech, is not in itself a guarantee that Wales will last for ever. Her will to live is as strong today as it ever was — in a loyal remnant of her people — but the forces that would destroy her are also stronger today than they have ever been. The English are not only on the other side of Offa's Dyke[3] but in our midst. The English language is not just the medium of school instruction for seven hours each day, but an ubiquitous voice throughout the day on radio, in newspapers, and on the television screen. Wales is no longer a haven beyond the mountains, but an open playground for hordes of motorists and cyclists and hikers, and an experimental field for the Government's technology. The teeth of her defensive mountains have been drawn, her valleys drowned by the English, and the innards of her rural society ripped out. She now stands naked before the world.

It is this nakedness which burdens me and all my kind. And since I am a writer by nature, above and before everything else, what I write and the way I write must somehow be a medium for extending the life of Wales, the country to which I owe everything. And because it is her own language that is the fount of her Welsh identity, to write more clearly and with greater liveliness and variety in that language is my non-combatant's way of waging war on her behalf.

I wasn't brought up on the slopes of Arfon, where a quarter of a century ago English was heard only by chance, but two-and-a-half miles from the border with England, where all communication outside that narrow, Welsh-speaking valley meant English. That is why, I think, 'the language struggle' has penetrated the very marrow of my being and is therefore a condition of my writing. It's something that writers and critics brought up in the heart of Gwynedd or Seisyllwg — or outside Wales — cannot easily understand. There's no point in trying to reason with me that a concern for Welsh-speaking Wales is having a detrimental effect on my work. Every writer is formed during the first ten years of his life, and I can't alter the first ten years of mine. The border is in my blood.

I'm not so naive, however, as to believe that the survival of the Welsh language and the Welsh identity depend solely upon me and my generation. It once depended on William Morgan[4], Williams Pantycelyn, and O.M. Edwards, and in a century from now it will depend on whoever will then be expressing Welsh thoughts in the Welsh language. The battle for Wales is a relay race, and it's hard to believe there will ever be an end to it. So much greater, therefore, is the responsibility upon us not to let the torch fall into the mire, after so many have borne it and handed it on for so long.

Of course, it would be better to be able to write without any awareness of battle and crisis. It would be splendid to be locked away in Gwales[5], to play about contentedly like a dilettante with writing and literary ideas, pretending that there's no difference between being a Welsh writer and an English writer, or an American or Russian writer. But in an ivory tower like that, as in the Mabinogion[6], would the literature we produced be any the better? I don't believe it would.

Fy Nghymru I (gol. R. Gerallt Jones, Gwasg Gee, 1961)

Disenchantment

R. Gerallt Jones

I was born at Nefyn in 1934, a clergyman's son, an only child, and a monoglot Welsh-speaker, in so far as I had any language at all at that time. When I was ten years old I was sent, to my dismay, to an English school in Shrewsbury. I went from there to a minor, English, Anglican boarding-school in Staffordshire. In 1951 I returned to Wales, to read English at Bangor. Then, having graduated, I began to take an interest in Welsh literature, tried to write in Welsh, and while doing research into English poetry, found time to begin familiarizing myself with the literary traditions of my mother-tongue. That was a sure way, probably, of bringing up a schizophrenic, but be that as it may, I regard Wales and Welsh nationality today under the influence of that mixed background.

When I was a boy at school Wales was for me a hearth, a home, a playing-field, the seaside, a father and mother, a wonderful world, hidden, separate from the world of school, a proud possession of my own, a secret room that my English friends knew nothing about; Wales, if you like, was for me at that time of my life a status-symbol. Many Welsh-speaking Welsh people, I know, say they have suffered scorn and mockery in England on account of their Welsh identity; I must say that was not my experience. No one else spoke Welsh at school, so I tended to be an object of some curiosity — I was an odd creature, one who spoke a strange language at home and used to receive letters written in it every week. On Mondays I used to get *Yr Herald Cymraeg*[1] and *Y Cymro* for the previous week, and these papers would be passed around from hand to hand among my class-mates. In time some of them came to use the Welsh language as a kind of code in which to send secrets from one to the other, since certain among my closest friends had picked up a few phrases by now. I was received into school society as a peculiar foreigner, but was shown every kindness and courtesy; I heard not a word of mockery from start to finish.

The consequence of all this was to make me think of Wales as very important in my life, because it was my Welsh identity, and nothing else, that made me the object of so much interest to the other children.

But it also made me form an inaccurate picture of Wales in my own mind. It made me look upon her as a kind of Utopia, a faery-land where it was always a white Christmas, or summer sunshine; this was a dangerous picture, of course, but an advantageous one, too. The dangers will be evident to every Welshman now in 1960, but perhaps the advantages are not so obvious: it created in me a lasting love, a love real and profound, for one particular part of Wales, the land of Llŷn.

I never felt, from my school days on, any happiness comparable with what I experienced at term's end while travelling by train across the border between England and Wales; the feeling was purely sentimental, of course, but at that time I *was* a lump of sentimentality, and there's a lot of it in me to this day, I know. But if it was sentimentality that made me shout hallelujah on crossing the border from English Cheshire to Anglicized Flintshire, it was nevertheless a sincere feeling, that growing excitement which caused me to move about restlessly from one part of the train to the next as it drew into Bangor station, and the most important part of my journey began. From Bangor on, everywhere was sheer paradise. Eifionydd was my mother's home and my tongue was familiar with all the names of the sleepy villages that slipped by in the feeble, reluctant, Spring sunshine, or in the exciting dark of the days before Christmas: Llanwnda, Penygroes, Ynys, Pant Glas, Bryncir, Chwilog, and in due course, the old, single, wind-swept, draughty, glorious platform of Afon Wen. I used to enjoy Afon Wen best on a dark winter's night, with the eloquent wind from off the moorland making me turn up the collar of my coat and seek the shelter of some shed or other. There, under the dull lamps, and looking out into the darkness, I could imagine the warmth of Christmas, football games in the village, shyly meeting my first sweetheart (without her or anyone else being aware of it) at the children's service in the vestry on Tuesday evening, and all the buttermilk life and the sea-wind and country quiet of our district in the days before television came to break it all up and keep everyone in their burrows like so many frightened rabbits. I was able to construct my world before I had reached it, and go to live in my splendid ivory-tower without moving an inch from Afon Wen.

After such a start, my holidays were usually as full as my dreams of them. I had, as an only child, created a personal life for myself, and I was perfectly content to be left on my own in my favourite places, to be allowed to go on living in that world. I created flowery romances around Melin Fadryn, in the mill itself, all about the lake, in the wood beyond, on the slopes of the Garn, and then, later on, I managed to recreate an imaginary, paradise world among the trees and wild-flowers of Plas Gelli-Wig after my parents had gone to live in that old mansion. All things considered, although I shouldn't wish anyone else to be an only child if it were possible for him to belong to a larger family, I had the kind of childhood for which I shall be grateful for as long as I live. The contrast between holiday and work, between Wales and England, between school and home, was so complete, so black-and-white, that it made me regard Welsh-speaking Wales in that period of my life as if it were heaven on earth. But, alas, everyone has to put away childish things sooner or later, and that's what I did in coming face to face with the facts about Wales for the first time at the University College of Bangor. That was the beginning of the disenchantment, probably.

Fy Nghymru I (gol. R. Gerallt Jones, Gwasg Gee, 1961)

The Hiring Fair

Ifan Gruffydd

One of the great occasions of my life was the day I was allowed to go to the hiring fair at Llangefni for the first time.

I set out early on a May morning in the year 1909 in the hope of finding a place for myself. I strode like a two-year-old foal through Rhostrehwfa, delighted to be looking forward to the day that was about to dawn when I should be allowed to wear corduroy trousers, bell-bottoms and London yorks, with shining buckles and the straps fastened on the outside in a curly link at both knees. Many an old inhabitant of Rhos looked pityingly at my small, puny build, unable to believe that I was ready to go out into the world, and Mary Price the Coal tried to persuade me to look for something better than serving farmers. But there was nothing could stand in the way of my determination to be able one day to follow a pair of well-fed horses from headland to headland, turning the peaty bog of Morfa Deugae into long furrows ready for sowing.

There was nothing for it but to walk every step of the way, of course, and the three miles to town was nothing to us in Llangristiolus, anyway. I had been there several times before, either driving cattle for threepence or sixpence, or else helping to carry baskets of some neighbour's chicks for twopence, and I had been glad of the money, which I took to Nan Roberts the Shop towards a pair of new boots.

But when that great day arrived for which I had been yearning so long, I felt a degree of independence and put my mind on being respectable from now on. People would soon forget that I was such a naughty boy once I had started working, and perhaps they would come to see that I was as good as most lads my age if only I were given a chance to prove it, and it was my intention that morning to seize the chance if it came my way.

I put myself on the market, as it were, in front of the Bull Hotel, among scores of the county's young men, as was the custom at the hiring fair. It was a lovely experience to feel as if you were someone who mattered in the agricultural tradition, and I thought myself to be among those who made the world go around. The farmers, great and small, walked at their leisure through the ranks, weighing up the size and strength of the prospective employees as was necessary. If it was a bailiff a man wanted, he had to have one who was capable and clever in his work, who was prepared to rise early and retire late, one who could keep himself in good order and take a keen interest in his master's affairs. If it was a horse-handler he wanted, well then, a strong young man was required, with broad shoulders, a cap on the side of his head, and a straw in his mouth. The same qualifications, more or less, were needed in a feeder and farmhand, namely that they were prepared to turn their hand to anything — and to some things that would degrade a bailiff or a waggoner, perhaps, but which were necessary to make a team and ensure a successful season for the master.

The hiring had been brisk and had been going on for hours before anyone noticed that I was there at all, and although I stood up straight and stuck my chest out as best I could, somehow or other they all passed me by. Plenty wanted bailiffs and waggoners, but almost none seemed to be looking for a farmhand, and I was so willing.

I began to lose heart, fearing that I should be left 'on the clout', as Anglesey people say. A man from Llangristiolus came by, one whom I knew well, whose children had all made their way in the world.

'Are you hired?' he asked.

'No, I'm not,' I replied.

'You're too much of a scalliwag, my lad, aren't you, who would take you on?' Perhaps I should be ashamed to say it, but for the rest of my days I never had much liking for that man.

If it had started badly, my subsequent fate at the fair turned out to be even worse. Perhaps that man had spoken truly after all, and perhaps he, and others like him, had warned the other farmers not to burn their fingers by hiring a wastrel like me.

It was now late in the afternoon and most of the lads had been hired; the ranks had thinned, and only about three or four were left on the square waiting for someone from somewhere to take pity on them. The street was beginning to empty, the farmers' wives, having filled their butter-baskets with goods, were making for the stables at the back of the Bull, and Huw Jones the ostler was attaching the horses to traps, and the pig-carts were hurrying off home. I had never felt so lonely: there had been such brisk hiring all afternoon and I had been rejected. I would sooner have gone to Davies the Kennels to clean out the hounds than be without a place to serve in, because it wasn't respectable in those days to be left out. I saw Dafydd Evans of Tyddyn Lleithig coming — towards whom, I wondered? Yes indeed, it was in my direction he was coming, this short-legged, fine-looking smallholder who had decided, he said, with his air of authority, to employ some slip of a lad to do the running about for him now that he was getting on in years. With him was Owen Evans of Penrhos, an old neighbour of ours who had showed a bit of fatherly concern for me, fair play to him, and this is how the conversation went from that moment on.

'Here's Ifan, Dafydd Evans, he's very keen to find a place and I've no doubt he'll be just the right lad for you.'

'But I hear he's a bit of a rascal.' He turned to me and asked, 'Are you really a rascal?'

Because of my guilt about a few pranks that I couldn't deny, I was unable to say anything, but lowered my eyes and scraped my toe-cap on the edge of the pavement. But I ventured to raise my head on hearing Owen Evans say, 'No, he's not, this lad's all right, a bit mischievous perhaps, as some strapping lads like him are when they haven't any thing to do. Give him plenty of work and he'll soon settle down.'

Dafydd Evans paused, and then asked, 'If you're allowed to come to my place, will you promise to change your ways?'

'I will,' said I.

'If I speak to you sharply, you won't answer me back?'

'I won't,' and before I had a chance to finish, Owen Evans broke in with, 'No, he won't ever, even if you kick him he'll only go off like a dog with his tail between his legs.'

'H'm,' said the smallholder, 'I'm glad to hear that about you.' He put his stick under his arm, and reached for his cherry-wood pipe and filled it with Amlwch tobacco, and as he threw away the match after lighting up, he asked amid a cloud of smoke, 'After finishing your work, will you help the girl with the hens and chicks of an evening, and not go larking about with those daft boys up the lane?'

'I will,' I said once again, lest I be without a place. He drew himself up and pushed out his stomach as if he were the owner of a thousand acres: 'Well, I'll give you two pounds this first season, and if you behave I'll raise it by five shillings by the time winter comes, what do you say, Owen Evans?'

'Well, yes, but aren't you a bit hard with the wages, Gaffer?'

'Hard? What's the matter with you, man? Isn't it enough for him, and he'd have his belly full of food into the bargain? What else does the little bugger want? I don't know what these lads think they are. Where do they expect a farmer to get money from to pay them?'

In the end it was agreed on two pounds, with a down-payment of sixpence to clinch the bargain and all the conditions that went with it. So about eighteen pence a week was my wage when I first found employment, and I was glad enough of the job.

Gŵr o Baradwys (Gwasg Gee, 1963)

The Man at Chapel House

Gomer M. Roberts

Jenkin was living on his own, in Llety Siencyn, when I first came to know him. He was on the dole at the time, and his only delight in life — apart from reading — was wandering the slopes of Mynydd Penrhys, with a big black dog at his heels. He was a short, stoutish man, with broad shoulders and a large round head. His thick crop of yellowish-red hair was beginning to go grey. It must have been very difficult to put a comb through it, I should think, since it was so frizzy and disorderly. 'My head's a bit like heaven' he used to say, adding in English, 'for there is no parting there!' There had never been a hat or cap on that head of his, for the simple reason that

hat-makers had never imagined there existed heads quite as big as Jenkin's. There was a nasty scar across his forehead. He got it when he was a lad in the pit. While walking out of the drift one day he had grabbed the tail of one of the ponies, but instead of pulling him up the incline, the horse had kicked him. His forehead had been split open by the horse's hind hoof, and for a few days Jenkin had been in danger of his life. They had put straw on the road in front of his house to keep down the sound of traffic. The doctor had put a silver plate in his head, and later on that was to give Jenkin the chance to boast, 'There may not be any silver in my pocket, but there's plenty of it in my head!' He suffered terrible pains for the rest of his life as a result of that accident.

Jenkin was his parents' youngest son. One of his relatives was John Lewis of Margam, one of the ablest deacons among the Methodists of Glamorgan in his day. His mother, Marged Lewis, was a remarkable woman. She was one of the stalwarts of the Sunday School, and quite outstanding when members took oral examinations in the Scriptures at Jerusalem Chapel. Jenkin had inherited this interest from his mother. His brothers, Thomas and John (the latter a grandfather of the popular singer Ivor Emanuel[1]) were both married men, and Jenkin and his mother were quite comfortable in each other's company at the old family-home. Great was Marged's solicitude for her son. She had a good deal of admiration for the Old Connexion[2]. Indeed, the other denominations didn't count at all in her sight. Once, about the time of the big Baptist meetings at Bethel, Jenkin had a cold and was being kept at home by the fireside. 'You could easily catch pneumonia if you went there,' said Marged. Then who should call after supper on the Monday but their neighbour, Wil Beti. 'Jenkin,' said Wil, 'So-and-so (naming one of the Old Connexion's lynch-pins) is preaching at Gwarycaea — do you want to come?' Whereupon, before Jenkin had a chance to say anything, Marged said cheerfully, 'Yes, my boy, you go with Wiliam, and have a bit of a stretch.' Marged firmly believed that neither pneumonia nor any other ailment lurked within the walls of a Methodist chapel.

Like Dai, in the poem by J.J. Williams[3], Jenkin was 'quite a good scholar, who read a bit'. The scope of his reading varied — commentaries on the Yearly Syllabus, political pamphlets and books with some substance to them, of a philosophical and theological nature. He had come under the influence of the teachings of Annie Besant, and begun to take an interest in eastern religions. He even claimed to have proof of an earlier existence, and some vague, faint memory of having walked upon earth previously in some form or other. Such revelations used to astonish some of the ministers who visited the Sunday School.

On the first Sabbath I took the service at Jerusalem, I recall seeing Jenkin sitting to my right up in the gallery, and noticed him while the congregation was singing. I have to say it, he wasn't much of a musician. It was the words counted in his view, not the hymn-tune, and he was looking all about him while the congregation sang. But suddenly, on coming to a phrase in one of Pantycelyn's[4] hymns, Jenkin began singing with all his might, his eyes shut. When the preacher started on the sermon, Jenkin too was by now taking a lively interest in it all. He was leaning forward, with his two elbows on the gallery's rail. He was listening intently, his face the living expression of the interest he took in the truths proclaimed from the pulpit. And whenever he heard delicious things of the kind he loved to hear, he would study the faces of others — William Hughes or John Thomas — to see what effect the message was having on them. Yes, Jenkin was a listener second to none, and during the week he would ruminate, as it were, in readiness for the Fellowship meeting on the Thursday evening.

He was very fond of Sunday School and Bible Class. The way he went about it was this: he would wait to see how the wind was blowing, and after listening to the opinion of the teacher, and to everyone else's, he would argue against them. And then, tally-ho! fervently and loudly, until such time as the Superintendent rang the bell to bring the Sunday School to a close. I enquired of him once, 'You don't really believe what you were saying today, do you, Jenkin?' This was his reply: 'The great thing is to have discussion, and something to argue about,' and there was a twinkle in his eye. To corner him in debate was as difficult as catching an eel under a stone. He would stick to his point of view and never concede that the argument had been lost.

During week-day meetings in the first year of my ministry at Jerusalem, Jenkin used to sit in a seat at the back of the little vestry, getting to his feet now and again to bear testimony, and always in his inimitable style. He had a good memory and could remember the more incisive observations of all the preachers who had ever been in Jerusalem's pulpit over the years. Something along these lines, for example: 'I well recall Peter Hughes Griffiths[5] from London saying once at a big meeting,' 'Where do you keep Jesus Christ — in your head or in your heart? If He's in your head, it's look-out, my lad, because someone will come by one day with a better head than yours, and you'll lose your Saviour. But if He's in your heart, He'll be safe in there, and you'll have Him for all eternity.' 'Yes, friends, Jesus Christ is safe enough if He's in your hearts.' And with such sayings as this, he kept our lively interest in the Fellowship.

Dafydd Jones, one of the old deacons, was not content to see Jenkin getting to his feet so boldly, and one Thursday evening the old fellow expressed his disapproval, while standing on the pavement outside the vestry. 'If you won't go down on your knees occasionally in the Prayer Meeting, don't you go getting up on your hind legs in the Fellowship!' Jenkin took the rebuke mildly. But after he became a deacon he would always come forward, and was often called upon 'to work' — the local expression for taking part in prayer. If Jenkin was argumentative and had a lot to say when on his feet, it was different when he was on his knees — he was then solemn and humble, like a child. His favourite verse, sung in his own mellifluous dialect, was:

> The heat of day it is so fiery,
>   My passion's strength is like a fire,
> And empty things are all about me
>   Preventing me from reaching higher;
>   Give me shelter,
> O Gentle Jesus, at noon-day.[6]

He was just as fervent in spirit outside chapel. A Socialist by conviction, his great hero for a while had been Ramsay Macdonald, the Member of Parliament for Aberafan. After that politician's demise, his political idol was Aneurin Bevan[7] from Ebbw Vale. He was in his element at miners' meetings, and in the end was persuaded to contest a seat on the Neath Town Council. But he soon grew tired of councillor's work and turned his back on it.

Just a few years after I first knew him, Jenkin married one of the girls from the village — to everyone's great surprise. Then, before very long, he and his wife went to look after Chapel House. And so a new chapter started in his life. I dare say that nobody was quite like the man at Chapel House. He had a high opinion of the preachers of his denomination, and he took delight in their company, both old and young, from one Sunday to the next. He would insist on arguing with them, each in turn, although the skirmishes were always friendly. 'Great was the argument'[8] in the parlour of Chapel House, but all in a brotherly spirit, of course.

The high point of the year came with the Annual Meetings at the beginning of May. Two preachers, of course, one from North Wales and the other from the South, as a rule, and the meetings lasting from the Saturday to the Monday evening — *seven* meetings in all. Of course, there was no question of going to work on the Monday of the Big Meetings. I remember one Saturday evening in particular. About a fortnight before, Jenkin had received an injury to his hand at the coal-face, and had been paid compensation, as was the custom — the colliers called it 'the compo'. The festival's guests were the Reverends William Morgan and Emyr Roberts, and one of them had preached at the first meeting. There were about ten of us at the supper-table, deacons and ministers. Grace was said, whereupon Jenkin in the middle of the silence that followed, exclaimed, 'Well, now then, boys, pitch in — nobody works in this house except me and I'm on the compo!' I am sure that the two delegates from North Wales won't easily forget the mirth of that supper for as long as they live.

Yes, Jenkin had a happy time at Chapel House, and he went on taking the means of grace at Jerusalem as the years went by. He sat the Sunday School examinations regularly from one term to the next, and always attended the Summer School that the Sunday School used to hold regularly at Aberystwyth, making new friends every year from all parts of Wales. He never missed a meeting on Sundays, except when he was taking the service at one of the smaller chapels. For in his last years he had developed into a lay-preacher. I don't know what sort of preacher he turned out to be, but I was assured by many who had heard him that nobody preached in precisely the same way as he did. He had something of Siencyn Penrhydd[9] in him — another man from the same district, as it happens. He went faithfully to the District Meeting and to the Monthly Meeting, and he became president of both in turn. I heard that he had given new deacons some wonderful advice at one of these services.

At last the time came for Jenkin to go the way of all flesh. He slowly faded away, and everyone was aware that he was being gathered. The end came one Sunday afternoon. He had been at the morning-service and taken his usual place in the afternoon as teacher of the women's class. He opened the discussion, then sat down to allow the women to air their views about the matter under discussion. The blow fell upon him unawares during Sunday School. He was carried home and died there quietly and at peace. The district had lost one of its most remarkable characters, and I an amusing and kind-hearted friend. I trust that now and in the years to come Glamorgan will continue to produce men like Jenkin to enrich the life of the old valleys that have contributed so much to the religious and social life of our country.

Y Genhinen (Gaeaf, 1967/8), *Cloc y Capel* (Gwasg Gomer, 1973)

Question and Answer

Kate Roberts

In the 'twenties I had a small nephew living in Liverpool who was very fond of listening to stories from anyone with the patience to tell him one. As children will, he would ask questions of the story-teller as he went along, eager to know the fate of the characters in the tale, not wanting to know what would happen to them but what they would say. If you paused for a moment, the question would be on the tip of his tongue, 'And what did he or she say?' And so on, right to the end, and of course there never was an end to the story, because you always had to think up a reply to the question, 'What did he say?' I never once heard him ask, 'What happened next?' For him, what was important was what was said, not what happened.

The boy died in 1925 when he was only eight-and-a-half years old, and after his death they came across some little stories he had written. Although he had never been taught Welsh, except for a little in the Sunday School, and though he had heard only what was spoken in his own home, his Welsh was perfectly good. He had used to spend his summer holidays at Rhosgadfan and it was there all his stories were set. One was about a boy skating on the frozen brook near his grandmother's house, our house. In this story there was a dog with the boy, running at his side. At the bottom end of the brook the ice gave way and the boy went under. ' "Bow-wow," said the dog, but he got no answer.' That's how the story ended. The answer was important for bringing the story to an end. It was what *proved* to him that the boy had been drowned. Someone older than a child would have been content to say merely that the boy had gone under.

I remember an old preacher who came to preach occasionally where we used to live. He was doubtless a godly man, but he was also a very feeble preacher. One Sunday afternoon he had been preaching on 'the best of meats and the finest of wines'. It was too warm an afternoon to pay much attention to such delicacies. The sermon turned out to be as inept as ever, and as we made our way past the deacons' pew on our way out, and the old preacher was coming down the steps of the pulpit, we heard one of the deacons say to him, 'You were pretty good, really': one has to be hypocritical sometimes. And the old saint replied, with the sound of great weeping in his voice, 'Only trying to say something, you know.' I can still hear the sound of that lamentation. The dear old fellow knew full well that he had not had much success, but he also knew something else. He knew that he could 'say' much better (that was his word for it), because he had tasted of 'the best of meats'. He had been attempting to express his *experience*, but something had prevented him from telling it as he had wished.

Is that not the experience of all people who speak in public or write? They have something to say but find that they are not able to say it as they would wish. Yet not everyone weeps like the old preacher because he has failed.

All that came to mind while I was thinking about the interrogation of writers that goes on so much these days. They are always being questioned about their work: how they go about it; how they get ideas; whether they first make notes; how many times they re-write a piece of literature; and so on. And there's every kind of question to be answered for television and radio and magazines. I don't know why people have to make these enquiries; some probably out of curiosity, others wanting to know as a help for their own writing. Looking into other people's affairs is all very interesting, of course, especially when the authority of some television or radio company is behind the questioning, and then it's not considered so impolite. But the answers aren't so interesting, nor so easy. If someone asks you as an author, 'When did John Jones from Such-and-Such-a-Place die?', you can answer immediately, 'On such-and-such-a-date,' But when you are asked, 'How did this story first come into your mind?', it's not so easy to say. Sometimes a sentence spoken by someone, or even a single word, on the street or bus or anywhere, gives you an idea, but you could never tell someone else how the word became an idea, nor along what paths your thoughts had to travel in order to find material for the story after the word had suggested something to you.

A question that is often asked is, 'How much of what you yourself believe is to be found in your work?' Exactly as if you used a story or poem as a means of preaching what you believe. Some part of your work might express your credo, but you can also express an opinion that's completely contrary to what you believe. After all, a writer's function is not to give lessons or teach morals of any kind, but to say how you see life. It can appear like this in the life of some of your characters, and like that in the life of others; like this today, like that tomorrow.

Miss Victoria Sackville-West has written a book about the two saints, Teresa of Avila and Thérèse of Lisieux, under the title *The Eagle and the Dove*. It's a splendid book and the two saints come alive for the reader — one, the eagle, going like a spinning-top all over Spain as a missionary, and the other gentle and quiet in the convent. The author has been accused by some of her best friends of being about to convert to the Church of Rome. There isn't a word of truth in what they say. But since she has described the two saints with understanding and sympathy, and there was bound to be sympathy if her understanding perceived the truth, then some people just had to say that she was about to turn Catholic.

Margiad Evans[1] says that belief has experience of unbelief in a way that unbelief can never have, and that the words of an atheist are the best and most consistent expression of God's presence.

There's plenty of question-and-answer in Welsh literature: in the Black Book[2] and in the works of poets like William Llŷn.[3] But the questioning and answering there is *a means of creating* literature. In the question-and-answer we get nowadays, it's the thoughts of people who have already created that are being examined. The *act* of creating is one thing; an inquest on the creating quite another.

Now the most important question for a writer is, why does he write at all? And here we come to a punctuation mark. It's almost impossible to say; you grow shy when trying to explain to other people that certain things are troubling you, and that in order to be rid of them you have to create. It's true that story-writers (and poets, for that matter) write about people, since it's people who cause them pain, and worry, happiness, and joy. These are at the very heart of life; things worry them, and because of that, if we have any sensibility at all, we worry on their behalf. The opposite is, perhaps, even more true: we transfer our own pain and joy on to others in order to be rid of them.

But is that all? Are we not also searching for something, for some mystery in the creation and so in people? Are we not trying to provide an answer to the mystery of life and, in the end, searching for God by describing His handiwork in people, though they be poor creatures often enough, and quite unworthy of their Creator? We are burrowing after some mystery, trying to discover the truth; sometimes in people, and sometimes in ideas. 'Opening a gap out of the grave', says William Llŷn in one of those dialogues at the grave of his friend to which I referred earlier. That's what writers try to do, 'to open a gap out of the grave', although they speak to the living and not with the dead.

If I may quote Margiad Evans again, 'To me it appears as if Nature and creative art, meditation and religion, were God itself and that there is no separating the prayer from the answer, the accomplishment from the desire.'

There, like the old preacher, I've tried to 'say' something, and failed. The asking was right enough, but the answer is inadequate and perhaps quite wide of the mark.

Y Faner (8 Awst, 1968)

The Little Llandeilo Boots

Dafydd Rowlands

The children don't understand the relationship. But they will one day. What mystifies them is the fact that a child so young could have been an uncle. After all, it's not easy to think of a two-year-old as uncle to a man of forty. But perhaps I had better explain.

I'm not one of those fortunate people who are wealthy enough to accumulate rare and costly treasures — the original oil on canvas, the small piece of carved marble, the first edition of an antiquarian book. I was tempted, some years ago, to buy a clapped-out old car at the wheel of which, so it was claimed, Lloyd George[1] had once sat. But it was the same old story — I'm not one of those fortunate people who are wealthy enough to accumulate . . . And yet I do *possess* a few odds-and-ends that I should be sorry to be without — the bric-à-brac of the years that have some personal significance or family association. The picture of Leusa'r Injin, my grandmother's grandmother, hangs in the dining-room, her traditional Welsh costume coloured by the diluted, insipid oils of some long-forgotten artist from Neath. On the mantelpiece stands the brass kettle in which my forebears used to boil water but which is now nothing more than a cold ornament, a mere memento of many a cup of tea and a chat. And a host of other things, relics of the blood and family roots, symbols of an undeniable belonging. But among all the treasures in my home, the little Llandeilo boots are by far the most cherished.

My grandfather, on my mother's side, was — like Naaman the Syrian — 'a mighty man of valour'. A man of strong physique, he spent his days, and sometimes his nights, in the heat of iron-furnaces. And on Saturdays he would go down into the heat of the scrum on the rugby-field, in the days when players of that game sported moustaches and wore long trousers. Every photograph of him, in the football team, in the Sunday School[2] class, displays the strength of a man familiar with handling heavy metals. He had a son — John, his only son, who was two years old at the turn of the century. I have three sons, one of whom is also now two years old. I have seen him on more than one occasion taking the little Llandeilo boots and trying to put them on his feet. I always have this feeling of anxious dread whenever I see him loosening the leather tongues and forcing his feet into the boots. These were John's boots when *he* was two years old. They were made in Llandeilo by a craftsman-shoemaker, and the tiny, brightly shining nails bear to this day no traces of rust.

My grandfather was a devoted and meticulous gardener, and John was his helper. When he worked with his father in the garden, running along the open rows, weeding between the thriving vegetables, and tormenting the occasional fat worm between his fingers, the little Llandeilo boots kept his feet snug. But it happened in one of the gardening seasons that John fell ill, weakened, and unexpectedly died before his third birthday. After the funeral, my grandfather would go quietly into the garden and stand on the path to look at the living vegetation. And there in the soil were the imprints of little boots, the small footprints, the shallow impression of his son. The father, as was his custom when the time was ripe, dug the garden over, but he couldn't bring himself to apply the spade to that bit of ground where his child had left his mark. The wind and the rain granted him their favour.

The little Llandeilo boots are here now, important to me, less so to the children who regard them as mere playthings. For me they are Uncle John's boots — uncle though he died when he was only two. And the children don't understand. Every so often one of them will say, 'Tell us the story about the little boots.' And once again the tale is told of the small child in the garden's soil.

I'm not sure which of my three sons will inherit the boots. Who knows whether there will be in the veins of any one of them the awareness I have of belonging to those footprints in the garden? Perhaps I romanticize too much, turning my very breathing into the rhythm of some fanciful poem, yet I can't help feel, when I remove the dust from the leather and polish the black boots, that those two years of a frail child who died are part of me, and part of my sons, too. But it's not only his footprints that lie in the soil in which my roots were nourished. It's fascinating to look at those footprints which can be seen in some parts of America fossilized in rock under shallow water — the tracks of some huge creature that grazed the submerged forests a hundred million years ago, a creature whose bones lie unseen between the strata of lost time. A descendant of that creature must exist somewhere today. And when I go walking on the beach at Llansteffan, across the wet sand that gives under my feet, it's not only my own weight that presses my shoes into the softness of the sand.

> Our forebears are within us,
> Sinew and blood and tallow,
> A vitality in our bones,
> An energy in our marrow.[3]

In my chromosomal pattern are John and his father, the innocent child and the hard man at the open-hearth furnaces. In the genetic tapestry is Leusa'r Injin, an old woman in her Welsh costume standing at the wooden stile in Cilybebyll.

I was once asked by someone who had heard that I'm one of those strange fellows who write the occasional verse whether there was a poet lurking somewhere in my family's past. And so far as I knew, there wasn't. But I was later enlightened by a relative who lives in Trebanos. He knew about Leusa'r Injin and my grandmother's family, and he has in his keeping two objects that I should dearly like to get my hands on — an old Bible and an old bell. The owner of both these things was a great-great-uncle of mine, of whose existence I was unaware until quite recently. He, it seems, was the local town-crier — hence the bell — but he was no ordinary crier, and his medium wasn't prose. He used to announce his news by singing it in verse, or at least in doggerel. And so now, when the question is asked about a poet in the family, I offer a different answer. And that rhymester hides somewhere in the genetic weft of my sons. So it would be no surprise to see one of them some day as a newsreader on the television screen. But his broadcasting wouldn't be in the traditional metrical forms of Glamorgan.

'Tell us the story about the little boots.' They enjoy the story, but they can't understand the nature of the relationship between the child and the middle-aged man who tells the tale; they can't grasp the chain linking the generations. But they will come to understand it. When that day comes one of them will inherit the little Llandeilo boots; they will be important to him, less so to his children who will regard them as mere playthings.

Ysgrifau yr Hanner Bardd (Llys yr Eisteddfod Genedlaethol, 1972)

My Last Day in Prison

J. G. Williams

Perhaps those who lived in this cell before me used to feed it, because it comes to the window every day at about dinner-time. I have heard of prisoners making friends with mice, spiders, and all kinds of the most unlikely creatures, and not only with birds from the outside. So I began to save crumbs of food and share them with the grey pigeon at the window, and it's here now, fluttering about, alighting on the sill, and peeping in. There's a little redness in its grey feathers as it settles and presses up against the window-pane, as if it wants to warm itself in this cold weather. It probably can't make out what I'm doing here at this time of day, sitting in my cell like this at mid-morning, instead of being at work in the workshop with the others. It has no means of knowing that I have to stay in my cell this morning, while waiting to see the doctor before my release tomorrow. I shall have to try and bid it farewell somehow or other today. I managed to shake hands with Hooper and Summer this morning in the gully, and said goodbye to them, the only two of the seven who will be staying on in this place after I'm let out.

A feeling of guilt comes over me, and I can't help myself, as I take my leave of them all. I feel that I have no right to be leaving and that from now on my place is here. And though it will be marvellous to see my own clothes again, and to step out through the Main Gate as a free man, something is preventing me from rejoicing as it smoulders away inside me. Many's the time I was unable to understand the words when my father read them: 'It is better to go to the house of mourning, than to go to the house of feasting . . . Sorrow is better than laughter: for by the sadness of the countenance the heart is made better . . . The heart of the wise is in the house of mourning; but the heart of fools is in the house of mirth.' I would take up the Book myself and puzzle over those dreadful words. And I once had the feeling that perhaps Jac Penyrallt had hit the nail on the head when he said light-heartedly with his customary wit, in the middle of a spell of unusually bad weather, 'Well, at least there's one comfort, we'll have fine weather next.'

One of the things irritating me now is the feeling that I haven't really achieved anything worthwhile, that I haven't suffered half enough, and that nobody and nothing will be any the better for my having slaved away like this. Yet there's no way of knowing what will happen either. I shall probably be back here again one day soon, and again after that. And the war will come to an end sooner or later, and perhaps things will then return to normal, if there is such a thing as normal. But the Graves of the Living will remain, full of their terrible wretchedness. And our war will never be at an end. Our war will intensify and last for a long time to come.

I have one very small source of comfort. I can claim that I have now set my foot on the two lowest rungs of Hoppy's erudition. I am able to claim acquaintance with at least two of hell's staging-posts[1], and run a critical eye over them. I feel now that I should be able to contribute just a little to the discussion should I ever find myself in Hoppy's incredible company again. And I fall to wondering which of the two prisons I should choose to stay in, if I had a choice. This one is fairly clean at any rate, although its atmosphere is a lot more inhuman. Unlike in the other gaol, I haven't seen any sign of bombing here. Every building here seems intact and in good order, and it's easy to understand what an advantage that is when it comes to running the place with a reasonable measure of discipline and cleanliness. The other gaol had suffered so much bomb-damage that it might have been thought something of a miracle that men were able to inhabit the place at all.

Somehow or other I find myself tending to choose the first prison, the one that was old, dirty, and damaged. There were fewer prisoners there, and it was much easier to know what was going on. For some reason or other it was a lot easier to understand the orders. Even to this day I have difficulty in understanding the barking in this place. Perhaps I should give an account of my inability to comprehend the barked, reproving English that's to be heard here, but it's only with a certain amount of prejudice that I'm able to think of the mistake I made on the first morning, that very first morning as we all stood in our doorways waiting to leave our cells to go about our various duties. As I listened to the orders, I made a mess of things and found myself marching behind the others down one staircase after another, through the hall and the doors and the gates, until we had reached the exercise yard. After walking round and round for some while, I noticed that two or three warders had appeared on the scene and were behaving rather oddly. They were looking closely at each ring of prisoners and at every prisoner within the ring. And then they came to the one where I was, and right up to me. They asked for my name, read the number on the tab of my coat, and then snatched me out of the ring, while the others watched in astonishment as I was marched off between two warders, no doubt a dangerous fellow.

As for me, I thought I was being taken off to the dark-cell and a regime of bread-and-water, because they had been given evidence that I was an unheeding and disobedient prisoner. But I found myself instead in a huge room, where the six others were sitting together, awaiting their turn to go before the Chief Warder. I was delighted to see Green there, too, and he'd got his cap back and was wearing it with some dignity, re-arranging it all the time and patting it affectionately on the side of his head. By this time old Green had a host of other complaints, and was mumbling and muttering to himself and everyone else about his deprivations.

One other thing tends to make me favour the first gaol. There I had no trouble in keeping in my cell the Bible that Olwen had given me. But here it's been different. I had to make a special request to go before the Governor to ask for the Bible, and on finding myself in his office, all I got were three questions. Did I have an English Bible in my cell? I did. Wasn't that good enough for me? It wasn't. Was I able to read English? I was. End of interview. I wasn't allowed the Welsh Bible.

Yet there are several warders in this prison, just as there were in the other place, who sometimes behave more like men than warders, and they can communicate with you in some strange ways, smoothing your path and making you feel that life is well worth living after all. I was given the privilege of working in the workshop with two conscientious objectors, both Quaker lads, John Ward and Harry Wilson by name. John was let out yesterday and Harry says he finds it very depressing now, since I too am about to leave and he's going to be left on his own.

I never had the privilege in this gaol of going out to work, but I've been on several strange journeys inside the place with a warden from the engineering department, mending and winding clocks and things like that in the various halls. And I was shocked once to see a hall full of women busy at their sewing-machines, and several newly born babies lying in their cots. It was in church on the first Sunday morning I was here that it dawned on me that there were women in this place. As we stood singing a hymn I began wondering whether I could hear female voices coming from somewhere or other. During the next hymn I was certain that I could hear them. But there wasn't a woman to be seen anywhere. There was a curtain between them and us, and this had the effect of creating a certain other-worldliness that was rather curious. It was as if we were caught up in a scene from

Wagner, with enchanting mermaids wafting the sound of their music towards us while at the same time they kept out of sight in the stage-wings. There too I caught a glimpse of Bryn Evans and we managed to exchange a brief word, arranging to take each other's addresses before we left prison. But things were not to work out for us.

At the very time when it would have been possible for Bryn and me to meet in the church, or in the exercise yard on a Sunday, the Works Party had to turn out for some urgent job or other. This meant that we weren't able to see each other, and it's unlikely now that we shall ever have another chance. But working on a Sunday, in the wash-house, was an interesting experience. The two Quakers and I were engaged in woodwork, reassembling some large tables, pulling them apart and then re-setting and re-joining them on a smaller scale. The electricians were re-wiring the place, an Englishman, an Irishman, and a Scotsman. I found myself working with Bruce, a large cheerful Scot, a ship's engineer who had got himself in here for something or other. In these circumstances we had some interesting conversations about our respective national movements.

One of the warders looking after us was a Mr Barrat. I hadn't seen him before, but had heard about him from the Quakers. It was said of him that he was particularly hostile towards conscientious objectors, and that it was his habit to put them to the test at every opportunity, and that he had the knack of being able to knock your guts out and destroy you completely. But during my time in the wash-house Mr Barrat was always pleasant and friendly. He even looked kindly and cheerfully on Bruce when he was up to some mischief in the wash-house that Sunday. One of the warders had taken Bruce and the Irishman down to the kitchen to fetch our dinners, and when he came back Bruce started taking pieces of bread and bits of margarine out of his shirtsleeves and sharing them among the rest of us. No one asked from where, nor how he had acquired them.

I often marvel at the knack some people have of getting their hands on things like that. I had seen only one other prisoner like Bruce before and that was a chap called Dic Tyddyn Sianel. I saw Dic on more than one occasion taking a dozen or more potatoes out of his sleeve after coming into the workshop, handing them to the man who worked in the smithy, and when they were roasted sharing them out among us to eat before going back to our cells. No one asked from where, nor how.

On one occasion I'd been thinking it would be good to eat a potato just before retiring for the night, and had stuffed it down my shirt before leaving the workshop. And as we were being lined up in the Centre and Mr Waller was searching me for weapons, his hands came upon the lump under my shirt. He looked stunned for a moment, but then his eyes lit up and he whispered, 'Oh, your spud.'

The grey pigeon is still perched near my window and the time has come for me to give it a few crumbs. From the last meal. Not that anyone here ever refers to a last meal. Cocoa is the tally that prisoners usually count by. A man says he has twenty cocoas still to go. Ten cocoas left. Five, four, and three as his last day within the walls draws nigh.

I'm going down the metal stairs, down to the next landing, down again to the bottom floor, and then to the workshops, for the last afternoon's shift. The vision comes over me like a shower of rain. It occurs every now and again, making familiar things seem different at moments like this. Since this is my last afternoon in gaol the stairs seem very strange. The large, long, dark hall appears to be a long, long way off. I never saw it like this before, it looks so unfamiliar. I take a second look about me, and I'd swear that I've never been here before. The warders seem strange, peculiar, superfluous creatures as they stand about here and there. They can't possibly be needed, so many of them at every corner. Everyone and everything has lost its meaning for me, all of a sudden. Harry Wilson appears from the direction of his cell and under the supervision of a warder we go together into the workshop. Nor does Harry look quite the same Harry, nor the warder.

I take up my mortice-chisel and sharpen it. If all goes well I shall be able to finish off the window before the end of the afternoon. I wonder who it'll be fixing this in position with Harry next week. Harry is going to be here for many more weeks yet, and a lot of new windows are needed here, so they say. I know only too well that Harry is anxious about who's likely to be his new mate in the workshop, because he has said so many times these last few days. He looks as if he's thinking it over this very minute.

We've been at it diligently throughout the afternoon, without chatting very much, and the afternoon is now starting to draw to a close. At the bench nearest to me Harry is hard at it with his plane, and the pensive look is still written across his face. I too am at the same juncture on my window and eager to put the edge of my chisel to it now that it's been sharpened. As I begin planing I hear a rustle at the far end of the workshop. There's the sound of keys in the door and warders greeting one another. I hear the one coming in go through the ritual of calling the roll as he always does whenever he's responsible for bringing in newcomers. 'Three on, sir,' he says. I wonder who these are now. Harry has stopped planing and calls over to me quietly, 'Watch out, Jack, he's coming for you. And I thought you'd been let off.'

I see Mr Barrat coming in, walking slowly and deliberately towards me. With him are three members of the Works Party. In the middle of the floor, in a clear space, Mr Barrat orders the three to place two sawing-benches against each other, looks around him for a moment, straightens himself up, then turns round and shouts at me, 'Right — you. Come here. Sit on this bench.'

I put down the plane, placing it on its side among the shavings on the bench, and think what a pity it is that I'm not going to be finishing the window after all. I go up to the benches and sit down, feeling that this is rather like going to one's execution, like putting one's head on the block. Every slightest detail now seems vivid and important, every chip and shaving on the floor, every speck of white paint that's been spilt at one time or another, with a little sawdust sticking to it, or a shaving of pinewood. When I heard the 'Three on, sir,' I was planing the window, working at the pleasurable task of putting a finish to it, and thinking whether it would be fair of me if I were to give the plane the name of Jumper; it would be a pity if a name like that were to be consigned to oblivion. Mr Barrat has sat down on the bench in front of me, about a yard or so away. The afternoon is growing dark and shadows are starting to form all around me. Harry and Bruce are seated on benches near by, the Englishman and the Irishman and the other warder opposite them, forming a kind of circle. The vision persists. The workshop is transformed and looks like a huge, dark cave. The faces of the lads around me look pale and white, and Bruce for once seems to be very earnest. This isn't Mr Barrat. This isn't the man who was with us in the wash-house that Sunday. He was a man then like Mr Waller, and Mr Henley, and Mr Miller. Now he's sitting quietly, with a kind of menace in his posture, clutching a piece of wood and holding it with one hand at each end across his knees.

Mr Barrat's voice grows strident and raucous. He asks me to state my reasons why I'm not fighting in the war, and starts on the clever business that's become so familiar to me of making a man feel execrable and a disgrace in his own estimation. As I listen to him I feel that the only substantial word with any kind of meaning to it is Jumper, and I can't for the life of me rid myself of this word. I should like to start expatiating on it, with a great zeal, but who here would understand? I try my very best to put my thoughts in order, and all the various reasons I have heard from the Socialists, the Jehovah's Witnesses, the Church of Christ, the Plymouth Brethren, and the

Quakers, all get jumbled up with one another in my mind, and I know only too well that I'm looking pretty daft at Mr Barrat by now, just as I used to at the minister in the prayer-meeting when I'd forgotten my verse. I feel very, very lonely, and I hear the word Conchie among the things Mr Barrat is saying. Mr Barrat is now asking me whether I've been before the Tribunal, and what I said to them. I see the face of Sir Thomas Artemus Jones[2] looming large in front of me, and hear him reading a sentence from my statement . . . 'I refuse to recognize the right of the English Government to impose military conscription on Wales . . . I refuse to enlist in the armed forces of the King of England.' Sir Thomas asks me whether I have any other reason to offer him, and when I tell him that I haven't, he says, kindly enough, that's all then and for me to go back to my place. Back in my place, Ben Owen[3] appears from somewhere, slaps my back and says, 'Oh boy, oh boy, oh boy . . .', and shakes my hand.

And now here comes Ben Owen, in this very room, standing behind me. And J.E.[4] at his side, looking like J.E. when he's spoiling for a fight. And there are the Three Men of Penyberth stepping out of the shadows and standing at my side, and Jack Dan and Wil Berry and Fred Jarman and Trefor Morgan, they are all here. I know full well that Owain Glyndwr and the two Llywelyns are here too, and I hear myself raising my voice and thundering at Mr Barrat, condemning England's imperialism and asking him who the devil they think they are taking over the countries of the world and pushing everyone around and making them fight in their old wars . . . They were always the same, using Welshmen to put down Ireland and Scotland, and today there are thousands and thousands of Welshmen in every part of the world fighting in the name of all kinds of grand ideas like civilization and peace and democracy, and you ought to see the kind of democracy that goes on in Wales these days . . . Penyberth, one of our most venerable homes, demolished for ever so as not to disturb the ducks somewhere in England . . . A whole community of Welsh-speaking farmers on Epynt[5], who had been living there in a civilized way for centuries, being uprooted and swept away like a load of weeds, and it's going on all over the country and the English are taking over, taking over, and usurping everything . . . They are stealthily taking Llŷn and Eifionydd from us under our very noses, and how on earth can any Welshman wear the military uniform of the King of England after what's happened to Penyberth?

Mr Barrat is smiling. Surely he has changed again, and he looks like the man who was with us in the wash-house the other day, kind and reasonable. I am surprised to hear him say that he has a good deal of sympathy for the Welsh and their troubles, and that he knows all about Wales, the most beautiful country he's ever seen . . . I get exactly the same feeling as when I saw the hurt look in the eyes of the bull as it turned its nose away, the piteous feeling that perhaps I've been too discourteous to him, and that I shouldn't have been, and yet instinct tells me that it was either him or me. Hearing the word 'homogeneous' was what drove me completely beserk. Mr Barrat is at it now, preaching in a fatherly, kind sort of way, about the homogeneous amalgam of the British Isles being fused and made into one strong nation, and that everything is sure to be all right in the end, but that we have to stick it out for the time being and win the war, and that the important thing now is to beat Hitler. I'm not sure whether it's Ben Owen or Jack Dan or Seus or myself I can hear hard at it now, causing Mr Barrat's kind enough face to fall, and making him look somewhat confused . . . The only thing that ever counted with you was keeping your grip on the world through your empire, and maintaining the balance of power in Europe . . . In doing that it's made not a jot of difference to you how many wars there have been, you always had plenty of people to fight on your behalf, and you always had a scapegoat . . . the Pope or Napoleon or Cronje or some other worse rascal was always to hand. I grab hold of the word 'predator' from somewhere and I hear myself calling England the most rapacious nation in the world . . . It's easy for the crocodile to tell the kid-goats not to struggle and not to worry because in the end things will be all right . . . But what consolation is there for the goats in staying silent and content when they are going to be chewed into small pieces and become a homogeneous part of the big crocodile? . . . You've been at it for centuries, trying all sorts of violent and cunning tricks to kill us off . . . You just can't tolerate the fact that there's another, different nation living on the same island as you, and we were here first anyway, and the fact that the Welsh language is still alive is an irritation to you . . . But John Bull, the biggest bully the world has even seen, has at last met his match in India in the shape of Gandhi, the greedy maniac has bitten off more than he can chew this time, and what's more he's going to choke . . .

Mr Barrat is on his feet. He kicks away the bench and looks down at me severely, and yet not altogether unkindly. He holds out the piece of wood towards me, as if pointing straight at the tip of my nose, and he says, '*You* are not a Conchie. You're a bloody rebel, that's what you are — a bloody rebel!'

Before long now it will be light. The night has been long and I was tossing and turning for most of it. I knew full well that the last night would be a sleepless one. The lads who know about these things had told me about the mental excitement of the prisoner on his last night.

When the cocoa came I broke off bits of my bread and stood on the chair by the window and shared them with the grey pigeon, feeling that we were celebrating a sacrament, the two of us. As I took my leave of it, before pulling down the blind, I felt as if I were about to betray the bird by leaving it here in the wilderness of the city's bricks. I had already said goodbye to Harry and wished him well, and had talked about the possibility that we might very easily bump into each other again soon in the same old place.

After drinking the cocoa and eating what was left of the bread, and washing the cup for the last time, I sat down on the chair and slowly became aware that I was feeling uneasy about something. I set myself to stitching sacks, determined to stick at it, stitching and stitching until the very end. That seemed preferable to sitting and staring at the walls around me. And I felt myself growing more and more uneasy.

It was nearly time for bed. And then it grew dark. And the uneasiness was still troubling me. I fancied that I was still at Mr Barrat's tribunal, and still had the feeling that I'd been too severe, that I'd lost my temper and hurt people. Perhaps I had even hurt Harry. He's so quiet and gentlemanly, like all the Quakers I've met here, and some of the others too. But I'm sure he's wise enough to understand. It was the Machine I was attacking, the Machine that he and his friends refuse to acknowledge and to have any part in, the Machine that the rapacious nations create for themselves so that they can suck the life's blood of the smaller nationalities into their own veins, the Machine which knows only too well that its demise will be imminent when each of the smaller peoples escapes from the clutches of the great empires, and sees through the conspiracies of Mammon.

The cloud's shadow spreads over all. Although the night is dark I can feel it enveloping me as I think about being a free man when the light of dawn breaks presently, and I shall be going home, to see the snow on the top of Craig Goch as the train pulls out of Caernarfon. I know that I should be dancing with joy, and that's exactly what half of me is doing with some abandon. But the other half is like lead. Because I know that I shall be returning to a land where a nation is imprisoned, having languished in captivity for centuries, having so grown used to its condition that it's gone quiet and is content at being chewed and swallowed up by the crocodile. Before long all its vitals will be smoothly absorbed into the crocodile's veins. It's the Almighty's doing, they say, the smaller creature feels a thrill, an indescribably gorgeous sensation when it gives up the struggle for its own life, feels the teeth ripping into its flesh and tearing it apart and crunching the bones. That's the ecstatic state I've noticed in the

Welshman who has given up and at last decided to be an Englishman.

Before coming to prison I was so familiar with hearing speeches and reading articles about the effect of four, five, and six centuries of living under oppression. But I hadn't once fully grasped the terrible truth until I saw the process working on the minds of men in gaol, and I was stricken with horror by their readiness to adjust to their captivity, and to grow content — and waste away — although they still existed.

But I must try not to look at it like that. I must be brave. I mustn't worry about whether I've hurt Harry or anyone else. I know that Ben Owen would have done the same. Come to think of it, I'm sure Ben Owen would have hit out much harder. I was doing it for the life of Wales. Hitting out on behalf of the spirit. And if you're fighting for your life you have to hit out without pity. It's either the other man or you. So I shall cheer up and not worry about yesterday. Nor about tomorrow either. There are so many of us now. So many with the spirit in us. So many that we shan't be absorbed and grow content at being extirpated. And there will be more and still more. And the future will be exceedingly bright, and our lives shall have meaning.

I leap up off the bed as the cell starts to grow lighter, and I begin folding my clothes neatly and getting the place ready for my departure. Things will happen in quick succession now, according to the lads. As I stand in the middle of the floor with a bundle of bed-clothes ready under my arm, I hear the sound of keys in the door. I wonder whether the gaol's regime is working well enough that they will remember that I am to be released today. But there's no need to worry. The machinery works without a hitch every time. The warder stands in the doorway looking at me, with a paper in his hand, instead of moving on to the next doors and shouting 'Slops out!' as he usually does. 'Come on,' he says.

I follow the warder along the landing and pass the other warders at their task of shouting 'Slops out . . . Slops out . . . Slops out . . .' The prisoners hurry out of their cells, each carrying a pot and bucket to the gully, and so another day starts. I follow the warder round the corner and into a hall that I haven't been in before, with scores and scores of prisoners hurrying back and forth, and the warders standing around and watching, watching, watching. Every cell has its door open. In a moment every one will be slammed shut and they will all be washing down the floors, the tables, and the chairs.

'Cheerio, then, Taff.' I hear the voice and turn to see Bruce in the doorway of his cell, grinning broadly. I hear myself shout back, 'Goodbye, Scotland,' and I raise my hand in farewell. As I walk behind the warder I look back and see Bruce still standing in the doorway. I wave to him. He too raises his hand with an even broader smile. I feel as if I am a leaf being borne along by the stream's current: I shall surely never see Bruce again.

Down in Reception there are about fifteen of us eating porridge. We change into our own clothes and put our belongings into our pockets. I get Olwen's Bible back at last. We stand in a row in alphabetical order, and for the last time I find myself last in the line, walking in the darkness towards the Main Gate under the warders' supervision. The small door in the middle of the big gate opens, and each one of us steps through it, one after the other, into the darkness of the great outside.

Maes Mihangel (Gwasg Gee, 1974)

A Discovery

R. Tudur Jones

It was one evening. An evening in early September. What year? I don't know what year. Not last year nor the year before that. A quarter of a century ago, perhaps. But it might easily have been yesterday evening, except that it's now March. For time has nothing to do with it. It's an important part of the story that it can't be connected with any one specific day on the calendar.

But it was an evening in the month of September, for all that. A still evening without a leaf stirring. The kind of evening the sun hangs red and hesitant above the horizon and, in delaying its going down, persuades us that it's a sad thing to see the end of that particular day. And the smell of late hay lingering in the air and the bramble-bushes black with fruit. A cow's lowing mingled with the buzzing of small flies.

It was an evening that invited a spin. And so off I went across the Menai into Anglesey. The great bustle of summer and its visitors was over and the Anglesey roads empty. Turn right. Turn left. And within the blinking of an eye I was lost. But there's one splendid thing about the Isle of Anglesey. If the unfamiliar wayfarer gets lost, he knows that it's on Anglesey he's lost, and not that he's lost Anglesey. In

Caernarfonshire it's possible to be lost and then discover that you are lost in Merioneth. And then you have lost Caernarfonshire. But in Anglesey every road will sooner or later take you to a cove and beach. It's a pleasant way of getting lost, a sort of being lost in safety. And so I was.

And then, completely unexpectedly, I discovered it. It's not a huge place, crouching in the shade of its tall trees. And that evening they were very tall: their lower trunks were in shadow and their topmost branches catching the last rays of the sun. The church of Penmynydd.

I ventured in through the iron gate. I paused a moment to read the notice on the board outside. There was a proclamation on it, in Welsh as well as in English, to the effect that 'This Church is the seat of the divine presence in this parish.' Those were not the exact words but that was their meaning, because I've been back there several times since to check them, for fear I had dreamed them. But no, that was the message. And I accepted this curious theology as part of the discovery, that evening in September many years ago. I opened the door and went inside. By now it was too dark to make out the architectural and decorative details of the church. And the sound of our footsteps was ringing round the shadowy walls. While outside I could hear the impatient croaking of the crows as they raced the sun to bed.

A cold shudder came over me. Not an angel flying over my grave, as the old saying has it, but the stirring of Anglesey's long dead in my imagination. And I vividly recall why the dead of Anglesey should have disturbed me.

I had been preparing lectures for my students in time for the new College session that was due to begin within the month. The topic was the Protestant Reformation. In order to illustrate the dissolution of the monasteries, I had been intending to describe the demise of the priory of Llan-faes, and the facts were already set out in my notes. The date had been the middle of August 1538 when Richard Ingworth, the monks' Lord Visitor, had arrived at the priory. This was the priory that Llywelyn the Great[1] had raised over the grave of his wife Joan, and to the glory of St. Francis of Assisi who had died ten years before. But by 1538 all that was in the distant past and the day of the priory's closure had arrived. At Ingworth's heels were Mr Thomas Bulkeley[2] and two bailiffs from Beaumaris. The priory bell was rung and the handful of brothers gathered together. Ingworth was the messenger of Henry VIII, with a document in his hand ordering the house's reform — or its dissolution. The brothers admitted that they should reform according to the king's summons, but how could they, in a world so weak in religion? 'In that case,' said Ingworth, 'I shall have to confiscate the house in the name of the king.'

And so he did. Ingworth and his friends pocketed the ready cash and the Communion vessels. An inventory was then made of the priory's possessions, and that list cannot be read without feeling sadness at the circumstances — the altar-cloths, the candlesticks, the crucifixes, the bells, and the books; the vestments from the vestry, the flock beds, the pillowcases, the blankets, the feather beds, the sheets, the kitchen utensils, the cooking-pots, the dishes, the saucers, and the fire tongs. And the whole lot was sold and the house let to Sir Richard Bulkeley. And on the twenty-fourth day of June 1540 the workmen arrived to start demolishing the memorial priory of Siwan, stone by stone.

I had stepped from that story into the midst of Penmynydd's crows, in coming across the old church for the very first time. And as I stood in the gloaming of its interior I could only sense that Thomas Bulkeley and Richard Bulkeley—not to speak of Ingworth—together with a host of Anglesey people, were hovering between me and the door. Not that there was any terror in the place. A man who spends his life studying and teaching History is not frightened in the presence of the past. On the contrary, if Richard Bulkeley himself had stepped into the church that evening, I should have been in the right frame of mind to have put a few quite intelligent questions to him.

No, it was quiet in Penmynydd that evening. A heavenly peace, in fact. And 'the divine presence'? No question about it. Were not bushes burning here, too, without their being consumed? And so out I went through the door, closing it gently after me. By now the sun had set and the crows' croaking eased. And the waves of Anglesey's quietude were all about me.

I know nothing so mysterious as this kind of discovery. And only once does it happen. I've been back to Penmynydd many times since then. Hardly a year has gone by without my calling there. But there's only one discovery. The provocative church proclamation on the noticeboard has been removed. I, too, have changed. The hedges have been trimmed five times or more since that evening. And Anglesey's dead were not present in the church during any of my subsequent visits. The discovery was made once and for all time.

But it doesn't matter. For as long as I have a memory, I shall be able to recall that marvel. The sounds and smells and colours, and the close connections with the dissolution of Llan-faes priory, will come back to me. That's why I say the date of the discovery is neither here nor there. If I were a Platonist, I should say that it's an eternal reality. And indeed, perhaps, in some sense, that is what every such discovery is. Opening a window on to the eternal.

Y Cymro (26 Mawrth, 1974)

A Land of Romance

Alun Llywelyn-Williams

One of the great privileges that my father quietly bestowed upon us children, without our fully appreciating at the time how fortunate we were, was the family holiday. He was a man of generous heart, and adventurous at that. The venturesome spirit must have been part of the family's inheritance. Two of his brothers went overseas as young men, one settling in South Africa and the other in the United States, and my father himself had wandered much of the world before marrying. He was never to buy a car, that's true enough. When still a comparatively young doctor setting out on a career as a health officer in Wrexham, he insisted on acquiring a motor-bike, and so I've heard, made quite a name for himself with this early machine as he whizzed gleefully on his rounds, a danger to the life of man and beast in those pioneering days. But by the end of the first world war, when he had once more settled in Cardiff, he was nearly fifty years old, and his eyesight too poor for him to drive a motor-car, and so as a family we were deprived of the privilege of enjoying an occasional trip into the country of a Saturday or Sunday afternoon, as did some of our friends who could afford to follow the new fashion. It was on foot that I had, as a boy, to get to know the countryside around Cardiff, and today I'm very glad about that.

But this didn't mean that we children hadn't plenty of opportunity for setting out from home to see the world. Whenever my brother and sister were home from boarding-school, my father would hire a car to take the family to visit some remarkable place or other in the vicinity, and we were taken, each in turn, to spend a few days in London, like that time I accompanied him to see the Empire Exhibition at Wembley. He took care that we all spent time fairly often with our relatives in north Wales. Later on, he encouraged me to go with my schoolfriends to the summer camps organized by Tom Ellis and Phil Burton and other brave men under the auspices of the Welsh Schoolboys' Camp Movement, which had nothing to do, by the way, with Urdd Gobaith Cymru[1]. With the Welsh Schoolboys I first crossed to the continent, to Germany, to stay in the old town of Andernach on the banks of the Rhine — that was a memorable experience for more than one reason. My father's generosity in this respect was to continue long after we had left school. He paid for my sister Enid and myself to accompany him on some of the Urdd cruises; my mother wouldn't come because she was afraid of the sea, and by this time my brother Eric was too busy with his own work. But without a doubt, when we were all children and the family still together, our greatest privileges were attributable to my father's unshakeable faith in one of the most amiable habits of the middle-class at that time. He believed in proper holidays, not a measly week here and another there, but really long holidays for the entire family in the good old unstinting Victorian style. Every summer we used to go off for a whole month at a time, either to the seaside or to the country. As a rule it was to England that we went for our holiday by the sea, year in year out; whenever we went to the country, we would stay in Wales.

That is how Cornwall became for me as a boy the very mirror of heaven. For our seaside was in Cornwall, and more particularly in the small town of St. Ives. In chronological order, it was the country holiday in Wales that probably came first in our family; I was about ten or twelve years old, and about to go to the grammar school, before we were to set out for St. Ives. Whichever it may have been, I was young enough to be utterly seduced by the place's charm.

Even in those days, nearly half a century ago now, St. Ives was a popular resort for summer visitors, but the town hadn't yet been overwhelmed by tourism. The large hotels of the day were almost all on the outskirts of town, especially on the pleasant slopes above the most sheltered beach facing the bay, and it was of particular interest to us, by the way, to note that many among them had strange names in a language which seemed curiously like Welsh. But the old town around the harbour was, one might have thought, exactly as it had been for hundreds of years. And this part was the seamen's quarter, their very own grey fortress on the narrow promontory between Porthmeor, where the Atlantic waves beat relentlessly on the white sands, and the quay nestling in the shadow of the Island. The plain, stoutly built houses in the narrow streets that spread in a mysterious labyrinth on the rock floor were seamen's houses. The plain Bethels that stood up here and there from the labyrinth like ungainly boxes were where they worshipped. The stalls on the quayside where mackerel and herring were sold, freshly wet from the sea, were their market-places. The whole harbour was taken up by their busy boats, and the quayside loud with the cries of seagulls and the shouting and talk of the men who went out into the deep waters off Cornwall's wild coast to earn their living in fair weather and foul. All this was long before artists discovered the place and destroyed its romance by trying to capture it in paint on canvas, and before the visitors became settlers and began buying up houses for conversion into summer hideaways. Today the little houses have a much more cheerful look to them, it must be admitted, with their doors painted in every colour and flowers hanging from their windows as one sees in Mediterranean villages, but for me in those days their incomparable charm lay in their uncompromising lack of decoration.

One of my chief pleasures was to wander the winding streets of the old quarter, but sooner or later I would find myself at the quayside by the harbour, watching the boats and chatting to some of the seamen. One among them became a great favourite of mine and the family's, a middle-aged man, tough and rough in appearance, but always ready to do a kind turn, who had sailed the oceans and could spin countless yarns about his adventures in far-distant lands that Joseph Conrad himself would have been glad to claim as his own. Henry Peters was his name, if I remember rightly, and in those days I had no cause to doubt his veracity. I used to listen to him as the boy Walter Raleigh listened to his sailor in that painting by Millais. But Henry Peters had things even more exciting to offer than the telling of tales. He had his own small sailing-boat and every now and then I was allowed to go out fishing with him in the bay or around the point of the Island in the direction of the Five Headlands and the terrifying cliffs of Gurnard's Head. Sometimes we would go out to try our luck off the Godrevy rocks where the lighthouse stood, the beams from the lamps of which we used to see flashing at us at night from the far side of the broad bay. There was a good haul to be had off the island of Godrevy, although there was no artistry in the kind of fishing that we went in for. You cast a line overboard, often not even with bait attached to it, and then waited until you felt the tug of the fish as it took the hook — that's all there was to it. And you could manage that lazily enough while basking in the sunshine stretched out in the prow of the boat and enjoying a soaking every now and then from the spray that the waves threw up. Years later I tried creating poetry from my memories of those trips to Godrevy in Henry Peters' boat. At the time the poetry was in the sea-journey itself, and I didn't know that Virginia Woolf just about then was writing her novel *To the Lighthouse* and that it was my lighthouse which was the inaccessible destination for the yearning of the holiday-makers in her imagination.

It wasn't only the sea that kept us amused and charmed us. Of course, there were always the sandy beaches — the quiet, sheltered beach of Porthminster and the stormy beach on which the huge waves broke so savagely at Porthmeor. Our favourite was Porthminster, naturally enough, because though Porthmeor was splendid to look at, we thought it far too dangerous to go bathing there. There was no such sport as water-skiing in those days. Besides, it was above Porthminster that we used to stay, not in one of the grander hotels but in guest-houses on the Malakoff where the entire family could be comfortably accommodated at reasonable charge. We could be on the beach in less than five minutes, and that's where we went each morning without fail. My mother's idea of pure enjoyment was to hire a small tent for the whole holiday and sit placidly in front of it, in a comfortable chair, knitting or sewing or striking up a conversation with like-minded neighbours from the other tents near by. We children, and my father too sometimes, would muster energy to swim in the bay or stroll and play about the place. The beach was a very friendly spot, and what's more, my brother and sister, both of whom were quite a bit older than I, had the happy knack of making friends. Often we would be a fair-sized crowd, a mixed gang of visitors' children, some of whom were already acquaintances of ours from Cardiff or Wales, and others the children and young people of St. Ives itself. Among the natives we had two special friends, a brother and sister by the names of Cyril and Irene, both terrific swimmers, particularly the girl; it was she who usually won the main swimming-race at the annual regatta. And it was Cyril and Irene who introduced us to the land of Cornwall.

I had already fallen in love with Cornwall before ever going there. Not that I knew anything about the place, but Cornwall and Devon, all of western England, were among the most splendid landscapes of the imagination for a boy brought up on popular adventure stories like *Westward Ho!* and *Treasure Island* and other such tales, and on stories about adventurers in the golden age of Elizabeth, Drake and Hawkins and Raleigh, and their feats in putting the Spaniards to flight and opening up the seaways for Britain to conquer new continents. Since Somerset and Devon were on our doorstep in Cardiff and in daily view across the Severn estuary, the spell of this heroic west appealed to me all the more strongly. And as for Cornwall, it was a land out yonder beyond mortal gaze. But it was there. It floated in an enchanted light created by reading the books of Quiller-Couch and some of Hugh Walpole's early tales, and there every beach and cove and every secret valley on that rocky coast would bring to mind the feats of smugglers and pirates and sailors from the exciting days of yore. But it was also a land where once giants of a very different kind had walked. It was with Cornwall, rather than Wales, that I associated King Arthur and the Knights of the Round Table. I don't quite know how this came about. Maybe it was my brother Eric's influence that coloured my ideas about Arthur. He was a great romantic, and at the time he was immersed in the work of Malory and Tennyson. He knew large parts of *The Passing of Arthur* by heart, and never tired of reciting them. I would listen intently, especially to the sad tale about the battle of Camlan that for us was located at the far end of Cornwall — 'the sunset bound of Lyonesse.'

> 'So all day long the noise of battle roll'd
> Among the mountains by the winter sea:
> Until King Arthur's Table, man by man,
> Had fall'n in Lyonesse about their lord . . .'

On the shores of that 'winter sea', with the ghosts of Elizabethan sea-captains, there roamed the mighty shades of Arthur and Medraud and Bedwyr, and of King Marc and bold Trystan.[2] Dead Man's Rock looked down upon the lost strands of Lyonesse. Cornwall was indeed a land of romance.

But it was Cyril and Irene who also taught us that Cornwall was a real land of special importance. Although prosaic enough in their attitude to the world, they were conscious of being Cornish and regarded with some suspicion anyone from beyond the river Tamar, as if he were a stranger from another country. It wasn't that they were in any sense nationalists. They knew only that they were different from the rest of the English. This was an unexpected discovery on our part, yet although the feeling of separateness was quite obvious, the difference was difficult to define. One thing at least was certain: it had nothing to do with a difference in language. There were plenty of Celtic place-names all about us, and of course my father would talk to us about them and compare them, as far as he was able, with the Welsh. Cyril and Irene took them pretty much for granted, with no wish to find out what they meant, nor with much interest in them at all. The only Cornish words we ever heard from them, as far as I know, were '*Kernow bys vyken!*', which we understood to mean 'Cornwall for ever!', a saying they would use in order to rally each other whenever the need arose at games. Of course, this was long before *Mebyon Kernow* and the recent revival in Cornwall. There was, at that time, it's true, a handful of Cornish people who were enthusiasts for the language, though I knew nothing about them. We learned that there was a Gorsedd of Bards in Cornwall, because my father insisted on dragging us one wet and windy day all the way to the summit of Carn Brea between Camborne and Redruth to see the Gorsedd going through its rituals, though not, I'm afraid, 'in the eye of light' on that occasion. But, like me, Cyril and Irene had little interest in games of that kind. Now that I come to think of it, although I was so bewitched by Cornwall at the time, the attitude of brother and sister towards the manifestation of the locality's peculiar character must have done me tremendous harm in my attitude to my own country. It was perfectly evident that good Cornish folk didn't have to be attached to their language and culture. So why did a Welshman have to worry about his?

Nevertheless, this indefinable difference existed, and it was to be seen and felt in people other than Cyril and Irene. Among the fishing community, for example. Something very exciting happened during one of our holidays at St. Ives that furnished us with proof of it — I don't recall when exactly it was, but it must have been at some time in the late 'twenties. I can't say whether Cornish people were religious or not. The Nonconformist denominations were very strongly represented there, particularly among the seafaring folk. My father was always keen to make sure that we were taken to a place of worship on Sundays, to the parish church, to the Wesleyan Methodists' very proper chapel, or to various seamen's chapels in the old quarter that belonged to all kinds of sects that were strange to us, where the singing was marvellously spirited and the wooden seats reeked of Lifebuoy soap, as was no doubt appropriate. Wherever we attended was usually full to capacity in those days. And St. Ives on a Sunday, apart from the places of worship, was like the grave, very much more so than Cardiff or anywhere else that I knew of at that time. The inhabitants, moreover, obviously wished to keep it that way. One innocent fellow tried to open his café on the quayside on a Sunday afternoon. The place was smashed to pieces by an angry crowd of seamen. That was exciting enough but there was more commotion to come. There arrived another venturesome chap, from London it was said, or at any rate from beyond the Tamar, who had a new-fangled motor-boat with which he planned entertaining the visitors by offering to take them on pleasure-cruises across the calm waters of the bay at some astonishing speed. All right. This was a new experience in those days and many people found it a very acceptable addition to the summer attractions of St. Ives. The boat's proprietor had a successful and profitable week. And come the Sabbath, there he was taking his boat out of the harbour and on board a crowd of blissfully ignorant sinners. When he came back to the quayside after about half-an-hour to pick up another lot, the seamen were waiting for him. All excuses and arguments and pleas were in vain. The transgressor was unceremoniously hurled into the harbour and his boat broken up. He went back in haste to where he had come from on the other side of Tamar, and the Sabbath peace returned to St. Ives. At the time I took this as an unmistakeable sign of the seamen's religious zeal and their determination to keep their local tradition free from stain, but it could nevertheless have been economic considerations which, in fact, had caused their strong action. Whichever it may have been, these people behaved very differently from any others I knew.

But ultimately what Cornwall gave me as a boy was a sensuous experience of a new environment, and it was in the country itself, the sight of the green land and particularly the mighty waters round about it, rather than in the people, that I came to perceive the particularity of the place. And that was the favour which our friends Cyril and Irene did us as a family, they showed us the land. Not that my father didn't have his part to play in educating us. He had been used to travelling the world and was fond of exploring new territories. It was he who took us on long journeys, to Penzance and Land's End, to St. Michael's Mount and the Lizard, to Falmouth and up the wooded river on the little steamer to Truro, to Newquay, and on one especially memorable trip to the wondrous castle of Tintagel, 'the high fort above the sea'[3], than which no more wonderful and fitting embodiment of the romantic dream can be imagined. Splendid journeys one and all. Cornwall's splendour lies in its shoreline, the golden beaches and stunning cliffs around its coast. Its countryside is not so remarkable. Years later I discovered that there are, at the edges of Europe, other peninsulas very similar to Cornwall which reach out into the western ocean, and that Pembrokeshire and Llŷn and the promontories of Brittany, as well as the extremities of Ireland, are every bit as interesting, and perhaps even more remarkable in atmosphere. But it was in Cornwall I first experienced the charm of the free breezes that blow at land's furthest bounds and sensed something of the primitive world. And it was while tramping the country around St. Ives in the company and under the instruction of our two native friends that I began, my brother and sister too, I suppose, to grow acquainted with these delights.

Usually we would go everywhere on foot, carrying our food with us, though this wandering didn't take us very far. In time the journeys developed into pilgrimages, annual rituals. We climbed to the top of the old fort at Trencrom and spent a fine sunny afternoon lying on the sward or circling the hedges and enjoying the splendid view over the countryside below, from sea to sea, from the foam-white beaches of the familiar bay that stretched northwards as far as Godrevy, to the smooth blue that surrounds St. Michael's Mount and the Lizard to the south. Or else we walked along the coast on the path that runs above the edge of the the cliffs and over to the Treveal valley, where there was no need to bother about a packed lunch because the farmer's wife was famed for providing an incomparable tea, one of those truly Cornish repasts with a dish of huge dimensions that brimmed with a thick-skinned cream which was mixed generously with homemade strawberry jam and spread on a long, tasty bun. And after the feast, we would walk down to the cove at the mouth of the valley to watch the seals basking on the rocks or sporting amongst themselves in the waves' swell.

Perhaps the most pleasant outing of all was our trip to the church and small village of Zennor. Not that I had a high opinion of churches in those days. Once again it was the journey itself that counted with me, the physical exercise, feeling one's feet firm on path and road, the experience of the sun's warmth and energy on the face, and the breeze on the nape of one's neck, hearing the buzz of bees in the heather (or coming from the fuchsias in the garden at Treveal), feeling the glorious and boundless freedom of the cloudless blue sky and the mighty restless sea, from the pounding of which there was nowhere any escape. And as far as I knew, Zennor's was quite an ordinary little church, despite its antiquity. It was a grey, plain building, of rather poor appearance, with a sedate little tower to it. But it was situated in a beautiful spot between sea and mountain. And there were two curious things about this church that we never tired of noticing and wondering at. The first of these was an inscription in Cornish on the outside wall near the porch, a quotation, I think it was, from the Book of Proverbs, in memory of someone of that parish who had been one of the last native-speakers of the language. That was a curio. The other odd thing was that on one of the seats inside the church there was carved in the wood the image of a mermaid with a comb and mirror in her hand. Here was something much more serious. What was an image from the pagan and superstitious world of the past doing in a Christian church? The story, Cyril said with an innocent grin, was that a handsome young lad had used to sit in this particular seat. He had a splendid singing-voice for which he was famous thereabouts, and many a girl had lost her heart to him. But one day a mermaid heard him singing and she too fell in love with him. She swam up the small stream from the sea to hear him singing in the choir, and in the end she persuaded him to follow her. The lad was never seen again, but the old folk used to say that his voice was sometimes to be heard singing to his wife, like the bells of Cantre'r Gwaelod[4], deep beneath the waters. Having been used to believing that it was the lure of mermaids' singing that drew poor sailors to their watery graves, it seemed to me that there was somehow a hint of truth in the Zennor story that had turned the temptation on its head. As I came out of the church and looked about me at the quiet hollow and the cluster of ancient houses that huddled there, and then towards the inviting blue sea that filled the far horizon, I could almost have believed that every kind of magic and fantasy was a daily possibility in Cornwall.

Gwanwyn yn y Ddinas (Gwasg Gee, 1975)

Hi-ho!

Urien Wiliam

I'm old enough now to be able to begin cherishing my memories, and to bring them to mind with a delicious feeling of nostalgia. And in living them over again I sometimes find myself following a pattern or sequence of images that are connected in some way or another. One of these came back to me vividly the other evening in Llandrindod[1], through which I happened to be passing on a short holiday with my family.

The very name of the place, Llandrindod, brings back a host of memories from the days of my childhood. An aunt of mine had lived there for quite a long while and I used to spend many a happy week in her home being pampered in all sorts of ways, wandering through the parks or practising what passed for rowing on the lake, chasing after the red squirrels that swarmed in those days in the wood near the lake, or taking the tasteless waters of the Pump Room[1], where to this day the glass that was used by some prince or other in 1910 can still be seen.

But as far as I know, there's no place in these particular memories for caravans.

Nor do they figure in my recollection of the other holidays I spent with other aunts and uncles, and since not even one of them lived in a caravan, that's not at all surprising. Indeed, I was probably somewhat dismissive of caravans in my early days, in so far as they entered my head at all, for the reason that the only experience we had of them as a family was as awkward, unsteady things that swayed dangerously and held up the traffic on main roads. Or else we would hear someone deploring the long rows of caravans that disfigured the shore-line of Rhyl and Prestatyn by attracting all sorts of dubious people from places like Liverpool during the summer months. Or again we would come across a band of gypsies on the common between Killay and Cefn Bryn, poor in appearance and low in morals, or so it was said. They must have been dangerous people if they were so fond of stealing children from the farms and clean washing from the back-gardens — and of buying little children, if we were to believe my mother's threat that, if we were naughty, she would sell us to the gypsies.

It's true that she once dragged me to look at a caravan and to peep slyly through the windows at the cramped tidiness within, but I half-suspect that the motive for that visit was sheer curiosity on her part — perhaps a fleeting glimpse would be a better description of our visit — rather than the proverbial restlessness which is so typical of our family. It's this restlessness, by the way, that is responsible for my frequent dreams of foreign parts and sunny climes — of paté in Périgeux, pizza in Portofino, sangria in Spain — and for the low spirits that come over me every November and remain with me until winter's end, when they vanish once more with the coming of April's flowers.

I had an opportunity of satisfying this restlessness and craving as a student at college. Since the grant was ridiculously small, in summer I had to go selling ice-cream on the beaches of Swansea, or turn my hand to gardening and look after the clock made from flowers in Victoria Park, in order to scratch enough to be able to bike around the country, sleeping in a tent, later on. Then I became a schoolteacher and owner of a very old black Austin that took me, and the tent, to the Continent, to wander through France and sunbathe on the beach at Cannes, to breathe the fresh air of the Pic du Midi, and to gaze in astonishment at the pilgrims in Lourdes.

That was when I discovered caravanning and took it up seriously for the first time. Who can beat the French at making a religion out of the custom, displaying their endless diligence and ingenuity in bringing a houseful of furniture and living-equipment with which to adorn their mobile summer-homes? They must have completely stripped their houses of all movable things, as if they had to have them about them in order to find comfort so far from home. I learned it was not lightly that the French spent the month of August under the scorching sun of the Midi — the mothers perspiring over feasts for lunch or up to their elbows in soapsuds, the kids climbing trees, or swimming, and the fathers playing boules, and everyone in their element from morn to night.

I know now that what I had remembered about the French on holiday stuck vividly in my memory during the years after I became a schoolteacher. Those were full years — meeting my life-partner, courting and marrying her, and then raising a family, all experiences that are so particular to me and yet common to most men. And among those experiences and the most obvious lessons learned was the awareness that the homes where you are always welcome had by then grown fewer in number, and that there's a limit even to the patience of Grandpa and Grandma as they see their restless grandchildren rushing like a whirlwind through their house and leaving havoc in their wake.

It's true that we had a package-fortnight in Spain, thanks to the planes from Rhoose, and us pretending we were wealthy for once in our lives, but the main consequence of that holiday was to empty our pockets and rekindle the old wanderlust worse than ever before. And that was the moment there flowed back into my mind the memories of those French caravanners and their healthy children playing in the sunshine — and of the fond aunts, and the Urdd[2] camp, and the tent and bike.

Considering the various degrees of expense and inconvenience that go with family holidays, it isn't surprising that I've followed the French example. Not entirely, perhaps, because I've never taken a mouth-organ, let alone a piano, with me on a caravan holiday, nor anything at all that might remind me of home and work during the weeks of the great escape. But I believe that a little of the *joie de vivre* comes with us on our travels for all that.

Not that everything goes smoothly for every minute of every day, mind you; with five of us on our own from dawn to dusk, there's an incomparable opportunity for quarrelling just now and again. But a caravan is a good place to get to know other members of the family — a splendid way of coming together as a close, harmonious, family-unit. This feeling of togetherness grows gradually, of course, after days of learning to be old hands at this caravanning business. But little by little a man learns how to pack food, and remembers to shut the lid of the toilet before going off on a trip, and to keep spare wicks and matches handy, and after he's adapted to this way of life, he begins — to his great surprise, perhaps — to *enjoy* it.

There are very many advantages to the caravanning life — visiting other parts of the country, and for a Welshman that means his getting to know Wales and her history better, meeting friends old and new, and feeling that you are widening the children's experiences by taking them to different places, and to different countries.

Some pompous ass once gave us what I consider to be a mocking nickname — 'middle-class gypsies'. Be that as it may, I know there wouldn't be any hope of our 'travelling the world, its length and breadth' if we had to rely on hotels and guesthouses, and if we had had to, our children would have been a lot less aware of the cultural heritage of western Europe than they are now.

Soon it will be the Easter holidays and there are already plans spinning in my head; the memories of those French caravans have been awakened once more and I feel the itch of the old craving. Come to think of it, it would be nice to be lazy this summer and stay for quite a time in just one or two places, instead of rushing around too much, and besides, petrol has become so expensive. It would be good to sit in the sunshine in a comfortable deck-chair or two. They say that an awning gives a caravan warmth and shelter from the wind. And after all, that's the fashion in France these days. I think it's high time that we too bought an awning.

Ysgrifau Heddiw
(gol. G.R. Hughes & I. Jones, Gwasg Gomer, 1975)

Ancestors

Glyn M. Ashton

They'll never make a Yankee out of me. I am unsuitable in that I lack one distinguishing mark, or rather, one particular characteristic, namely a keen interest in my ancestors. Of course, I sometimes try to half-imagine what they were like as people; and what's more, I occasionally wonder in a superficial, flitting sort of way what their opinion might have been, or is, of me. Rather low, I fear. Could it be some sinful indifference in me that's the reason for my not letting such things cause me pain and uncertainty, as I rush headlong to live as I please?

I went so far, years ago, as to ask my father and mother about their lineage, but I didn't get all that much out of them, because it was the recent past which filled the horizon for them. They gave me a pile of names, but there were only two interesting characters among them — Owen Davies on my mother's side, who was responsible for starting the first Sunday School at Llangurig, and on my father's side, some old country-doctor from Llanidloes who, as a fervent supporter of the Chartists,[1] had let off terrible threats against the authorities. But when the military came to town, he had stayed safe in his medical cabinet, not uttering a word.

The only distinction I can claim is that Davies is the sole Welsh surname in my family-tree, as far as I am aware. The rest are Ashtons, Beedles, Chapmans, Cleatons, and Millses — again, so far as I know. Although there's not the slightest note of music in my head, I can innocently boast of my connection with the musical Millses — my mother's mother was a sister to Richard Mills.[2] My father wouldn't have claimed any relationship between us and the wretched Charles Ashton[3], but I don't see how it can be avoided, though it's a distant connection, no doubt. Indeed, on three occasions recently I've come across people from Montgomeryshire, and after much questioning and puzzling, we have come to the conclusion that we are related to one another — distantly, that is. But not 'in a sense', as Dewi Wyn o Eifion[4] used to say — 'In a sense, we are all brothers from the same womb.' For if we were to go back far enough, we should all discover that we have many blood-connections about which we knew nothing. A good deal is heard about country people's ability to trace their ancestry back for generations, and to explain the relationship of such-and-such a man to such-and-such a woman. But not often does this happen in city or town, since we are generally people without roots, townspeople more often than not. And yet some echo of our rural past is to be heard whenever we refer to the living-room as the kitchen, which to be precise is a room for cooking in, but also, in a farmhouse, a room for eating and living in. Kitchen was the word we used for the living and dining room in the house where we lived, but it was in the back-kitchen that the food was cooked. The pretentious terminology of estate agents for these ordinary rooms hadn't penetrated our world, and we were surprised to hear the words 'drawing-room' or 'reception room' being used to describe 'the front room'.

Although we lived in a town that had been developed only in the recent past, we felt that we were people from the country, and that it was definitely there, or so we were given to understand, that we had our roots. And it was a grand feeling to know that we belonged to a particular district, which was a paradise for us children, in the very heart of Wales. After all, it's easier to grow fond of stream, farmyard, and hill than of a lamp-post on a street corner. And there's an indescribable difference between a gentle, well-bred sheep and a street-mongrel with no pedigree.

For months we used to look forward to the annual invitation to spend the summer-holidays in the country, and the waiting before our departure was for us delicious agony. The journey on the old Barry Railway, the Taff Vale and the Cambrian Lines took ages before we made it from Cadoxton to Llanidloes, and the very length of the journey used to make me think that the distance between those two places was almost without limit. In those days there was a station at Rhaeadr, and I remember my surprise on one occasion that we had seemed to reach it so soon. Poor little chap . . . it was only Radyr.[5]

Today it's at best a journey of about two hours by car. Yet despite the brevity of the journey nowadays, Llangurig is further away from me now than ever before, for to a very large extent it's people who make a place. I was in the old home recently, and though the furniture was the same, and the house's particular smell, and the view across the moor and river towards Moel Llangurig, it wasn't nostalgia for it that I felt, but the echo of nostalgia. With my brother I used to go out across the field as far as the stream. Once, when I was a lad at school, I wrote a lyric for the school magazine. The only phrase that has remained in my mind is 'the white ribbon of the brook'. An exaggeration . . . This was the centre of our world. The foot-bridge was still there, and the water changed its speed and appearance at that point just as it had used to, frothing under the little waterfalls and running bright over the pebbles that had a smooth layer of furry peat sticking to them. That was the coldest water in the world in which to bathe. When you looked up the rushy, peaty valley, more or less in a westerly direction, there were long but comparatively low ridges on one side and the other, which met on the horizon. Over there, beyond 'the old, distant line'[6], lay Cist Faen — the name of a place rather than a natural feature of the terrain. Only once did I ever walk the three rough miles as far as the high cairn of grey stones in the middle of that gloriously lonely moorland. There were Bronze Age remains at this spot, or so it's said. There's also a tradition in the district of some bloody battle taking place here, — although they don't go into detail as to when and between whom it was fought. It's maintained that the victorious chieftain placed his foot on one of the boulders and that the mark's still there. It's been pointed out to me several times, although it's a bit of a strain on the imagination to recognize it as a footprint.

I sit upon the pile of stones. To the south lie the frowning hills of Radnorshire; before me, westward, the wild moorland away in the direction of Pumlumon; and behind me, my forefathers' native ground. One or two suspicious sheep stare at me stupidly. If I had any imagination I should see coming towards me a man and a woman, both of them bare-footed — my mother's ancestors on a Saturday afternoon pilgrimage to Communion at Llangeitho under the ministry of Daniel Rowland.[7] When they drew near their Mecca, they would put their boots back on, go to take Communion with the crowd, then turn towards home, taking off their boots again at the same spot where they had put them on, and walking home silently over the hills and moors. They wouldn't say a word all the way from Llangurig to Llangeitho and back again, lest their speaking turn their thoughts in a direction other than in that of the formidable Communion.

The wind is sweeping heaven and earth, and I turn back along the ridge. The altitude causes a certain amount of pleasant lightheadedness. Down in the valley on the left are the ruins of Pantyrhelyg. There, in times gone by, lived two lovely people, Abraham Davies, known as Bugail, and his wife, distant kinsfolk of ours. They had no children of their own and in their will they left me ten pounds. I have no recollection of them but I shall always remember them. A white barn-owl bursts silently out of the ruins, eying me defiantly. I venture hesitantly across the swamp with its powdering of cotton-grass. When I saw its heads for the first time I thought they were balls of wool until I had examined them more closely. I then follow the stream down the valley, though I frequently lose it between the rushes and mosses, until I arrive at a small pool where I had placed a number of white pebbles in the water the previous year, and feel some innocent thrill at finding them in the same place still. I try rather crudely to think about the passing of time, and to guess how long they will remain there before they are worn or borne away — by whom and why I have no idea — and whether it might be by geological change or human agency in that lonely valley. As far as I know, the white motionless pebbles remain in the water to this day, unlike the people into whose midst I now had to return, for they have one and all gone into the parish's gravelly earth.

I was at the verge of more cultivated land, where the rushes and coarse grass had to some extent been tamed, and found myself in a pleasant meadow where once I had an experience that was quite upsetting. I had been wandering through the fields, and was coming back at my own pace over the meadow towards the house when I saw a determined little pony galloping towards me. There was no mistaking his intention. I didn't wait to try and reason with him, but hurried back in an undignified manner towards the stream. Half-way across the foot-bridge I paused to weigh up the situation. The pony wouldn't venture on to the narrow bridge, which had no hand-rails, but the whites of his eyes were enough to persuade me that it wasn't out of affection he was coming in my direction, and the gnashing of his teeth was obviously unfriendly. We stared at each for a brief moment. But when I withdrew to the other bank the little fiend trotted up his side of the stream until he had found a convenient point at which to ford the waters. And now he was on the same bank as I. He stormed at me with all his vigour but I promptly retreated over the foot-bridge to the opposite side, and it was then I realized I was much too far from the safety of the gate at the top end of the field. Fortunately, the geography of the horse-ring was in my favour. I hurried down the opposite bank, much to that peevish beast's frustration. But then he galloped back to his fording-place and crossed to my side of the stream, making for me again. But I managed to reach a spot where it was easy for me to cross the stream but which, for the vicious little animal, was an insurmountable barrier. He paused in fury for a few seconds, and then charged back after me across the ford. I leapt to the other bank . . . This went on for quite a while. But all the time I was going further downstream, and soon I was in an adjacent field of oats, and when I reached a spot nearest the hedge (an earthen bank about four feet high, with three or four strands of wire between short poles on its top), I had some idea of how far I had come. I waited until the enemy was almost upon me, then jumped across the stream at a point where it was impossible for his nibs to follow, and ran to the hedge. The hoofed devil discovered my intention in an instant and outdid himself in his most determined efforts to reach me before I had a chance of hurling myself over the hedge to the safety of the next field. As will be evident, it was I who won in the end. Now then, as a rule I'm kind to animals. I greet them politely and ask after their families. But not this time. I had tremendous fun hurling stones and insults at that vicious horse. I jeered at him mercilessly, insinuating all manner of unpleasant things about his ancestors.

Ancestors! If any of mine had been witnesses to that trivial incident, I'm fairly confident that some of them would have been making fun of me — especially the one who had split her sides with laughter at hearing (since she couldn't read) the story of Samson tying foxes' tails with burning torches between them and sending them into the cornfields of the Philistines. Yet it was she who had erred in my sight by selling a chestful of old Welsh books for a shilling. For her, paying her way, running a quite successful farm, and making money were far more important than anything to do with culture.

But I've been surprised by relatives of mine on more than one occasion. There was the cousin whose sons all became eminent doctors, who had no interest in anything, I had supposed, except farming and breeding horses. The last time I saw him was at a funeral. We were walking together from the chapel to the cemetery.

'You know what?' he said, 'There's nothing gives me more pleasure than a good *englyn*[8].'

And he began reciting one *englyn* after another, and his taste wasn't to be faulted. I don't know where on earth he had cultivated that knowledge. I knew of only one poet who wrote *englynion* in the whole parish.

There were saints and sinners, without a shadow of a doubt, among my ancestors. 'To shame our fathers in their coffins'?[9] Perhaps . . . But it's pretty certain that there were peasants among them, too, and I shouldn't be able to swank about each and every one of them.

What about you — can you say otherwise about your ancestors?

Ysgrifau Heddiw (gol. G.R. Hughes & I. Jones, Gwasg Gomer, 1975)

While Shaving

Gwilym R. Jones

At a quarter of a minute past eight o'clock this morning I half-opened the window of my bathroom in order to let in some fresh air that had not been in someone else's mouth. I stood there with hands at my sides and drew in a long, deep breath through my nostrils and then exhaled it from my lips after counting ten. I did this a dozen times, thanking the Giver of all breath for being allowed to see what the old people of long ago used to call in their prayers 'this new morning' on His fair earth.

That's just how a self-centred believer would see things, you might be saying, and the charge is true: in drawing those breaths I should have remembered that millions of my fellow-humans were cursing the same 'new morning', having been unable to take as much as a single draught into their lungs or drag themselves from their beds to a bathroom, let alone go through the ritual of physical exercise. I ought to have borne in mind that the ball of matter we call the earth-mother doesn't always spin to the advantage of countless numbers of my fellow-wayfarers.

But I had pushed these disagreeable thoughts to some obscure cell in my mind and set about the mechanical task of shaving. My grandfather from Llŷn would always 'cut his beard', and he cut it any old how with an old-fashioned razor which had a blunt blade. I myself use a smaller razor, although that too is quickly going out of fashion. And while carrying out this rather mundane task, there sometimes come into a man's head a lot of quite strange thoughts.

My father had a habit of saying, whenever he caught my brother or me staring at our own faces in the mirror, that we would 'be sure to see the old devil himself' if we kept on looking into that shining glass. While staring at my face in the bathroom mirror this morning, I saw no one worse than myself, though I peered hard and long, and yet the image I saw gave me quite a nasty fright.

The mirror draws a cruelly honest picture, but as I looked at my face in it I had the impression that someone completely unknown to me appeared there. I saw a surly, indifferent face and a pair of lukewarm eyes gaping from under the hood of the lids. And I remember them smooth-skinned as an August apple! Around the eyes and forehead I could make out new creases, some of which were deep enough to provide refuge for black-heads, and I was also starting to grow a double-chin.

Come to think of it, the marks of a man's past eventually congeal on his skin, and it may be that every worry and fear I have ever had is now engraved on the parchment of my face by the merciless hand of time. Time is something quite un- — un-what, would you say? I'm beginning to think that only the present moment has any significance: yesterday has been and its door is shut for ever, and we don't have any hold on tomorrow. We go through life from moment to moment as a man leaps from stone to stone while crossing a ford, and in between we feel that time is slipping by like the stream's current, as some hymn-writer or other has already said.

It's odd that we judge other people by their faces more than by anything else, especially those strangers whose paths cross ours from time to time. The shape of the face, the nose and mouth, and more than anything else, the way the eyes respond to us: these are the externals that convey a man's character. The shadow of a scowl, or that warm smile lighting up a man's countenance, it's these tell us a good deal about someone else's attitude to us.

The question I asked myself just now, while shaving my beard, was this: how could anyone like, let alone love, the owner of that mug which I saw in the mirror? How, indeed! It's a face with no virtue in it for those who like amiability, a face that shows the wear of the long years' wind and rain upon it. There's no ointment, oil, powder or paint from the chemist's shop that could hide its ugliness. It's a face into whose eyes I can't bring myself to look by the clear light of day. I sometimes wonder whether it's only 'the spirit of man', as the old theologians used to say, which can be unfetching? I can hardly believe that even the hippopotamus, the dear old clumsy long-nosed hippo, is an ugly creature. It's no uglier than other animals of the same family, and yet a man or woman can be more ugly, or more beautiful, than their brothers and sisters. There was once an old bachelor from Tal-y-sarn who used to advise us young men to get to know women 'before the dew of their innocence turns frosty, my lads'. But beauty is destroyed not only by time. From our forebears some of us have received only a very small phial of loveliness.

How many times, I wonder, has the blade of my razor been scraped over these jowls of mine? And how many tons of stubble have been been removed from this face since the days of my gooseberry-down youth? No one knows. I ought to be quite good at shaving by now, but find that I'm often pretty inept: some mornings I feel too bothered and there'll be a small sliver of skin on the razor's edge and a speck of blood reddening my cheek.

Another time the blade will be too blunt and leave the raw mark of its mean scratching.

Speaking of meanness, the worst example of stinginess I ever saw was that of an old quarryman from the top end of the village who would peel an orange in his pocket and slip a slice of it into his mouth surreptitiously, for fear his mates might fancy a bit of the fruit.

I often feel jealous of people who are better off than me. I know I shouldn't, especially after just reading such cynical words as these by Maurice Baring: 'If you would like to know what the Lord God's opinion is of money, you have only to take a good look at those who have it.'

Drat it! I cut my skin a moment ago while trying to clip a bristle on the lobe of my ear with the razor. So I've been searching frantically in the small drawer under the mirror for the tin of alum to staunch the flow of blood. No, there wasn't as much as a thumb-nailful of it left. But there was a small book, its covers gone yellow with the years, an old book made of fragrant silk-paper from which I used to see my mother tearing out leaves with which to rub her nose and cheeks. This, and a small scent-bottle, was the only cosmetic aid she ever used. How on earth had 'the book with nice smells' — our name for it all those years ago — been left behind like flotsam from the turn of the century on the strand of our bathroom? It ought to have been in some little perfume-box, with all the rest of my mother's trinkets.

But there was no point in trying to guess, and I found about four leaves of the little book a great help in the emergency of having to tend to the lobe of my ear. As I went downstairs there was still part of a leaf of the powdered paper sticking as prominently to my ear as a banner on a turret, which caused great mirth for my family at the breakfast-table.

It took me precisely ten minutes to adjust my countenance in readiness for the day ahead. I shouldn't have been a whit sooner had I been using my electric razor, and my skin wouldn't have been so clean afterwards. My jaw and cheek and the particle of skin under the nostrils and my throat were once again as smooth as a baby's, and the old-fashioned woollen flannel had done its job on the creases in the flesh of my forehead and temples. The morning's task had been completed by the subtly aromatic liquid that made my skin sensitive to the touch. I felt, after taking another look at my shaven face, that the day was off to a good start and that the first step had been rather a tidy one, despite the small cut on my ear.

For how many more mornings, I wonder, shall I be able to shave myself? Such was the question that came into my mind as I looked at my bold face in the mirror before going downstairs. Another question that came to bother me in the wake of the first was this: Why does a man go to the trouble of living? Some groggy mornings you feel that life is an unmixed weariness, a habit that has no meaning. But this morning, after coming across that little book with the sweet-smelling leaves, there flashed through my memory a picture of my mother at home on our farm. She had just found a hen's nest under the hedge, and was warming her hands on the eggs, and there were wild hyacinths in a blue haze all about her feet.

    Now that I come to think of it, that was the very moment my razor misbehaved in the vicinity of my ear.

Ysgrifau Heddiw (gol. G.R. Hughes & I. Jones, Gwasg Gomer, 1975)

Of Time and Distance

Dyfnallt Morgan

'To tell you the truth,' my mother said to me, 'I seriously thought that I'd never see you again.' She was an old woman by this time, about three score years and ten, although you would never have thought it from her bearing. And she went on looking younger than her years right up until her death at eighty-four. Perhaps an only child, as I was, is blinder than most children to the change taking place in his parents' appearance. That is, except when some cruel disease intervenes to cut a man down in the flower of his days, as happened to my father when I was in my twentieth year. Two years previously, on my leaving home for the first time to go to college, in the middle of the great Depression, he had been in tears for hours afterwards, from what I was to hear later. We were close friends, true enough. But the probability is that his illness (undiagnosed at the time) was already giving him trouble, and also that some instinct was warning him that he wouldn't live to see me finish my course; he must have felt, too, the abysmal sadness of sensing that there was something final about his son's leaving home on that occasion.

    My mother, however, went on living for thirty years after him. And just as I throughout all that time looked on her with a son's unchanging eyes, so she looked on me with the unchanging eyes of a mother. It wasn't that she was over-possessive, a charge much too often levelled against the mother of an only child; not at all. And the second world war saw to it that she couldn't be. Indeed, after finishing my college career, I didn't spend much time in the old home ever again. It was always a case of my coming and going after that. And if the French saying is true — *Partir, c'est mourir un peu* — the frequency of our saying goodbye in the course of the years was to cause quite a bit of wear and tear on the feelings of us both.

We must have long grown hardened to the experience. Not only I but my mother as well. How else had she been able to come to terms with the notion of never seeing me again? Nor is 'coming to terms' the right phrase, nor are 'content' or 'accept' or 'submit' the right words either. There was a far more positive and worthier attitude behind the notion, namely a readiness to let me follow my own path, come what may, because it was the right thing to do.

My own path, that's what I said. So I'm not talking about the compulsion that was upon everyone of my generation to do some form of 'national' service from 1939 onwards. It's true that I responded to conscription as a conscientious objector. The law of the United Kingdom allowed for that. I believe that my mother suffered more scorn than I ever did on this account, and sometimes from unexpected quarters. She learned to grow hardened in the face of this experience, too. It was enough for her to receive my letters regularly and be able to follow my adventures with the Friends' Ambulance Unit in England, Italy, and Austria. Not that there was anything heroic in them. Quite the contrary. I've always been a timid and over-anxious sort of chap and I couldn't have deceived my mother even in a letter.

The war in Europe eventually came to an end and the day drew near for my release from the law's demands. It was then I answered an appeal for volunteers to go out to work in China for two years. At the time my mother was staying in Cardiganshire, and there I was to spend the few days of freedom that were allowed me before leaving this country once more. Our farewell took place at the railway-station in Pontllanio this time. My mother was as self-possessed as ever, as far as I could tell, anyway. She knew the famous line by Ceiriog[1] full well, but not for all the world would she show such softness in her dealings with me. Her strength enabled me to face the journey with an easy mind. During the romantic journey to Carmarthen I was engaged in conversation by a talkative woman whom I didn't know. As the train pulled in I suddenly remembered the old joke about that leisurely line and said, 'Well, that's the worst part of my journey over.' 'Why do you say that, then? Where are you off to?' she enquired. 'To Shanghai!', I replied. The woman laughed heartily and I knew for sure that she didn't take me seriously.

As the ship made its way out of Portsmouth, I stood on deck looking to the north-west, remembering that my mother that afternoon was on a trip to Pembrokeshire. She, too, was gazing towards the sea, and it was that day she had in mind when she told me, years later, that she didn't expect to see me ever again.

Why, I wonder, did such an idea occur to her on that particular occasion? Why hadn't she felt like that during the years of the war? She was not sensing the end of her own sojourn on earth, like my poor father years before. She could hardly, either, have been worrying about my safety. After all, the war in the Far East too had ended by then. And she wasn't to know, any more than I did at the time, that as I reached Shanghai the civil war which was to last for nearly twenty years was about to tear China apart once again. And I was coming back in two years' time. I wasn't going out there for the rest of my life, like those dozen young Catholic missionaries from Ireland whose company I was to enjoy for six weeks or more on the passage to Shanghai. I was astonished more than once at the self-sacrifice of those men, who had no hope of ever seeing the Emerald Isle again, for all their love of it.

'You see,' my mother had said, 'you were going so very far away.' This, to me, was an explanation both revealing and intriguing. Was there, in my mother's mind, some moral or theological significance to it? Wasn't it to 'a far country' that the Prodigal Son had gone on his journey? I had never been ten thousand miles away from home before. And yet, throughout my time in the faraway country, despite the fact that the people, the language, the customs, and the culture, were all so foreign to me, and although the conditions there were so often horrible, I myself wasn't at all conscious of the 'distance'. The same sun warmed the day, the same moon lit up the night. Indeed, I should almost have said it was the same snow that fell in Hankow on the banks of the river Yangtze (the first that many had ever seen there) which caused such losses to the farmers of Wales during the winter of 1946.

Over those long months a stream of letters flowed regularly between us, each with a number on it, lest one arrive out of sequence, as sometimes happened. And indeed, they all reached their destination, in both directions, wonderfully quickly. I still have about a hundred of them, although I've never sat down to read them through. No doubt they contain some interesting things, like my description of the splendid Sun Yat Sen monument in Nanking, or of the service at the Griffith John Memorial Chapel[2] in Hankow which I was privileged to attend, though I understood not a word at the time. Yet I remember two things about that service. First, being introduced to an old man who had known the famous Welsh missionary well. The second thing was that I had been charmed by the singing, to the accompaniment of piano and organ, something I had heard only once before, at Capel y Wig when I was at the Urdd[3] camp in Llangrannog. Doubtless, too, I mentioned that I had been impudent enough to accept an invitation to preach one Sunday morning at the Hankow United Church to a congregation of Americans mostly. I had been given only a short warning, and I preached shamelessly, in English of course, as much as I could remember of a powerful sermon I had more than once heard being given in Welsh by a not uncelebrated minister back in 'the old country'.

There must also be in those letters quite a bit about my frequent and difficult journeys between Hankow and Nanking and Kaifeng, a triangle within which two conflicting sides were fairly equally matched, so that I was never sure whether it was Mao's forces or Chiang's who were all around me from day to day. That's the order, or disorder, of things in a guerrilla war. It's quite certain that I recounted our futile attempts at transporting essential goods for distribution among the population of Shantung province, with the Kuomintang aeroplanes bombing and sinking, before our very eyes, the barges that were to have carried us and our lorries across the Yellow River. All this despite the personal promise of the President himself that we should be allowed to carry out our duties, under the conditions agreed for the support services of the United Nations. I shouldn't be surprised if there were a reference, too, to the hideous cholera epidemic which some of us once helped more experienced missionaries to deal with in a place called Hsu-chow-fu.

In calling things like that to mind, and a host of other experiences, I find it possible to understand my mother's worst fears, at least as I look back over the shoulder of the years. Then there was the distressing journey home, before the two years were up. By air this time, since a bed was awaiting me in a London hospital. One of the plane's four engines exploded and caught fire soon after we left Cairo on the fourth night out of Hong Kong, and the clever Canadian pilot brought us and the flying-boat down safely on the waters of the Mediterranean. There was no mention of this in any of the London papers, as far as I know. Perhaps the reason was that one of my fellow-passengers from Rangoon onwards had been Thakin Nu, Prime Minister of Burma at the time, on his way to London to see Mr Attlee.

Yet more important and wonderful than all these adventures, in my mother's eyes, was the fact that I had returned to these islands at all. But as I have said, years were to pass before she admitted to me what her feelings had been that day I had gone away. I remember laughing and suggesting that it was only heroes, such as those missionaries from Maynooth who were willing to go into exile for ever, not creatures like me who were always sure to find their way home from anywhere, like a cat or dog which appreciates home-comforts in its natural habitat. But if I had ever been a hero, I told her, it had been that time when I was about eight years old. With my father ill in bed, my mother had asked me to take a letter to be posted (to Cardiganshire I warrant) from the post office at Penydarren. To do that you had to cross 'the tramway climbing from Merthyr to Dowlais'[4], and that main road was much busier then than it is today, what with the screeching trams, and the cars and lorries, and there was no such thing as Belisha beacons in those days. It was a nightmare of an adventure for a timid child like me, yet I carried out my errand successfully, though not without risk to my life. But it had hardly dawned on my mother then that she might never see me again, because I had been venturing no further than a mile from home.

If I had cause to curse the Post Office that day, I was to bless it for years afterwards. And our habit of corresponding went on regularly right up to the end. If my mother wasn't on one of her frequent visits to us in Bangor, I'd be sure to receive word from her about mid-week, and she would have had a reply without fail by Saturday morning.

Then, one Sunday morning, a few years ago now, I got an unexpected message to say that my mother had died. By the time I reached Merthyr that evening, the letter I had posted on Friday hadn't arrived. Once again I had cause to curse the Post Office. The letter was delivered on Monday morning.

After marrying, my mother had lived for fifty years in the same house, and she had died there, all on her own. It may be that I had gone off on my wanderings more than I should have done, and had thus neglected to ask her whether she could throw any light on two perplexing questions for which I still don't have any answers: What is time? And what is distance?

Ysgrifau Heddiw (gol. G.R. Hughes & I. Jones, Gwasg Gomer, 1975)

A Methodist Deacon's Advice

R. Emyr Jones

I don't really know when I began taking an interest in boxing; at some time during my schooldays, most likely, in the 'thirties, when men like Jack Petersen, Len Harvey, Larry Gains, and that tough German, Walter Neusel, were household names among a good number of civilized, Christian, Welsh people. My interest probably reached its peak that unforgettable night in 1937 when the idol of Tonypandy, Tommy Farr[1], fought Joe Louis, the Brown Bomber from Detroit, for the world championship. That was a night! What a contest!

Next day the fight was shown at every cinema in the kingdom, and the fans — both saints and lesser folk among them — flocked to see the film on screen. I well recall a man from Dyffryn Ogwen going to see it at the Plaza in Bangor three nights in a row, and when someone asked him why he was going a third time, he replied, 'Farr was close to winning the night before last, and last night, so perhaps he'll have better luck tonight.'

However foul and uncivilized it may be to set two fit and muscular men to face each other in a narrow ring and then, in cold blood, to pitch into thrashing each other mercilessly, it must be admitted that it appeals to many of us — proof, perhaps, that the beast is still strong in us, despite our having heard so many eloquent sermons on peace and kindness and brotherly love.

My father was a deacon with the Calvinistic Methodists, and he had not only heard hundreds of powerful sermons but had also found something engaging in almost every one. What he hated most to hear was criticism of preachers and preaching. For me, at that time, every Methodist deacon was a narrow, drily religious creature. Nevertheless, high though my father's respect was for the sermon, and for preachers, and despite the fact that chapel and religion were so dear and important in his sight, he also had a great interest in boxing. It's not easy to reconcile the two, and I have no intention of trying to do so now.

Only twice do I remember him offering me advice, and that was at a time when it was fashionable for deacons to counsel their children, and other people's children too, if it comes to that. No child ever had more practical, and more unexpected, advice from any

Methodist deacon than what I was given from my father thirty years ago.

We were standing on the platform at Bangor station one freezing January morning. The cold wind was whipping down from the tops of Eryri like a sharp knife to chill the marrow of the bones, and I remember to this day how I longed to see the train arriving so that I might shelter from the cold. There's no more miserable place than a station-platform when you are waiting for a train. Everything that is to be said has been said, and the small-talk for the last few minutes is just to pass the time. Indeed, both of us had been standing there silently for a long while that morning. We had had to be there in good time because I was setting out on such an important journey. Had not the King himself sent for me? Well, no, he had ordered me to join his army, and there was nothing for it but to obey. And my father, fair play to him, was losing a day at the quarry in order to come with me to Bangor — the Methodist deacon accompanying the eighteen-year-old youth who was about to leave home for the first time, to join the army.

'Listen,' he said, as if I had given him permission to quote a verse or two from Scripture, or to tell me about the experience of some hymn-writer, or perhaps to remind me not to forget my roots; that's probably what the usual advice would have been on an occasion like this. But then, as sober as any saint, he said quite casually, 'Now don't you go starting a scrap with anyone while you are away. But if you have to, see to it that you get the first punch in. That's what counts, every time.'

The advice was so surprising that it left me speechless. I nodded my head to assure him that I should bear it in mind. The train pulled in and I set off on my journey to a far country feeling glad that it had been the pugilist and not the deacon who had counselled me. It may be that he had enough confidence in me to refrain from offering the usual advice; I like to think that, anyway. However that might be, it turned out to be splendid counsel that he had given me at Bangor station. I acted upon it more than once. Yes, I did a lot of boxing while I wore the King's livery, and each time I heard the bell at the start of the first round, my father's words would come back to me, and many a bloody nose and box on the ear was avoided by my taking his advice: to get my blow in first. Well, there's more than one kind of advice, isn't there?

Rhwng Dwy (Gwasg Tŷ ar y Graig, 1976)

Of Violets and Bells

Selyf Roberts

The hospital in Parma was part of the University, but stripped of any vestige of academia and adapted as a refuge for the sick, some of them Italian soldiers but most of us prisoners of war. Bare corridors and rooms deliberately scoured to make them clinically clean gave the lie to the building's exterior with its walls and towers studded with splendid carvings as fine as any of the numerous proud buildings which adorn this city, one of the principal cities in the old province of Tuscany. All that I knew about the place was that it had been a great favourite with the thousands who had toured Italy before the war. I supposed the city had important historical associations, a famous gallery or two perhaps, housing priceless works by old masters, but I knew nothing at all about them.

It didn't, however, take me long to find out. Very raggedly, and by dint of questions by the score in my very stiff Italian, I became the willing pupil of Sorella Caterina, a nun who had been sent into this world to give succour to prisoners of war. She it was who looked after the ward that I was in, and who made it her business to convince me that I had now arrived in the most beautiful, the most important, the most gifted, the most brilliant, the most aristocratic city in the whole world. If I understood her aright, and it must be borne in mind that the only English she knew was 'yes', not even Rome, where reigned her Father in the Faith, could be compared with Parma. What comfort I drew from this knowledge was dubious, because there was no hope whatsoever of my seeing any of it, fairest city in the world though it may have been. The guards made sure that none of us put a foot outside the ward, and yellow jaundice, together with two or three other less serious diseases, ensured that I wouldn't budge from my bed for quite a while. So there was nothing for it but to go on chatting with the Sorella, about Italy, its people, its culture, and about Parma, the city that was a combination of all that was 'true, honest, just, pure, lovely, and of good report'.

It's true that in passing she mentioned the local woollen industry, and spoke ecstatically about the craft of the cottagers who worked in fine silk on the outskirts of town. Once she became mundane enough to speak of cheese and ham, the likes of which were not to be found on land or sea, but she didn't linger over these. Stars would come into her eyes whenever she began talking about the Cathedral and the many elegant churches around it, each consecrated to a particular saint and a treasure-house for priceless relics. She told me about convents and priories by the dozen, and explained their connections with these famous churches, and about the schools and colleges under their patronage, where the flower of the Tuscan and Italian aristocracy had received their education in days gone by. On the very spot where now I lay, who knows what young nobleman or prince from among the wealthy monarchies of Europe had not come to grips, at his teacher's feet, with the world's classics and all civilized learning? One evening — and that was when she was at her most eloquent, the heaviest of her duties done — she summed up her vision of Parma for me in a single sentence. A Cathedral, she said, and a family of churches at its skirts, a University with a family of academies at its feet, and for the rest, the palaces and courts of families whose history had been bound up with the fortunes of the Medici and Florentine gentry before Rome was exalted to the status of capital. That was Parma, said Caterina, and with a sly smile in her eyes, she added, 'All this, and violets, of course.'

In the old days a posy of Parma Violets had been synonymous with what orchids are in Britain today. They went with the special occasion, and were worn or carried by ladies of high birth. It was an unforgettable sight when these gentlewomen attended the opera or ball in their expensive clothes, aglitter with priceless stones. No other city boasted as many titles and orders as Parma, and it was the aristocracy's duty and delight to demonstrate this to the world at every opportunity. But amidst all the diamonds and pearls and costly gems, there were always the violets. No matter what jewellery a woman wore, at her ear or on her finger or round her arm, the whole would be crowned with a pale-purple spray of Parma violets in her corsage.

Hanover had nothing like these, nor Paris, nor Madrid, nor Alexandria. Violets were grown in Germany, it was true, and in France and Spain and Egypt, but it was significant that the name given to the species in whatever country it grew was Parma Violet. The Sorella Caterina hinted that she herself very much doubted whether it were possible to grow the genuine species in any other place, and that those of Egypt and France, and everywhere else, were mere imitations. But be that as may be, these violets belonged to Parma, wherever they might have been grown, and none but the ladies of Parma were entitled to wear these particular, these original, these authentic flowers.

Could not the wealth of French châteaux and the guile of its salons have bought the violets and brought them to be worn in their palaces? It may be that this question had been considered and discussed a hundred times, but to no avail. Caterina lowered her head to inform me, as though it were a secret known only to her and God, that Parma Violets could not be kept overnight in water because, if they were, they would lose their scent. That was why no one had ever succeeded in stealing them from the ancient city. Whatever damage Time had wreaked on its churches and colleges, the city still had its violets, flowers of one night and for one occasion only.

Caterina slipped from my bedside like a white ghost, with a prayer on her lips and a grateful, mischievous smile accompanying her *ave*.

I lay back in the clean white bed. It was the night before Christmas. It had grown late before any of us was asleep, and although everyone was quiet I could sense that some of the others were of restless mind, without knowing why. Expectantly awake, perhaps, because there had been talk going the rounds that next day there were to be Christmas parcels from the Red Cross. The evening hours slid into night, and I watched the stars move from pane to pane across the tall windows along one side of the ward. There had been a fall of snow the previous day and all that morning, but by now the leaden clouds had dispersed and the clear dark-blue firmament formed a fitting back-cloth to the silver and gold of the constellations. And as the clouds were driven away, the frost came — frost, and stars, and the night. And Christmas Eve.

I was nowhere near sleep when the bells began. They pierced the air without any warning, and for a while nothing could be heard save the careless confusion of their sound: the sound of bells from churches and convents and schools and colleges, all tumbling together like a cascade over the frost. But in a moment I was able to put an order to things and my hearing became a listening, so that the various bells were greeting me and I could distinguish one from another. I could hear the playful tunes of the church just up the street, and the more priestly boom of the Cathedral yonder; one bell was ringing out a single tenor note, as though it had escaped for the night from the accursed company of book and candle, and with its cheerful tinkling was interwoven the alto and contralto of other bells pealing in rhythmic dignity. A round of six was competing with another of eight, and yet another octave interfered temporarily to put them out of my hearing with a tumult of notes which seemed to be sent forth any old how. But the night ensured that the breeze would, every now and then, disseminate the bishop's sonorous bell, keeping discipline and preventing the rejoicing from becoming a carnival.

There was no war in the bells' world; there was no dispute among men to prevent the dawn of Christmas. There was no discord among those who listened to the anthem of gold, frankincense, and myrrh. Had they been listening, the bells of Parma would have been pealing in the ears of Hitler and Mussolini and Churchill and Roosevelt and Stalin, just as they rang out for me. For a few minutes I felt the situation to be too much for me. I couldn't understand how it was that the years had so injected poison into the veins of mankind as to allow the sound of gunfire to mingle with the ringing of bells. My leaping mind turned to my home in Wales, and I failed to understand what complexity of life it was that bade the bells of Parma ring so gleefully while the tongues of the bells at Llandrillo-yn-Rhos had been tied and were mute.

I gave up thinking about it, puny and helpless in my clean white bed. Soon afterwards I heard strange, new, different notes, as if at last they had succeeded in bringing the merriment to order. Some pretty carillon was sending messages over the city and they fell on my ears from the open window above my bed:

> *Adeste, fideles,*
> *Laeti, triumphantes,*
> *Venite, venite in Bethlehem.*

Perhaps this was Experience. If so, I had to make the most of it, for it wasn't likely ever to recur. The tender hands of the Sorella and her pride in her city, and Christmas morning, and the bells — they would never come together again. I could never hold on to them, to savour them again and again whenever the desire arose. For they were things that belonged to the moment, to one place. Flowers of one night.

Mesur Byr (Gwasg Gomer, 1977)

Remembering Mrs Newbould

Eirwen Gwynn

Often have I listened to panel members on a radio programme or in some cultural society having to answer the question, 'Who has been the greatest influence on your life?' I've admired them greatly for being able to give sensible impromptu answers, and been grateful from the bottom of my heart that I myself haven't had to answer such a silly question. That's how it seems to me, anyway, since I can't for the life of me think of anyone who's been a great influence on me — no one famous, that is.

Of course, the influence of my family has been very great: my father and mother, and particularly my husband — yes, and my son, too. The relationship between parent and child is important to the parent as well as the child. I have never been able to understand parents who send their children to boarding-school; it's a separation that affects growth in the personality of both parents and children. But there I go, after one of my favourite hares.

To return to my subject: the influence of a close relative isn't allowed as answer to the old question — not usually, anyhow. So whom should I choose, if I were to find myself in the position of having to reply? Some prominent figure from history? The only history I learned at school was all about kings and politicians and generals, British most of them, and I never took to them very much. I was never told about those rare souls who devoted their lives to the furtherance of learning and culture, or to improving the condition of society. And far too late did I come to be acquainted with the history of Wales for me to say in all sincerity that I've ever been under the influence of any of our great men.

Then what about the world of literature? No, I was middle-aged before I first met our great literary figures, too; nor did I learn much about them at school. Far too early I had to make that wasteful and unnecessary choice between Welsh and French, and as I had just come to live in Wales from England, my French was a bit better than my Welsh, so it was French that won. That was a loss, and one that I haven't been able to make up for to this day. So no writer. I've learned to enjoy the work of some of our best writers now, but I can't claim that any one of them has influenced me much.

But what about scientists, explorers, champions from the world of sport, famous people from all walks of life? I can't think of one, man or woman, on whom I should have liked to have modelled my life. I admire their skills and feats, but from careful reading about their careers it's clear to me that they are only human, all of them. Some have been more fortunate than the rest of us, or more privileged, if that's the right word, to have had some insatiable craving to attain a certain goal, never mind how purposeless it might have been, and a readiness to sacrifice everything else to achieve that end. I can understand this ambition but I shouldn't want to have been like that.

There remains an important sector that I haven't considered — religion. It's not likely that anyone has been untouched by the selfless example of people like Mother Teresa or by the conduct of men such as George M. Ll. Davies[1], but these too I came to know too late in life. And on the whole, I'm not excited by orthodox theologians, whether those of yesterday or today; too often their bombast tends to hide, I'm quite certain, the core of real virtue and vision that motivates them.

I'm sure that I've had some benefit from reading the work of the Bishop of Woolwich and our own J.R. Jones[2] and Gwilym O. Roberts.[3] They have definitely been of great help in my search for spiritual convictions. But I think I've had just as much of a lead from philosophers from the world of science: Heisenberg and Born, Einstein and Polanyii, and from others such as Mumford and Sorokin. Each has contributed to the synthesis of my own philosophy, however inadequate that may be. But I can't name any one of these, either, as the great influence on my life.

So who, then? I shall have to think of someone in case the situation some day arises that I have to answer that silly question. Who? Who?

I can, after all, I can name someone. An Englishwoman — yes, an Englishwoman. No, you don't know her; she isn't famous. She came into my life when I sorely needed the influence of her gentle, brave personality.

It was during the war and I was living in London, in the thick of it. This Englishwoman and her sister were living in a flat in the same building. Mrs Newbould was the widow of a missionary, a small, rotund woman, old-fashioned in her dress and with a compassionate turn to her mouth and humour sparkling from her little dark eyes. When I first met her she was in poor health but never did I hear her complain.

Her sister was rather a different character, although she too had her good points: she was an old maid who had retired from being headmistress of a secondary school, and the mark of a lifetime's authority was to be seen on her countenance and in her whole manner; but she, too, had a generous heart.

Both were exceptionally kind to a young couple trying to bring up a child in the severe and terrible conditions of the second world war; always ready to look after the child when it was too much of a risk to take him to the shops; generous with their advice and sympathy whenever the events of that confused and anxious way of life tended to overwhelm the spirit. And the unforgettable day when the war in Europe came to an end, there the two sisters were at the door, insisting on coming to baby-sit so that we could go out to celebrate our release from the tension and worry of those troubled times.

But not only that. At a time when there were no goods in the shops, nor money in the pocket, for that matter, Mrs Newbould insisted on selling, at too low a price, a carpet of hers with which to cover up the exposed baldness of our living-room floor. It wasn't a carpet with thick colourful pile, true enough, but rather a weave of something like grey string. But it made our life much more comfortable; before getting it, we could see daylight between the floorboards and a cold draught came up through the floor from the fissures where the windows had been in the flat beneath us. We also obtained from Mrs Newbould some sticks of furniture that it wasn't possible to buy; her good turns were innumerable. But that's not why she had an influence on me.

I have no idea what had brought the two sisters to live in the middle of London's danger. As for us, we had our livings there, as did millions like us. But there was no call for them to be there. They feared neither bomb nor fire, nor V1 flying-bomb, nor V2 rocket, nor any other devilish contraption that the mind of man could devise. The two of them remained cheerful and unperturbed through it all, especially Mrs Newbould. This wasn't the first time she had faced danger. She used to tell me terrifying stories about her life in Africa when she had been out there with her missionary husband. The point of recounting these stories was to entertain us, and there was no hint of self-aggrandisement in the telling.

When Mrs Newbould lost her sister, she faced up to that, too, with her customary unruffled courage; that was the moment I had a true glimpse of the depth of her character. By then she had nothing at all to live for — no children, no family or relative anywhere; and she was in poor health. Soon after burying her sister the fragility of her health meant that she had to be content to go and live in a home for the widows of ministers of the Gospel. But not a word of complaint was ever heard from her, and neither the mischievousness in her eyes nor the ready smile of welcome had faded whenever I paid her a visit there. I did that every week for a while and it was no hardship for me at all. This wasn't a drily religious woman; I don't recall her ever mentioning religion to me. I often found her listening excitedly to a boxing match or wrestling-contest on the wireless, responding with her sharp comments and urging the contenders on by cuffing the air about her. At other times she would follow a cowboy or detective story, listening intently until she was certain that the good guy had won — that was the usual kind of story in those days.

She took an interest in everything and her conversation was uplifting and a renewal of strength for one who was much younger and more fortunate in the things of this world than she was. I had the benefit of this relationship from week to week for several months and then, quite suddenly, the old lady was moved to another home a long way away. Out of necessity, my visits after that grew more infrequent, but each time I did manage to go that far her welcome was as warm as ever, although it was obvious that she was failing. When at last I left the city, we corresponded for a short while until I realized that I couldn't expect word from her any more. I knew for certain that, whatever her end might have been, she didn't complain.

It's now more than a quarter of a century since then, yet if someone had more than the usual influence on me, it was that little old lady, so cheerful, unassuming, and strong. I've had the privilege of meeting other people whose lives have filled me with wonder and admiration: an Anglesey woman who lost her sight but managed to re-adjust her life with courage and marvellous cheerfulness; another woman who gladly devoted her life to taking care of a brother who couldn't utter a word or move a muscle; and several others. But Mrs Newbould came into my life when I was, as it were, at a spiritual crossroads, when the hideousness and disillusion of wartime had put all faith to flight.

And today, although I am still much concerned with the work of great thinkers in the world of philosophy and theology and metaphysics, and continue to grope earnestly for spiritual conviction, because I had the privilege of knowing Mrs Newbould I know at least this much for certain: that there's comfort to be had in distress and strength to carry on. Yes, there's strength to be had — from somewhere.

Dau Lygad Du (Y Lolfa, 1979)

Good Morning, Lloyd

D. Tecwyn Lloyd

I was standing in front of the White Lion Hotel in Bala at about a quarter-past-nine one morning in the early summer of 1967. I was there to meet some people from the BBC, because that day and perhaps the next we had a television programme to make about the town and district, and especially about the people and places that had counted in my life there once and — if only in my memory — still count for something today.

As I stood there, expecting to hear doors opening, so to speak, and looking about me without thinking of anything in particular, I saw a stout, squarish, straight-backed woman stumping up the High Street, and immediately recognized the masculine, military bearing, the heavy tweed clothes, the substantial, unfeminine, brogue shoes, and the splayed feet that filled them. None less than Dorothy Jones, B.A., who had been headmistress of the County Intermediate Girls' School in Bala when I was a sixth-former in the Boys' Grammar School in the same town. She had been our History teacher, with a class of boys and girls, for the year 1932.

Now I couldn't recall ever having seen her to speak to since 1934, the year I had left school, and she probably hadn't seen me. It's a heck of a time, thirty-three years, a third of a century, and as she came towards me I hesitated for an instant, wondering whether she would remember me; and I also tried to work out how old she might have been. She must have been well over eighty, but before I could do my sums, she was upon me. I turned to her and greeted her. 'Good morning, Miss Jones.' She stopped and looked at me through her spectacles for a moment, exactly as I had seen her do when some distraction had interrupted her lessons in History all those years before; and then, without hesitation, she replied, 'Good morning, Lloyd'. At those three words, her tone and especially the bald, unprefixed 'Lloyd', the heavy rags of my years fell away and in an instant it wasn't the pavement of Bala High Street in 1967 that was under my feet but that of 1932, and instead of a man turned fifty, I felt once again as if I were a seventeen-year-old lad, one who hadn't won much approval from a headmistress whose iron rule had been more unremitting than that of any abbot of the strictest order. A formidable woman, indeed, the very archetype of every such woman who has ever been.

For a minute or two we had a factual, polite conversation, just as any pupil and headmistress would. Then she stumped off on her way to the shops at the top end of town. Although I couldn't have known it at the time, this was the last I was to see of her, for she died less than a year later.

Like every other headmistress in Wales in those days, Dorothy was a spinster. In the 'thirties and previous to that, I believe, a certain kind of spinster was usually appointed headmistress, and a psychological study of the *genus* would surely be of interest if one were ever to be written. They were all exceedingly authoritarian and many were masculine in speech and dress. Somewhere in their personal backgrounds it could be guessed that some excitement or confusion or emotional upset had taken place, causing them at times to go in for a sort of maudlinism that was very close to being lachrymose. Dorothy would have such turns when referring, in class, and very subtly, to the sacrifice made by her parents in the days when she had been an undergraduate at Aberystwyth. Many of these women were also very particular and keen to prevent all contact between the girls of their school and boys of the same age. So oppressively strict was their regime that it was often quite unnatural, as if they hated any sign of attraction or even family affection between the two sexes, finding it repugnant. Soon after she had arrived in Bala, towards the end of 1931, Dorothy was laying it down that none of her girls was to speak a word to any of the boys from the Grammar School, on the street or in any other place in town, even when a boy and girl happened to be brother and sister! It seemed as if all communication between the sexes were an offence worse than dishonesty. The only conclusion that can be drawn from an over-emphasis of this kind is that natural affection had once brought a bitterly disappointing experience to the maker of such rules, and that her real motive was revenge for some injury of long ago.

Dorothy was from Mawddwy. Going by her age at the time of her death, I should guess that she had graduated at Aberystwyth in the early years of this century, in about 1910 perhaps. Welsh, more than likely, had been her main subject. I don't know where she had had her first teaching-post, but before coming to Bala she had been in the County School for many years. The Girls' School at Bala was the only place she had been headmistress, and she was to remain there until her retirement.

Doubtless her restrictive, cold, and aloof attitude to children and adults alike was derived from the kind of social life she had known at Aberystwyth when she herself was young, a life in which no more than a completely formal relationship was allowed between male and female students, at least officially, a life governed by the chaperone, and one that's difficult for us to imagine today. It came to an end, in part, as Gwenallt[1] has shown in his memoir of Idwal Jones, when the ex-soldiers returned to the Colleges in 1919-20, shattering the convent-like silence once and for all. Alas, Dorothy had left by then, and she had spent the rest of her life according to the standards of the Victorian and Edwardian age, but without having had a whit of experience of the delight and charm of those privileged years that came to an end for ever in 1914.

I well remember the first time I saw her. As I have said, European and British History was the subject she taught, and as a sort of courtesy it was usual at the time for us sixth-form boys to take our lessons in this subject at the Girls' School. At the end of 1931 there was a shortage of space for these classes and the Girls' School had to rent two fine rooms at Church House in town. There, in a semi-circle around a long oval table, we sat to await our new teacher.

And she arrived, as square as a duchess. She had a mass of greying, cropped hair, a wide face and forehead, and the faint shadow of a moustache at each corner of her lower lip; she looked older than her years, but maybe her way of speaking and her mode of dress had something to do with that. Under her billowing B.A. gown (which was probably brandnew) she was wearing a costume of dark-green tweed; she also wore rimless spectacles, the kind often favoured by women in positions of high authority — just as colonels in the army used to choose to wear a monocle; a lense with no metal like this must have had some authority in itself. Be that as it may, she sat at the head of the table and greeted us — in English, of course — in a cold, headmistressly way, with the voice and register of one who wasn't at all fond of seeing boys or men on any occasion. Almost at once, we lads took a dislike to her, without any reason at all, just out of a kind of instinctive suspicion, a sort of subconscious warning or prediction that there was trouble on the horizon, the instinct that made Perseus unsheathe his sword before coming too close to the Medusa.

That's probably putting it too strongly. There was to be no trouble as far as we boys were concerned, and indeed, before a month or two was out, we came to realize that there was something rather comic about Dorothy at times, although it wasn't at all deliberate, of course. We had heard that she was quite good at delivering talks to cultural societies and religious gatherings, mainly under the auspices of the Independents. Without a doubt, she had the 'presence' for such work, and the vocal gifts, and she also had the knack of soaring above the subject of her talk to touch upon the Great Truths, while at the same time giving the impression of grave seriousness and high knowledge about such matters, not that many went home too clear in their minds what exactly those Truths might have been.

Although I never heard her at it on a public platform, my guess is that she had some fine, powerful addresses about the Protestant Reformation, its effect upon the world, on Christianity, and on the politics of the age, and so forth. The Reformation happened to be part of our syllabus at the time and as soon as Dorothy started on some of the characters from this period, her whole manner and delivery would change. Instead of a cold, pedagogical monotone, she became animated, and forgot that a class of nine or ten note-scribblers sat in front of her ('Introductory Notes' was what we used), and we would feel as if we were all sitting in the gallery of some Ebenezer or other, listening admiringly to Miss Jones addressing the throng from the pulpit on the Great Truths and the story of the Reformation. Of course, Welsh was the language in such a place, and this was what drove us to day-dream; for us, at school, the Reformation and the work of the reformers were something that had happened in English.

In addressing an unsophisticated audience or congregation, as every preacher and public speaker knows, you must take care to see that what you are purveying is finely ground, and if it can be presented dramatically, so much the better as far as the common folk are concerned. And that's what would happen to Dorothy's lessons under the influence of these turns. On one occasion she was discussing Henry VIII, Wolsey, whoever was Pope at the time, Charles V, and a few other such characters from the same period, and their political intrigues. Gradually, as she talked about Henry's ambition to become Holy Roman Emperor and Wolsey's brighter hope of sitting in St. Peter's Chair, Dorothy was seized by dramatic eloquence. In the excitement her voice rose and grew noticeably warmer. 'There was Wolsey,' she said (in English), noting with her finger a specific point on the blackboard in front of her, 'and there was the Papacy' — noting another point, nearer the centre of the board. Then, raising her finger and thumb to one of her bespectacled eyes, 'Wolsey,' she said triumphantly, 'had an eye on the Papacy,' and as she uttered this astonishing revelation, she slowly moved her finger and thumb from her eye and placed them on the exact spot occupied by the theoretical Papacy on the board. How indeed could the post ever after have eluded the scarlet Cardinal who had literally plucked out one of the eyes from his own head and placed it on one of the Vaticano's walls? It was quite a performance. We were busy scribbling all the while, of course, 'W. eye on P.'

It's more than likely that this quite terrifying act was one of the gimmicks she used to explain that particular piece of politicking to simple folk. Be that as it may, if Wolsey had lost an eye the reason for it has remained in my memory to this day, and what's more, when I happened to be working in the Vatican Library years later, I thought of Wolsey's eye and was rather tempted to ask the attendant whether it was on view somewhere. Such a question would make a good opening for a play in the style of Ionesco. Indeed, who knows what dramatist of the Absurd had been stifled in the folds of Dorothy's B.A. gown? Another of these illustrations, although not while discussing the same period, was the one about the difference to be felt in the atmosphere of an episcopalian church as compared with that in a Nonconformist chapel. The entire lesson on this topic came dangerously close once again to the Great Truths. Looking back, it might have been concluded that Dorothy herself, however staunch an Independent she may have been, came quite near on this occasion to a flirtation with Ritualism. Her point was that there's a sort of terror, some special mystery, to be felt in old churches that's not to be found in chapels. I shouldn't try to quote her in English, but here is her explanation as accurately as I can convey it: 'Now, you see, when you are in church, you can feel that some presence it watching you. You can't scamper down the aisle, or run up the steps on one side of the pulpit and down the other . . .' As she spoke of this sinful scampering, there came into her voice a bitter, scornful note, as much as to say, 'That's what you do in chapel before the service begins, isn't it, you scalliwags!' And then, going on about ascending or descending the pulpit steps (and in which episcopalian church are there steps on *both* sides of the pulpit?) she raised her left hand to imitate with her fingers the movements of someone climbing up and down stairs; all this, of course, synchronized with words.

We had a year with her. I have no memory of her ever discussing the Renaissance, although it was on the syllabus. But come to think of it, that great awakening would have been unlikely to engage her sympathies, for there were too many old paintings and graven images and nude women connected with it. Florence in the fifteenth century didn't wear suits of heavy tweed and strong, sensible brogues. And besides, the private lives of many famous people of the day were quite dubious; no, it wasn't suitable material for the examinations of the Central Welsh Board, Lower or Higher.

As far as her cultural inheritance was concerned, I should say that Dorothy's horizons were limited: like so many graduates of the University of Wales in that difficult and deprived period, she had learned enough European History to satisfy the examinations of the day, had crammed enough facts to go through the hoop and get a degree, but without really coming to grips with anything more than the Protestant Reformation — perhaps. For her it wasn't something alive. And yet it must be acknowledged that the school had flourished under her supervision, or at least had succeeded as far as examiners were concerned, and everyone was prepared to concede that she had 'kept order' over those in her charge. True, it was a convent's order, but one without a convent's spiritual purpose; it was this, I should say, which explained why so little creative work was ever accomplished by the pupils outside their formal courses. For the girls, as for us boys, Wales and its cause didn't exist, and all knowledge was utilitarian. There was one thing in particular that Dorothy used to do which was unpardonably bad: she would rebuke a young teacher in front of her class and criticize her in the hearing of her pupils, and even take over the class for the rest of the lesson. I heard several of the girls saying how she had turned on a teacher and made her cry in front of her pupils. I also heard contemporaries of mine in Blaenau say how glad they had been when she left for Bala.

Well, you might be thinking, this isn't a very pretty picture to be looking upon, surely there's something to set against all these dark and menacing hues. H'm, well, yes perhaps; she was, within her limitations, a good History teacher, and I can say sincerely enough that it was a loss to us all that we didn't have more than a year with her. It's likely that she was an efficient administrator; it's more than likely, too, that the fault was not entirely hers. At some time or another — and I haven't a shred of evidence for saying this — but at some time in her younger days, when she was inexperienced, and pliable, my guess is that she had had an emotional experience which had frozen her natural affections, perverting and distorting them ever afterwards. The masculinity and the aloofness were a kind of self-defence, a stride in the other direction, a way of vowing that none of 'the affections of the world and flesh' would ever again hurt her. If that meant going without feeling for other people and sometimes being unkind to them, especially to other women, then so be it. In its way, it was a kind of renunciation of the world and all its comforts, but not in the way a nun does it, not renunciation out of love and a higher commitment, or experience of spiritual elevation to a new world of light. That kind of renunciation always fills a person with love for humanity and an intense commitment to serve; it's a transcendence which opens out into forgiveness and utmost sympathy. This wasn't the path that Dorothy had taken; at least, this hadn't been her path when she was in her prime in 1932. In those days and thereafter, she had chosen to live apart from the community, geographically and socially; she had a nice house built for herself on the slope of the hill beyond Bodiwan[2]. In a word, she kept herself apart, and she was to have no more influence on the life of Bala and the district of Penllyn. She was a prisoner of her own past.

As I watched her shopping along the High Street that morning in 1967, I was half-hoping that she had changed, that the severe formality had thawed and become more flexible, and that after the age of three score years and ten, time had brought her reconciliation with a past that I could only guess at; in a word, I hoped that she had matured and, as Pantycelyn[3] put it, that she had 'conquered and passed through the tempests of fire and water'. It may be that my guessing was all in vain, my interpretation wide of the mark; anyway, in just three words the old woman put me in my place and back into the only time in which she was able to comprehend my existence, back at the table of the European History class in Church House in 1932. Nothing had changed, and so it was 'Good morning, Lloyd'.

Bore Da, Lloyd (Gwasg Gwynedd, 1980)

In Modesty and Trembling

Hafina Clwyd

I came up to London in September 1957, a young and innocent teacher full of confidence, energy, and ambition. There wasn't a white hair to my head nor any hint of crow's feet around my eyes. How are the mighty fallen! I had then a naive faith in human goodness and a healthy prejudice in favour of children. What I didn't know was that London children and the children of Dyffryn Clwyd were of different breeds, indeed, almost from different planets.

What worried me most was the thought that I shouldn't be able to speak English all day without breaking down, or drying up. As it turned out, I was surprised to find that there wasn't any need to have worried. I couldn't understand a word they said; this wasn't the English I had learned at school. It was an ideal situation: we didn't understand each other. If you have watched the television programme *The Sweeney*, you'll know what I mean. Cockneys, like the people of Caernarfon, have a lingo of their own, as you are probably aware, only theirs rhymes. It's an argot devised by coster mongers to swindle their customers. For example, apples and pears are stairs, whistle and flute is a suit, elephant's trunk is drunk, and so on. Usually only the first word is used and you have to guess what the second might be and then rhyme it. It's very cunning. And other words are made up with every day that passes, which makes for a lively and colourful way of speaking. When they realize that you've caught on to their secret language, they change the idiom. Cockneys are very crafty people. Unless you have the key, you won't be able to understand *The Sweeney* properly. Sweeney Todd was a barber in Fleet Street, and owner of a chair that would swing back and hurl the customer head over heels into the cellar, where he suffered an atrocious end, poor feller. There I go, I've got the rhyming bug now! So what rhymes with Sweeney Todd? Flying Squad! And that's what the programme is all about.

In spite of receiving a good education, I wasn't ready for the agony I had to face in London's schools. Oh, the foul language, the discourtesy, and the menace. Any lesson could easily deteriorate into a shambles. I said to someone recently that I hadn't really relaxed for twenty years. And now I'm completely unshockable. I fear, too, that my influence upon those children was very small. I met one of my former pupils the other day. 'Hello, Miss Jones,' said a voice behind me, and although I dropped that surname almost fifteen years ago, I still respond to it sometimes. She said, 'I'll never forget you.' I stood there preening myself and beginning to think that it hadn't been in vain, after all. 'Yes,' she went on, 'Your hair was always so nice.' Collapse of stout party.

It'll be astonishing news to some of my readers that the subject I teach is Scripture. I shan't go coursing after that particular hare now. I remember a dramatic classroom interpretation of the story about Jesus Christ scouring the temple. A loud-mouthed lad had insisted on playing the part of Christ, with a ruler in his hand. He stood in the middle of the Temple (a square yard in front of the blackboard) and shouted, 'Get the 'ell outa 'ere an' take them bleedin' lambs wiv ya!' It wasn't blasphemy on my part, but I laughed until I cried.

As I look through my diary for that first year, that baptism of fire, what appears in it day after day is: tired; no money; have had a bellyful; going to the Club. Despite the shortcomings of the London Welsh (and I'm aware that we have some deadly enemies), a sense of fair play obliges me to put it on record that the Club really was a refuge in those days. I think that, without it, I should have been lost.

I had good company and there was singing and dancing in the Club; I would have the occasional invitation to supper and there was always ready help to be found there in any emergency. There were many English people from faraway places who had come to London as teachers, some of whom were lonely and dispirited because they had no place where they could meet. You can't expect to have an English Club in the capital of England, now can you? And yet, come to think of it, I can remember there being a Welsh Club in the capital of Wales. Still, those exiles from York and Devon and Gloucester were very envious of us Welsh who had a haven of our own in the Grays Inn Road.

A gang began to form that met on Friday evenings, and this developed into a Noson Lawen[1] company, which in turn became a branch of the Urdd[2] with a hundred and fifty members at one time. Welsh classes were started; a Welsh School was opened; a Writers' Corner flourished, and an eisteddfod met with some success. That was the Club's golden age; the splendour has now passed. It's my opinion that if some student looking for a subject on which to do research were to think of studying the history of the London Welsh, there would be material in plenty. Those old dairymen are dying out now and their reminiscences should be written down before it's too late.

About fifty of us had come up from the Normal College that year, and going to a dance at the Club on a Saturday night was just like walking into a College hop. Only three of us are left up here now. The rest have disappeared, mostly back to Wales where they are a great asset to many a school and local society. I miss them but I don't begrudge Wales having her children back.

By immersing myself in the activities of the Urdd branch and the Drama Group, the Cymmrodorion[3], the chapel and the Book Club, I was able to forget the unremitting problems of school. At the same time, as my confidence increased, I came to be acquainted with the exciting life of the city. I would go to Cy Laurie's jazz-clubs and the coffee-bars that were so popular around Soho during the 'fifties. In those days it was perfectly safe for two girls to walk through the dingier streets of Soho and Piccadilly without having to be afraid of anything. Today it's very different: I can't leave the door of my own home; I have to depend entirely on the motor-car.

According to the statisticians, London teachers don't usually reach their allotted span of years, and the Government makes a profit out of us by channelling our pensions (which are taken from our monthly salaries) in other directions. At our school a gallon of jelly was poured into the piano one Christmas and when I sat down to play accompaniment to the carols, all that came out was a kind of harsh sigh. The Headmistress and the row of Governors were watching me like hawks. But the keys of the pianoforte had congealed and my fingers were sticking to one another. Even so, the story of the jelly fades into insignificance when I recall the great day we went on a trip to the Zoo. The zebras all had hysterics, every lion and elephant went mad, and feathery pandemonium broke out in the aviary, but what crowned everything was the discovery, on the bus going home, of a penguin tucked under the arm of Billy O'Brien. Billy is for ever seared into my soul. He's no longer with us. After he stole that penguin, dropped milk-bottles from the seventh floor on to an old lady's head, opened every gas-jet in the laboratory, choked the goldfish from the pool in the yard, kicked a ladder from under a window-cleaner, and burned the research work produced after months of hard labour on the part of the science teacher, it was decided that Billy wasn't too happy in our school. He's now in a safer place. 'And after battle . . .'[4]

I suspect that it was he, too, who telephoned the school one lunch-hour to say that there was a bomb in the office. 'Are you sure?', asked the Headmistress. 'Yes, miss,' said the voice. Poor Billy. (Isn't it easy to say that after getting rid of him?). I called at his home once to have a chat with his father and see whether we could help the child in some way. I had never seen such a home. The floors were bare and there were only two pieces of furniture — a huge armchair and a colour television set. The father was lolling in the chair and the mother and her ten children squatting on the floor. The kids were eating off metal plates on the floor, with their fingers, and there was neither knife nor fork to be seen. It was no wonder that Billy had pinched a penguin from the Zoo and throttled the school's goldfish. Not only was he wanting food, he also needed to be noticed.

Having had to deal with such children for more than twenty years, I can assure you that the statistics I mentioned don't lie. I should have listened to my grandfather after all. When he heard that I was off to London, he said I was going to a place that was so very far from everywhere. How right he was.

Defaid yn Chwerthin (Gwasg Gomer, 1980)

Christmas in the Valley

Rhydwen Williams

Life was hard enough in the Rhondda Fawr and Rhondda Fach throughout the 1920s, as the civilized world, and the uncivilized, came to know full well. Unemployment became the pattern of men's lives, and the despair of those years was plain for all to see in the listless eyes and colourless cheeks, and quite a few slashed throats up on the mountainside. And there was hardly a Christmas, despite the ringing bells and steaming puddings and the stockings tied to bedposts like the wares of Johnny Onions,[1] come over to Llwyn-y-pia from Brittany, that didn't mock a small child's dreams and expectations.

For all that, I can't say that I ever failed to enjoy any of the Christmases in that far-distant childhood of mine, nor that I had to go without anything. Of course, neither my nose nor my senses had been trained to expect any special kind of luxury or delicacy, and I almost always had everything that was within the compass of my taste and desires.

The fact that I was brought up within a kitchen's snug walls was responsible, I'm sure, for the contentment I felt at the simplicity of the fare and fun. The word 'snugness' has a very special meaning for anyone who was familiar with the shelter provided by a collier's kitchen in days gone by — the special warmth from a coal-fire, a grate full of red-hot cheerfulness, when the dozing cats purred like a choir in four parts and the kettle whistled as merrily as a row of sailors just landed on a quayside.

On Christmas morning, like any other morning, one of the homeliest features of that long-ago snugness was the large frying-pan hissing fat as it prepared the bacon and eggs for us. The festive meat — whether pork, chicken, turkey or goose — could scarcely have tasted better between a child's teeth, and the bacon and eggs far excelled any slice of bread with honey on it.

Those things we tasted in our early years were probably the nearest we ever came to a culinary thrill, something between palate and tooth, a sensitivity of the stomach, that a man never quite loses for the rest of his life. I don't want to suggest for a moment that such sensitivity was uppermost in the life of child or grown man in those days, that wouldn't be true by a long chalk, for a growing child and the mature man grow familiar enough with the sweet-tasting fruits of the tree of knowledge, even if it's only 'Rhodd Mam'[2] or the memoirs of Rhys Lewis.[3]

But thinking of Christmas morning in times gone by brings back to me, more than anything else, the aromas of a busy, happy kitchen, with Mam getting us ready for chapel, my father in his white apron ('to save your suit'), and a spit hanging over a large fire, and the goose or turkey on it, a bunch of sausages dripping from the chains into the ashes, and a huge plate catching the fat. My father sweated before the flames even more than the bird. The wheel went round like a clock slowly turning, until the fatted goose was drier than the cork-stoppers of Mrs Evans Small Beer.

Whenever we look back like this and start talking about 'the old days', nothing is likely to be emphasized more than the poverty and hunger and misery of those years. And yet, when we go into more detail, the most lasting impression is of a festival of tremendous eating, when we stuffed all sorts of delicacies into our bellies — Welsh cakes, bread pudding, apple tarts and rhubarb tarts, not to mention pea soup, bacon baked with cheese, liver and onions, and the thick gravy tasting better than the rice pudding, almost. I feel sorry for those wretched people from North Wales who know nothing of these dishes but who are inveigled by the smiling courtesy of Hywel Gwynfryn[4] to demonstrate their ignorance of things culinary on 'Helo Bobol' with recipes for meals that are a mess of grease and vegetables and hot curry, though they are acquainted only with takeways from a Chinese restaurant. When I was a child in the Rhondda a Chinaman's only function in the community — with all due respect, for I have fond memories of old Harry Sing — was to iron shirts and collars. Now they starch our food as well.

The only bird that managed to escape its fate for a while was the one my parents refused to feather, let alone put to the knife or throttle, and that was because of the great commotion the Christmas before. We had a large goose, which we'd been keeping in the coal-shed for weeks, and the creature had begun waddling into our kitchen and making itself at home in front of the fire. We had all grown quite fond of it and been amused at some of its tricks, swearing by the sounds it made that it was answering us in Welsh, duck-Welsh, until by the day of its execution it had become like one of the family. When my father, after long argument, came to wring the dear little thing's neck, the bereavement and our sense of loss overwhelmed us, so much so that none of us was able to put a morsel of that gander's flesh into our mouths. That was the kind of palaver associated with our feasting in years gone by.

I've already mentioned how we used to hang our stockings on the bedposts, staying awake for hours in the hope of catching a glimpse of Father Christmas coming down the stairs, despite the fact that I don't recall a time when I ever believed in him, preferring to think even as a very small child that it was really my father. All this goes to show that childhood, Father Christmas or not, wasn't so deprived that our stockings weren't full to their tops, even if we had only an orange, an apple, and nuts to rejoice about, and that Christmas wasn't so short on goodwill that we didn't have presents galore — a Meccano set, a magic lantern, books, a paint-box, dominoes, and all as precious in our eyes as gold, frankincense, and myrrh.

It may be that the highlight of every Christmas was the postman at the door and the arrival of Gran's parcel, a generous hamper of luxuries that were beyond the reach of our parents' purse and imagination — toys, clothes, shoes, chocolate, puddings, money, and every year a diary for me, the John Letts Diaries, that I still have, in which the years are chronicled in great detail: January 20, No school. Too much snow. Wil Pigs killed in the Swamp (the local pit); February 19, Next door's cat killed on the railway-line; March 5, Treorci beat Maesteg on the Big Field. Dai Rees scored a try. Wil Pengam found hanged on Pentwyn. A diary full of exciting entries, enough to inflame the imagination and warm the heart of any child.

School, too, was something of a centre of merriment and joy at Christmas-time. The teachers taught their pupils to decorate and paint the windows with a drift of snow at the bottom and a Father Christmas on all the panes, with a beard made of cotton wool and a red nose like that of Davies the Road. We children would be herded into the main hall, our headmaster, Gwilym Ithel, who was a bit of a musician and the son of the famous conductor of Côr Mawr Treorci[5], taking us through carol after carol. He was a staunch Methodist, but I remember that he was fond of the occasional Church chant, and he taught us more than one Latin hymn and a number of old Welsh carols, though never one in English. Mr Hanney, Mr Tewkesbury, and Mr Salter would stand against the far wall, monoglot Englishmen rigid with the boredom of it all. A carol service was also held on the last night of term in one of the local chapels — Moriah, Seilo, or Nasareth — and Mr Hanney, Mr Tewkesbury, and Mr Salter would stand uncomfortably frozen like men lost in a snowstorm, while the conductor, oblivious to the world and any Englishman in it, would be absorbed in the act of praise as his baton (which had once belonged to the Great Choir) inspired in us utter bliss.

Another Christmas treat was to go to the Workmen's Hall near Ystrad station to see a film and receive an apple, an orange, and a bag of nuts, all of them free. Usually, it was a cowboy film, with Hoot Gibson or Tom Mix, or else a chapter from the romance of Pearl White. I recall being in something of a quandary at about the age of nine in trying to decide whether I was in love with Miss Jones, our teacher, or with Pearl White. I may as well admit, whatever implications there may be in the confession, that I saw nothing wrong in wanting both of them at the same time.

Like everything else in the life of the Valley, Christmas came to an end in the chapels. Most of the villagers would go to a service, the 'listeners' (a breed apart from the 'members'), as well as absentees of long standing, would find a seat at the back or up in the gallery. One old tipsy fellow always pursed his lips and breathed in through his nostrils as he squeezed past the saints on his way to his seat, lest his breath cause eyebrows to be raised and eyes to flash. All the laughter and fun of Christmas would be stifled under a load of solemnity, like my father beating the bonfire out with his spade. But the festival's aromas would go on wafting through our nostrils for a long while afterwards, as real as the smell of the leaves and branches at the top of our garden.

And it's more than likely that a whiff of that long-ago world has brought these few memories back to mind now, and perhaps it's best to leave it at that. No one can be sure where such reminiscences might lead.

Barn (227/228, Nadolig 1981)

On Stammering

John Gruffydd Jones

I've grown quite used to my stammer, and it's only occasionally that a twinge of self-pity comes over me, and that soon disappears in the light of other people's problems. But I'd give a lot to have a month of being without it, all the same.

I well remember when it began, or rather when I first realized that

I had a stammer at all. A cluster of new faces in a class-room and every window closed, and my first day at grammar school had started. The warm sunshine of early May was filtering in and falling on the nape of my neck, and the smell of new leather satchels was strong in my nostrils. The room, like a beehive, was teeming with adventure and apprehension, with hope and loneliness, and I searching for a familiar face among the unfamiliar.

As the door opened, the uproar became a murmur and then dwindled into dead silence, and only the sound of feet nervously scraping the floor was to be heard. We were then asked to stand up one by one and call out our names to be put in the register, beginning in the far corner of the room, and I had to listen to names that within a week or so were to become as familiar to me as the Lord's Prayer, before the boy sitting behind me got to his feet. I rose hurriedly, feeling my throat to be as dry as flannel, and the words locked up somewhere so that I couldn't get them out. Quiet laughter rippled round the class until it became a roar in my ears. I gripped the edge of the desk hard, until my knuckles were white against the black of my new coat and I felt the cold sweat running down my back, before shutting my eyes tightly and taking a deep breath.

The words rushed out all at once, like water from Llyn y Felin when the flood-gate is opened, and I sat there limply with every eye an arrow sticking in my back.

As the weeks went by, the laughter subsided and the sympathy grew, but the experience will be with me for the rest of my life, and that's why I'd give a good deal for that month.

It would be a busy month, of unfettered utterance, of getting out and about and going to eisteddfodau, and of cutting through the old cords of frustration. A month at the beginning of the year perhaps, when there'd be a drama-week in the village, and I'd have a chance to take part instead of sitting there half-enjoying other people's performances. I'd take quite a prominent part, too, so that I could savour the taste of the words, and I know they'd be as sweet as heather-honey on warm bread. I'd make a speech, perhaps, with plenty of words beginning with 'd' and 'l', just to hear their sounds breaking from my lips and be avenged for the hundred thousand times those two consonants have stuck tight to my tongue. I once saw the river Horon frozen over, and everyone was standing on the bridge and gazing down at the captive water, and the teeth of the icy stalactites were like derisive laughter under the arch of the bridge. When the thaw came hardly anyone remained on the bridge to watch the water flowing smoothly and without hindrance, as it usually did. A stammer is something like that. When the words are in full spate nobody pays the least attention, but when they are blocked everyone notices it, some out of sympathy offering their words to fill in the silence, and others, in their embarrassment, trying to change the subject in order to bring down the tension.

It would also be a month for travel, and of daring to strike up conversations. Not that travelling is difficult in the company of a friend or someone you know; it's the lone journey that causes the tension. The memory of squeezing pennies and silver coins between my fingers until their grooved rims left a red pattern in the hot flesh, out of fright at not being able to get certain words out and name my destination. A long queue of passengers waiting impatiently at the station-entrance on a warm August afternoon, the holidays and the end of a day's work taxing their patience as I tried to say Pwllheli, and the name taking as long to come out as the miles between me and that distant town.

It would be fine to forget the tricks and break the rules for breathing. To run one line of conversation into another without having to change the word-order so that pronunciation comes more easily, and to tell a funny story without the stunning dénouement's being met by stony silence, and the humour turning into embarrassment. To be able to look straight into the pupils of people's eyes while talking things over, without having to turn away out of fear that they will notice the nervousness.

Perhaps I should choose the month of August, and be part of the serious discussion on the Eisteddfod[1] field, instead of chatting away within the close circle of my friends. To dare to be a member of a team in bardic contest and able to rattle off lines of verse to the audience, and to get up and ask questions and express an opinion when the Literary Pavilion is heaving under the weight of its Welsh culture. Not that anyone would find my opinion nor my line of verse memorable — except me. I should treasure that moment unto my last breath.

Yet it's a great thing to grow accustomed, to get used to something, and life has to have a dream or it would be very disagreeable. So when November and December are shortening the days, and the enjoyment of poetry and the music of words, I shall break the silence and in the quiet of my own room recite the lines and sentences aloud, and glide over words without either the slightest impediment or chilling fear, and I shall know at such times that I too have my part to play in the order of things.

Cysgodion ar y Pared (Llys yr Eisteddfod Genedlaethol, 1981)

Butlins

Gwilym Tudur

When Sir Billy Butlin died the other day, I'm sure some people would have been surprised to learn that I felt a small pang, not of grief, since I never met the man, but of botheration, as on losing some very familiar object, such as an old penknife. Surprised, because I don't have all that much to say to any sir, still less to any Welsh sir, and especially to a poet who sells his soul for a knighthood. The little man with the moustache and expensive suntan was a typical Englishman, yet the Gorsedd of Bards[1] might well have honoured him if only they had known about his achievement, his creation of something that's pure poetry. For that's what Butlins, or Bucklings as it's known to local people, is.

When a war-time navy camp was foisted on the tranquillity of the Penychain headland, not far from Afon-wen, and later turned into a holiday-camp, it was only to be expected that some of the proud inhabitants of Llŷn and Eifionydd would feel anxious. Not everyone; some saw an opportunity for making a living, and who's to say that they weren't right? I would go so far as to claim that the old Camp — which is a quite awful sight for the unsuspecting traveller — has turned out to be almost as crucial as the Rhyd-y-gwystl Creamery in keeping people at home for two more generations, thus keeping a community going on a far, unremarkable peninsula, thanks to Sir Billy's genius.

His first inspiration was to realize before anyone else that the worker needs a holiday just as we all do; that if only a large, paternalistic operation were to be created to take care of everything, a whole family could have the time of their lives for a week or two, far from the tyranny of kitchen and factory — and the organizer would make a fortune as well. Mind you, as a child I didn't take such a philanthropic view of the place. There would be twelve thousand of the poor souls there in mid-August. A not insubstantial number would manage to lose their way about the district every Saturday morning, and I fear that naughty children like me were responsible for some of their confusion. If a car stopped to enquire the way to 'Chillywog', 'Penny Chain', or 'Pulley Welly', rather than to Chwilog, Penychain, or Pwllheli, it was in danger of being sent in the direction of Nefyn, that way. The children of 'Betsy Code' very probably did much the same. Thankfully, those other weary thousands would pour into Penychain Halt by train.

Sir Billy's other stroke of genius, and one for which I'd have given him a lordship, no less, was to have the said twelve thousand penned inside an enormous fence made of wire netting. No one, except the youngsters who were familiar with the coves around the coast, could go in or out without permission — without the Pass, the famous document with your photograph and number on it, and the legend 'The Camper is Always Right'. Very seldom did the folk from Bolton and Bradford venture through the main gate at all, except to Pwllheli market on a Wednesday afternoon. Bus-trips were arranged, of course, but neither the splendours of 'Snowdon and the Welsh Alps', nor the 'Lovely Lleyn Peninsula' came anywhere near competing with the facilities inside the fence. There they had swimming-pools like blue seas, and pretty girls, snooker and tennis, and a beach, as well as crazy-golf and sweet-scented gardens; they had the biggest shops and pubs in creation, bingo and cinemas, and dancing until dawn. And a zoo, and in that zoo, in days long gone by, an elephant which gave rides to children, led by John Bach with an enormous shovel to clean up after it. And yes, really, you had Ringo Starr, a big white stripe in his hair, sending them all silly with his crude and powerful drumming; he was there with Rory Storm and his Hurricanes from Liverpool, before he joined the Beatles. (I heard them too at the Cavern, but that's another story.)

And yet, across the main road there stands Brynbachau Chapel, as it has always done. It was an odd experience, of a Sunday in summer, to see those two peoples, the English and the Welsh, the former half-naked peering through a fence at tweed-clad Calvinistic Methodists, just a beach-ball's throw away. I once witnessed something similar on an island in the Mediterranean, except that I was on the side of the damned on that occasion; at Butlins I'd be on the fence, as it were. Lest I romance too much, I must admit that the Chapel's congregation would have had quite a few relations who were sunbathing on Afon-wen beach at the time, and that the church in the Camp was never empty; the job of Vicar of Llangybi and Llanarmon paid well while it lasted.

So because of the fence, and since the campers were ordinary folk, all clearing off home at summer's end without a thought for buying a second home or swopping their country, tourism of this kind bred in us neither loathing nor servility. I'd almost go so far as to say it's a pity we ourselves didn't open holiday-camps all the way from Anglesey to Pembrokeshire; perhaps the visitors wouldn't have become unwelcome neighbours if only we had treated them as an industry and run it ourselves, as other countries do. For that's how Butlins is regarded, at any rate by the army of local people who work there, even though they don't get a big enough share of the profit.

I spent two or three seasons there, working — if that's the right word. The aim of all casual staff was to acquire as much of a suntan as they possibly could, by doing as little work as possible without getting the sack. This was a skilful business, and you weren't long in learning how to climb higher and higher, like Joseph in Egypt, or a bank-clerk. The worst job of all, and the one with least sunshine to it — and the one from which, naturally, I got my first sack — was that of Assistant Slicer in the Sandwich Department. This was lorded over by one Mrs Hall, of immortal memory to Ioan Mo and Hafan, Gillard and me, four novices on the bottom rung of the Butlins ladder. If ever Thatcher loses her job, or gets captured by the Russians, my advice to the Tories would be to send for Mrs Hall. Perhaps she was under the misapprehension that the place was a war-camp still — some Penny Chain Archipelago — and fair play to her, the inmates didn't ever stay long enough for her to get to know them. The work involved spreading butter on a myriad bread-slices and then filling them with an inordinate amount of ham. All day long. You either had to cultivate a soul of iron, and thus become a departmental head, or else crack up and have a bunfight. We cracked up. And after Glyn the ferocious butcher had chased me with his cleaver round the harvest table, that was it as far as I was concerned. After all, what was the point of risking my life if I wasn't going to acquire a suntan?

That was almost as bad as one of the strange stories I later had the privilege of hearing Waldo[2] tell about his wanderings. Once in England he was labouring at hauling buckets up a long ladder to the top of some frightful kiln — a lime-kiln, I think it was. The trouble was that the wages at the bottom of the ladder were very low, but that the man at the top was always in danger of falling in. And every time that happened, the others had promotion. The poet had left his job, he said, before reaching the pinnacle of his career.

I came to know how to grab the right jobs, like everyone else. I didn't manage to get the best one of all; that went to Ifan Afal and his friend Ses, the waste-paper men. They were supposed to walk around the camp, spear every scrap of paper with a spike and put it in a rubbish-bin. But since nobody was was ever able to count the bits of paper, either before or after they had carried out their task, they didn't actually have to collect any at all. It's true they would pick up one or two bits in the vicinity of women who were sunbathing. Girls in that state are quite defenceless, particularly if they happen to be reading a magazine or newspaper, and the thrust of that pointed stick was the most effective of all the numerous methods devised by the lovelorn workers at Butlins. And on unsuccessful days they would take a nap in the sun behind the privet hedges, with the result that they both became very brown.

By far the best job I ever had was on the cake van with Ron, another bronzed man, and a specialist in the aforementioned techniques. We interrupted the monotony of the sunbathing, whenever it became necessary, to deliver ready-made delicacies to the shops and the main kitchens. There were scores of cheerful girls, of every kind, in those kitchens, many of them nice Irish colleens from Liverpool. But Ron warned me to steer clear of the Catholics — they had too many principles; better the English women, especially those on the run from their marriages.

The real snag with Butlins was the private police force, the Security. Their purpose was to keep order, but they considered themselves to be guardians of morals as well, their calling in life to prevent anyone but themselves from entering the chalets of the female staff as night fell. The only way to deal with the Security, as with all their kind ever, was to keep on the right side of them.

Since due respect wasn't shown to the man on the cake van, I soon graduated to the Finance Department. The people there were of a different quality; it was their job to go round the tills, escorted by Security; but they were good old sorts, even the fierce Protestant from Belfast whose name I never caught because I couldn't understand a word he said. Our office, very conveniently situated next to the football pitch, was in the main building. There, in a prominent position in the vestibule, stood a golden statue of Sir Billy himself, to which Sgei and I used to genuflect as we went in or out.

Summer, like all good things, comes to an end. For a while the district reverts to being a homeland for the Welsh. Before the time of Thanksgiving for the Harvest of Wheat and Visitors, the great Butlins Eisteddfod takes place, and a curious crowd comes to stare. Over the darkened chalets now rise the strains of fair harpstrings. They are not heard by Sir Billy from his lonely pedestal in the empty vestibule, but he keeps on smiling, for ever brown.

Byclings (Gwasg Gwynedd, 1981)

A Millionaire

William Owen

Do you know where Cemlyn is? I said Cemlyn, not the Kremlin. You could hardly go anywhere more northerly in the whole of Wales. Turn to the right just outside the village of Tregele within about a mile after going through Cemaes at the far end of Anglesey. Follow the narrow road for another two miles or so, turn right again along an even narrower road, and you'll come across it quite easily. It's a place gloriously off the beaten track, not far from where the bone-setters used to live, with Mynydd y Garn imperiously casting its shadow over all.

And what's so special about Cemlyn? you may well ask. At first glance, next to nothing. A cluster of farms, a house with high walls around it at the water's edge, that's about all, except for the sea and a kind of bird-sanctuary — the last place on earth you'd expect to find a millionaire going to ground, and what's more, one with Welsh family connections who could speak the language fairly fluently and had some sympathy with the Nationalist cause, too.

Vivian Hewitt came from a line of quite well-known Grimsby brewers. He had been brought up in Bodfari and educated at Harrow. As a young man he had found fame as one of the early aviators. He had settled in Rhyl, renting land there on which to try out his experiments. Bleriot had set up a record by flying across the Channel in 1909, a distance of some twenty miles, but in 1912 Hewitt had broken that record by flying across the Irish Sea. He had set out from Holyhead and after encountering great difficulties in thick sea-mist, had managed to land safely about sixty miles away in Dublin's Phoenix Park. And as one of 'those magnificent men in their flying-machines' he had become a national hero overnight.

But his distinguished career was cut short by an accident. He was forced to give up flying and from then on put all his affections into ornithology, and his energies into studying creatures that were able to fly higher and better than he could himself.

He came into his inheritance at some time during the early 'thirties, and since he was so interested in sea-birds he searched diligently for a place in which to establish a sanctuary, in Gower, in Pembrokeshire, on the sand-dunes of Aberffraw, on Puffin Island, and the Skerries. In the end he came across Cemlyn. He immediately fell head-over-heels in love with the place. His adopted motto was *Je peux si je veux* — 'I can if I wish' — and since he was so wealthy he could as often as not do just as he wished. He bought the district up almost in its entirety and made his home at Bryn Aber, building high walls around it — a real Alcatraz — to keep out the world.

What a strange man he was! He would sooner have been hanged than take advantage of the usual amenities. He refused outright to install a telephone in the house; it would have been too much of an intrusion on his privacy. The place was lit by lamps and candles, there was a coal-fire instead of electricity for heating, no water-tap nor any sewerage system, and the lavatory was at the bottom of the garden. And you wouldn't have touched him with a pitchfork if you had happened to come upon him around the place. More than once he was given a tip for having directed visitors who were lost, because they had taken him for a tramp. And if the story's true, he wore the same suit for eighteen years. In comparison with him, Howard Hughes was normal. But if he was eccentric, fastidious, and headstrong, he could also be exceedingly generous at times. Every year shortly before Christmas he used to buy dozens of turkeys to distribute among those with whom he had come into contact — the policeman or postman, or anyone who had been to the house on some errand or other.

There was never a collector like him. He used to collect the strangest things. Perhaps there was nothing out of the ordinary about collecting stamps, but he also had marvellous collections of guns, steamrollers, and stuffed birds. He was thought to have the largest collection of birds' eggs in the country — half a million of them, all stacked in cases, one on top of the other, all over the house and filling the innumerable sheds outside.

And he remained a bachelor to the end of his days. He seemed incapable of loving anyone but the eight noisy parrots that always shared his study; they were his pride and joy. But he hated cats and the Income Tax people alike, the cats because they threatened the lives of his birds, and the tax-men because they used to pluck him so resolutely once a year.

Now every ornithologist worth his salt is sure to make it to Bardsey[1] sooner or later. Hewitt too spent a week there once but he didn't have much luck, unfortunately, only suspicious looks from the islanders. He was treated exactly as if he had leprosy when he went to buy milk in the mornings. He had probably given offence by going out with his gear of a Sunday afternoon, and he was never forgiven for such a wicked transgression. At one time he had even considered buying the island, but after actually going there and receiving such a poor welcome, he took the greatest umbrage. He wouldn't have wanted it afterwards, even if it had been offered to him, birds and all, for nothing.

And that was a pity, too, because he was such a generous fellow. If he had bought it, then perhaps he would have later presented it to the Urdd,[2] or to some other organization. And nor do I think that the saints who are buried on Bardsey would have been too put out if he had bought it, even though his family had made their pile by taking advantage of the thirsty people of Lincolnshire over many generations. The plans that a member of the aristocracy had for the place a little while ago were a far greater cause for their turning in their graves, I can tell you. And it would also have saved a lot of trouble for the Trust that's been trying to pay for the island these last ten years.

As his health deteriorated, Hewitt spent more and more of his time in the Bahamas, but it was in Cemlyn that the 'Modest Millionaire' (that's the title of the biography of him that was written by William Hywel of Cemaes) died. And it was there in his garden that his ashes were scattered. Nowadays the place belongs to the National Trust. Take the first opportunity you have of going there; it's a paradise for those who seek a retreat in which to lick their wounds.

How much did he leave, this wealthy man? Well, if what I hear is correct, yes, that's right — he left the whole lot.

Llacio'r Gengal (Gwasg Gomer, 1982)

A Scene from Military Life

Gareth Miles

Once upon a time, there was a very loose relationship between me and the English Army. It was in the days when I was a reluctant member of the Officer Training Corps at Llandovery College. I believe the College has become rather more civilized since the late 1950s — and grown seven times more snobbish at the same time. In my days as a pupil there, the place might have been described as a bourgeois, Anglican, Anglo-Welsh borstal on the banks of the river Tywi.

Now I was never a hot-headed rebel, nor did I go in for bold protest against the College's iron regime. I was much more like the poor Israelite who was condemned by the malicious whim of Jehovah to spend seven years of his life in one of the cities of the Philistines, and who throughout that time feared for his life, lest his fellow-citizens were to discover that he was uncircumcised. Even more depressing was the fate of the Philistine who pretended to be a Jew in the camp of King David.

With one or two other pupils of the same temperament, I bore witness against the School's totalitarianism in several subversive ways, such as starting a jazz-club, fostering the worship of Elvis, claiming that football was superior to rugby, and reviling the O.T.C.

My scorn for the cadet army was motivated by a combination of extreme nationalism, aggressive pacifism, and hatred for the ugly, uncomfortable uniform. During my last year in the Sixth Form, an Englishman, who also happened to be a teacher and lieutenant, discovered that I'd been contaminating younger boys by encouraging them to question the worth of the O.T.C. in the Age of the H-Bomb. From then on I didn't have to attend any of the gatherings of the boys' army, except for the Annual General Inspection.

This occasion was the high point of the military year at Llandovery College. A real live General — one year with his flies undone — used to come to run a hawk's eye over our uniforms, buckles and belts, and to praise our readiness to kill and be killed 'for Queen and Country'.

On the morning of my last Inspection, the General leapt from his car and strode straight towards me, of all people, with the College Warden (later to become Archbishop of Wales) and a retinue of teacher officers and some prospective heroes at his heels.

Now one of the virtues of the élitist private education system, compared with the common State kind, is that it teaches children to distinguish between those who have power and those deprived of it. I therefore understood instinctively that the General, although he was a Very Important Man in the English Army, hadn't the slightest authority over me. I also knew that my pseudo-military uniform was protection against punishment by the School, since the O.T.C. wasn't a constitutional part of its organization. So I stood there, almost as straight as a soldier, in the middle of a disciplinary no man's land.

'Good morning, Corporal!' said the General, in English, cheerfully but authoritatively.

'I'm not a Corporal,' I replied, in the same language.

'Oh, . . . but I see you've got a stripe . . .'
'I'm an acting Lance-Corporal.'
'Certificate A, parts one and four?'
'Part one.'
'Have you tried part two yet?'
'I failed it.'
'Going to try again?'
'No.'
'Any shooting badges?'
'No.'
'Been to Corps Camp?'
'No.'
'Ah well, do try your Certificate A, part two. You'll find it most useful when you come to do your National Service.'

I wasn't enough of an anti-hero to say, 'I won't be doing that either, if I can help it.'

Since military conscription had come to an end by the time I left University, I didn't have to choose between the English Army and clink.

I shall end this memoir by expressing my admiration for the handful of Nationalists[1], among them Hywel ap Dafydd, Chris Rees, and Emrys Roberts, who went to prison rather than wear the uniform of the English Army, and by paying tribute, too, to every worker and patriot who challenged that army in places a good deal more dangerous than the playing-field of a public school one morning in May.

BBC Cymru (23 Gorffennaf, 1982)

An Exile

R. S. Thomas

Whenever I hear the word 'Anglesey,' or 'the Isle of Anglesey,' the first name that comes to mind is Goronwy Owen[1], because for me he is the prime example of what it means to be an exile:

In sunny Anglesey, that is the best place,
Its people are merry, with many gifts.

In the place where I once played
There are men who do not know me.

Who cannot hear the anguish and yearning for his native place in such lines? And the latter couplet is quite prophetic, too. Everyone is familiar with what happened to him: he had to leave home and go to live in England and later the United States in order to earn a living.

Forgive me for being personal for a moment this afternoon. The subject of this short address is exile. And I too in my own way was once an exile on account of my inability to speak Welsh. My parents were English-speaking Welsh people from the Vale of Glamorgan, and as a consequence I was brought up as an Englishman from the start. I wasn't worried by the fact until I decided to prepare myself for the priesthood in the Church in Wales. Then, because I couldn't speak the language, instead of being accepted as a candidate for holy orders by the Diocese of Bangor, to which I belonged, I had to make a request to the Diocese of St. Asaph, in which the Welsh language was not essential. In due course, I became a curate at Chirk, and there once again, as a result of the new experience of starting a career, I had little chance of paying much attention to the change in my life. But when the time came for me to marry and try to find a house for my wife and myself, the only position available was one in English Maelor on the border with England. There, as I saw the hills of Wales some fifteen miles to the west, and listened to the wholly English accent of the local people, I realized what I had done. I had become an exile. And that was the turning-point. From that moment on, as it were, I embarked on the long and difficult task, as it is for a grown man, of learning Welsh in order to return to the real Wales and to a truly Welsh-speaking society. The first step on the way was Manafon, and although that wasn't a parish Welsh in language, it was in the hills and more Welsh in appearance than English Maelor. From that place I was able to come to grips with the language and so prepare for taking a Welsh-speaking parish later on. My wish was fulfilled. I was more fortunate than poor Goronwy. I could feel that I was on the way to Welsh-speaking Wales. But just spare a thought for him — the anguish, the longing, the yearning to be let back to Wales and to Anglesey in particular, into the bosom of the Welsh-speaking Welsh. And there were plenty of them around at that time, remember. His wife died on the voyage to the United States. He himself died there, an exile in every sense of the word. But there is also another aspect of exile.

In recent years I myself have had a new experience. Although I have won my way back among the Welsh-speaking Welsh, so that I might be admitted to any Welsh society, I have come to realize how easy it is these days to be an exile in my own country. As you will be aware, there are more and more strangers coming to live in Wales with every month that passes. The statistics are alarming for every true Welshman. There is also the fact that more and more of our compatriots are turning their backs on their language and heritage, to their great shame. It's too common an experience these days to knock at a door in the Welsh-speaking districts and see it opened by someone with the surly, inexcusable words: 'I don't speak Welsh'. So much can be achieved by money!

The writing is on the wall. Over the years we have seen the number of Welsh-speaking Welsh going down substantially. In future the bitter, shameful experience of being exiles in their own country will come to more and more of our young people.

A good deal of the blame for this lies with the English and the English system, with industry, and technology and big business, and without self-government there is little we can do to control the influx and ensure respect and justice for the language.

But — and I have to say this with the keenest sorrow — quite a lot of the blame lies with us Welsh, too. By their unwillingness to display and use the language, too many of our compatriots are putting Welsh down. I blame business for this, in the first place, more than certain of our public bodies, which (after prompting by the Welsh Language Society[2] from time to time) have shown an example to the rest of the Welsh people of how to give Welsh its proper place, an example, by the way, that they have been somewhat loath to follow. And then by their apathy, their spinelessness, and their snobbery and sloth in choosing to speak English, and by their support for English programmes, and English publishers, and English newspapers, at the expense of their Welsh counterparts, thereby losing their grasp on their mother-tongue, too many of our compatriots are fast creating a situation in which a Welsh-speaking Welshman will find himself not only an exile, but also an outcast and laughing-stock in his own country. Have not some of us had this experience already? What is the language used by people in authority in the hospitals, the telephone exchange, the railways, the shops, the electricity board, and so on, so that the Welsh-speaking Welshman is made to feel that there's something inferior about the Welsh language?

Here we are today a part of the family of Welsh-speakers. Welsh-speaking Welsh people every man and woman of us, gathered together in Anglesey, mother of Wales, to enjoy one another's company. I don't want to dishearten you and cast a cloud over your natural good spirits, but before I close, let me make this dire appeal. I am sure there are quite a few people among you today who have influence and energy. Take a vow before you go from this place that it will never be through you or on your account that any Welsh-speaking man or woman becomes an exile in his or her own land, but that you will do everything you can to help stem and turn back the powers and influences that are bringing this situation about.

Llawlyfr Eisteddfod Genedlaethol Cymru (1983),
Pe Medrwn yr Iaith (Gol. Tony Brown a Bedwyr Lewis Jones, Christopher Davies, 1988)

The Fox Under Glass

Bryan Martin Davies

Only once have I had the astonishing experience of seeing a real fox cross my path, although I've met many a human fox in my day. It wasn't one evening in July, as in the sonnet by the Poet of Summer[1], 'the sun bright and unsetting' summoning us on to the mountainside. It was Christmas time, some two days before the festival, a sunny, frosty day in the 1950s, and three of us lads from the village were making for Cwm Afon Pedol, the valley that divides Mynydd y Crugau. There was quite a big lake in a natural basin of that river, where we used to swim in summer, stark-naked, with none save a few nosy sheep to watch us, and in winter we went there to skate.

As in the sonnet, the three of us were paralysed for a moment as we climbed, by the sudden flash of red lightning across the white path, so close to us. He didn't just stand there, as in the poem, and we didn't see 'the two unflickering flames of his eyes upon us', yet the incident was caught as surely as by any camera, and it remains in my memory to this day as one of the most cherished Christmas presents I ever had.

It's hard to explain, but the experience of seeing that fox on the mountain has come to represent for me the rural and Welsh element that was such an integral part of life in our industrial community all those years ago. There was, after all, a quite definite duality about the place. Although we were 'boys from the works', that's to say from where the anthracite coal was mined, there was nevertheless a good deal of country life left in the district. It's true we were familiar with the blackness of the tips near the gaping levels of Blaenwaun, Pencraig, Yr Ynys, and Gwaith Godfrey as the places where we used to play, and yet the smell of cow-dung also stuck to our clothes. On the slopes of the hills around the Valley there were the whitewashed smallholdings of Y Foel, Bryn Pedol, Y Rhosfa, Pantyffynnon, Bryn Hyfryd, and Gorsto, like so many candles of solid Welshness challenging the gloom of English industrialism that had gripped the Valley so mercilessly in the previous century. It was to those holdings that we went at harvest-time every year to help with the hay.

In our village it was quite common for a man to run a smallholding as well as to work as a collier during the day. The produce was always a help in supporting him in the uncertain world of industry. The few pounds that he made from farming would come in very handy in time of strike or lockout. But I half-suspect that this working on the land was a deeper instinct than merely that of supplementing his income. Working the soil, keeping a cow or two and a pig and some hens, was a kind of release from the soulless grind that the collier had to endure at the coal-face. After all, many of the people who lived there had originally come from deep in the Carmarthenshire countryside, their forebears having been obliged to leave for the industrial Eldorado in order to earn a living. But the rural way of life had remained in the community's tribal memory, and as Gwenallt[2] said in one of his poems, 'Our recreation of an evening was in pigsty and garden, and with hammer, pick and shovel.' It was the first craft ever practised by man that brought us pleasure, whereas industrialism was some sort of vile foreign compulsion. But for Gwenallt the industrialism of the Swansea Valley in black Glamorgan had been one thing, and the life of the countryside at Rhydcymerau quite another. In our village, which was after all in Carmarthenshire, the two were one, and the experience of seeing that fox on Mynydd y Crugau was for us 'boys from the works' a reminder of the presence of the countryside, in such close proximity to the tips.

The rural Welshness of Carmarthenshire was an essential part of the social life of the industrial village. Take the public hall, for instance. Like every other village in the Valley we had our hall that had been built by the miners. Its chief purpose was to provide the local people with a means of celluloid escape every night of the week except Sunday. There, in the fourpenny seats, we would watch the heroic cowboys shooting the wild Red Indians by the thousand. Buck Jones, William Boyd, and Charles Starret were the Pwyll[3], Pryderi, and Llew of our Mabinogi, though the films had been made in Hollywood. There we saw the sagas of Al Capone in Chicago, with Cagney, Bogart, and Edward G. Robinson, taking the part of Efnisien in those legends. And though the tales were in English, it was in Welsh that we kids echoed in our daily lives the heroism or villainy we had seen on the screen.

The hall, moreover, wasn't just an ordinary cinema, I'm glad to say. It also had a good library, full of Welsh books as well as the classics of English literature. Welsh was the language of the library, and on its shelves I was to come across the novels of Daniel Owen[4] and T. Rowland Hughes for the first time in my life. The place also had a games-room, with draughts and chess and billiards. This room became a meeting-place for the young people of the village, and it was in Welsh that we used to quarrel and have furious arguments over the games we played there. In spite of the Anglo-American trash that was pumped into us like a drug night after night, to take our minds off the land of coal, our rural Welshness was quite strong enough to withstand such foreign influences in those days. In that hall I saw the talented company of Dan Matthews entertaining us with plays such as *Cyfrinach y Fasged Frwyn*, *Y Ferch o Gefn Ydfa*, and *Pobl yr Ymylon*. On this stage, too, our innocent eisteddfodau were held, chapel competing against chapel with enthusiasm, talent, and good humour. All this was the rural culture of Carmarthenshire continuing to flourish in the midst of the industrial haze, and there was a kind of unyielding tenacity to it in the days of my youth.

Only once did I see a real fox, and then only for a second or so, its unforgettable red pelt flashing over the icy path on Mynydd y Crugau that Christmas long ago. But on a visit to my old home two days after Christmas last year, I happened to call at the house of one of my father's old friends, almost the last remaining of his generation. He too had had a smallholding on the slopes of Mynydd Ddu, and though he has now given up farming the place, he still lives in the house. By way of marking my visit in the proper manner, he invited me into the best parlour rather than into the kitchen where I had used to go with my father in days gone by. It was then I was taken aback to see a large stuffed fox, arranged in a glass case, standing on a mahogany table in the corner of the room.

I don't recall ever before seeing anything so stone-dead as that fox under glass. The taxidermist had tried to arrange it in a sort of moving stance, for one of its paws had been made to hover in mid-air, as if the animal were in the act of trotting along. But the attempt had been a complete failure. The pupils of the eyes stared moribundly at me, and the mouth gave an unnatural, grotesque grin. Bits of straw had been made to look like grass, and there was tall fern for background, as if the poor creature were alive and well in its natural habitat. The red pelt, no doubt treated with chemicals, stood up like shining wires on its back, and the brush had been arranged like a piece of crimson linen around its hind paws. The idea had doubtless been to freeze the creature's vitality inside the glass case, but the finished article was entirely unconvincing. Where once there had been the muscular warmth of life there was now only the coldness of death, instead of the cunning hunter's energy and strength only the stillness of death, fixed for ever.

The real fox I saw on the slopes of Mynydd y Crugau is an image that belongs to one particular Christmas long ago in the days of my youth, but that dead fox under glass is to this day a new and terrifying symbol in my mind. The country Welshness of my old home isn't likely to flash across my path ever again, although the Welsh language is still sweet on the lips of children there, so far, at least. But the thought of the old rural culture's being stuffed and arranged under glass, to satisfy the curious eyes of generations to come, has been a nightmare in my consciousness ever since I saw that dead fox. It has become one of the most alarming symbols in my mind. I'd give the world to see the creature, by some wondrous magic, spring to life, break the glass into smithereens with all its force, and leap out of the parlour window and head for the mountain.

Barn (275, Rhagfyr, 1985)

A Doctor's Medicine

John Roberts Williams

For me it's been a week of seeing the mountains of my years being rolled back like a carpet, a warning that history isn't just something that happens between one Saturday and the next but some sort of strange pattern made up of various bits and pieces that are welded together to create what's called life.

On Monday I was taken back to some of the old scenes of Eifionydd that have lain unforgotten in the depths of my subconscious for such a long time — back to Bobi Bingo and John Price.

For a reason that's still a mystery to me, the third Monday in October is Thanksgiving Day throughout most of Gwynedd. Not that the custom's holding its ground, not by a long chalk, and the poor harvest we had this year isn't the explanation either; but rather it's the inexorable course of time that seems to undo everything, staying its hand not even in these parts. Until very recently the Caernarfon shops would be shut and the chapels full on this particular day. But this year the shops were open and the chapels had held the festival long since.

In the past even the offices of the County Council would be closed, whereas Dwyfor is now one of the last of the local authorities to keep to the old custom, and many a chapel in Llŷn and Eifionydd is struggling, in the worst of the long winter that's descended on people who go to prayer, to hold services for the handful who used to be a throng. But it was a fine day; every day was fine in times gone by, wasn't it?

I was at home reading *Doctor Pen-y-bryn*, the fascinating volume of memoirs by Owen Elias Owen,[1] that wizardly surgeon from Eifionydd. And thousands of you ought to know where Pen-y-bryn is because it stands on the land belonging to the farm, at the top end of town, where the National Eisteddod was held in Cricieth in 1975.

Owen Elias Owen is something of a god in Gwynedd, on account of his medical miracles and his common touch and his fervent Welsh feeling. He will tell you quite plainly that the old and sick must be treated in their own language. I'm one of hundreds who are thankful to him for being alive. And it's with great pride that I can also swank that I belong to the same family — the old family of Is-allt-fawr in Cwm Pennant — which has produced more than a hundred doctors in its time, or so they say, many of whom, like Owen Owen for example, are of great eminence.

My great-grandmother Elin — one of the Is-allt family — went as a maid to the Ring at Chwilog before the sun of Eifionydd's great bardic tradition had started to decline in the last century, and it was there she met my great-grandfather.

In reminiscing about his schooldays — and if ever there were naughty children, then they were the Pen-y-bryn children, but good naughty children, you understand — the surgeon talks about a custom that we too used to have. In Llangybi, at the other end of Eifionydd, whenever a child was caned at school, a pig's bristle would be put on the palm of his hand, in the belief that it would snap the stick. I never actually saw the trick work but we farm-children always had a bristle or two in our pockets ready for use just in case.

But it was the surgeon's story about his visit to an old man by the name of Robert Jones, who was on his deathbed at the Anglesey and Caernarfon Hospital, that stimulated my memory most. He had known the old man as a fellow-pupil at the Cricieth primary school, in the days when he'd been known as Bobi Bingo. Owen Owen remembered him as a backward child, not fully developed, who would bring pieces of wood to school and sniff at them in class.

As I read, I suddenly recalled going to Cricieth as a student-teacher — on 'school prac'. I remembered what a good and genial teacher Evan Davies had been. I could also call to mind a lad who, without warning, used to take a piece of wood out of his desk and put it to his nose, smelling it earnestly before putting it back again, to my great perplexity. I made some enquiries. I was given to understand that it was a piece of coffin-wood from a carpenter's workshop that this likeable lad had in his possession. Of an evening he used to go and watch every coffin being made, and would even leave school during the day in order to attend funerals, walking at the side of the hearse. Death seemed to attract him like a magnet. And his other great pleasure had been to chase butterflies on the hillock near the castle. That lad was Bobi.

The other prod I had during the course of the week was the news of John Price's death at the age of ninety-one. He was the last of the old gentlemen of the road — the real tramps. When I was a lad a tramp would call at my grandfather's farm every now and again, despite the fact that it was off the beaten track. But every one would turn out to be an Englishman — the first English people I ever saw in my life. But John Price was a Welsh tramp and he belonged to Llŷn and Eifionydd. The highlight on Radio Cymru during the past week was to hear a recording of his voice, and at the same time to receive a lesson in how to curse naturally in Welsh.

To hear someone say, 'I saw John Price over Liverpool way the other day,' was about as common as hearing 'I've just seen a cuckoo'. And back and forth he would go from 'that bloody old Shropshire', and so on. Just one story about him. A farmer suspected that milk had been disappearing from the churns that were left on their stands by the roadside to await the milk-lorry. One morning, what was there to be seen but a pair of legs, with a man attached to them, his head out of sight because he was inside the churn, and his screeching proof that he couldn't pull himself out. John Price had gone to take a little swig of cream and had been caught, in both senses of the word.

In the end the top of the churn had to be sawed off in order to get him free.

I can't guarantee that the story's true, but I hope it is.

O Wythnos i Wythnos (Mei, 1987)

The Little Huts

Eigra Lewis Roberts

A quarter of a century ago there were scores of little huts in the clefts of the cliffs above Blaenau Ffestiniog. Waterproof houses, the work of budding stonemasons; skeleton huts open to the proverbial rain, girls' toy-houses, and to every stone its place and purpose. Today all is in ruins. Not a shout or scream is to be heard, and the smell of burnt chips in a saucepan is no longer carried on the breeze. You won't see any gang in serried ranks on their way to the bloody fields of Cwm Bowydd, their pockets stuffed with the ammunition David used to bring down his giant enemy.

Where are they, the new generation, where are they hiding? Has the little hut, the most romantic of playthings, lost its charm? Toy-houses now come in kits — with a frame that's put up in three minutes, or so it's claimed, and packed in plastic. But these are summer-houses, of course, with colourful continental walls and corners that curl up in the wind; houses that mothers and fathers have to erect, one metal strip at a time, each piece interlocking with another, a task that's every bit as nerveracking as fitting an awning on a caravan.

Now that I call the little huts to mind, wasn't the greatest pleasure to be had in building them? And didn't we often knock them down in order to experience the thrill of putting them up again? Each hut was private property, and every tenant defended her, or his, own with an iron fist.

Childhood in those days stretched far into the teenage years. These days they just can't wait to grow up. What I remember most is the freedom of ankle-socks; legs blue with cold; bruises from a hockey-ball; scratches from nutting in the hedges and cuts from the slate-tips. Running and climbing, full of reckless daring, and the thought of growing up more painful than pleasurable. Playing at being wives and mothers without trying to comprehend what it was all about, and walloping the baby-dolls against the boulders whenever they were naughty. Boys were things to be avoided, nothing more than the sweaty smell of canvas shoes left in desks, snot on the sleeve, and horrible wet kisses at Christmas parties in the Women's Institute hall.

There was a rocky outcrop in Cwm Bowydd, a tower overlooking the wood, that seemed a mountain to us in those days. There we would lie flat on our stomachs, dropping pine-cones on to the courting couples in the ferns below.

Sailing home on the crest of a wave, after seeing Doris Day spooning on the screen of the Forum cinema, and forgetting all about the romantic moon and kisses as we watched the salt melting brownly into the drops of vinegar on the chips from the Bwlch Gwynt shop. Singing out of tune on the back-seat of the Sunday School bus-trip to Rhyl about roses and the bridges of Paris — children with their feet planted solidly on the ground, who were far more familiar with dandelions and thistles.

I was even fond of that shapeless cap, like a flying-saucer, and half-worshipped the gaberdine coat that had begun to go rusty with age. And heavens above, what schoolgirl these days would be willing to wear navy-blue knickers that you could pull up under your armpits when the weather turned cold?

New clothes were out of the question, even if we desired them, only the occasional outfit for the Gymanfa,[1] hat, gloves, and all. I renounced hats and gloves many years ago. But they were an essential part of that procession up Blaenau's high street, led by the band, the men from all the Sunday Schools staggering under the weight of their huge banners, and us with our rosettes and flags. That evening, I was there at the front of the gallery, singing soprano a key lower than the rest because I couldn't reach the high notes, even when standing on tip-toe. So quickly do experiences become memories.

I was in my late 'teens before I began to doubt and protest, and even then it was in reverent fear and trembling lest some retribution would, perhaps, leave me crosseyed. Now that I come to think of it, we must have been terribly innocent. Yet, although we were pretty clueless about the ways of this world, at least we did know how to play. There was a different taste to potatoes in a little hut. There was straw on an earthen floor to tickle our thighs and a warm smell to prick our nostrils. It was a time for playing, before responsibility raised its head. The years for falling in love and being loved came later; the years for discovering new wonders. The awakening was gradual, and the anxieties of our Puritanical upbringing were always present, curbing our desires.

I'm not usually one for looking back. Perhaps it's seeing my own children grow up so alarmingly fast that's made me rummage in old cupboards that it doesn't pay to look into too often. But I haven't quite lost the wish to build a little hut somewhere and curl up snugly inside, and I know that I should defend it with the same iron fist.

Perhaps I've taken too long to grow up — that is, if I've grown up at all. Or it may be that I've slipped, as others do, from my first childhood into my second. Shake your head as much as you will, I'm not a bit ashamed. Being a child, of any kind, helps you to see wonders and to delight in them. Once you lose that ability things no longer have much colour or flavour. I sometimes feel like telling children I see hanging round street-corners and trying to look old before their time not to be in too much of a hurry to grow up, and I pity them for being so eager to put their play aside and so lose the incomparable enjoyment of being tenants of little huts.

Seren Wib (Gwasg Gomer, 1986)

Three Heads

Prys Morgan

About thirty years ago, when I was a young lad, I happened to be staying at a convent in Rome. The attention paid in films and on television to the career of Casanova has tended to give a false impression of Italian nunneries. The nun's calling must have been on the wane at the time and the convents finding it difficult to attract young novices to their orders, since they were so ready to provide lodgings and extend a welcome to young pilgrims like me, thereby filling their empty rooms. Only female pilgrims were taken in by the Italian orders, but the Pope allowed young men to sojourn under the roof of orders such as the Order of Saint Elizabeth which recruited novices from Germany and from Switzerland. Since I had been wandering through Italy for weeks on end and living on a shoe-string budget, these convent houses were a great boon. The one in Rome stood opposite the large church of Santa Maria Maggiore, a pleasant old building from the Middle Ages, with shady gardens full of plant-boxes and seats made of stone and marble salvaged from the ruins of Ancient Rome. I used to climb up on to its flat roof of an evening, in order to watch the sun going down behind the dome of St. Peter's on the other side of the Tiber, and it was strange to hear the sound of the nuns praying and singing inside the convent's walls, though you would never catch a glimpse of them.

I remember, with a feeling of some shame, that I once tried to procure lodgings in the house for a friend of mine who was a descendant of Thomas Charles[1] of Bala and of Dr Lewis Edwards, a student who happened to be the son of a bishop in England. Earnestly and without thinking, I said to the mother superior (in German), 'But you must give him lodgings — he is, after all, a bishop's son.'

'I hope he's the son of a Protestant bishop,' she replied, laughing heartily, and off she went to find a room for him.

The reverend mother was a remarkably gentle and kindly woman, and I remember asking her to suggest how I might celebrate my birthday the following day. 'Well, the best thing to do,' she said, 'would be to go for a day's excursion to Castel Gandolfo and receive the Pope's blessing on your birthday. Such would do even a Protestant good. Usually I have a few tickets for people to go into the palace, but they're as scarce as gold, and every one has been given away. Go anyway, to see the countryside and the place itself, and perhaps, by striking up a conversation with someone or other, you'll somehow manage to get in to see the Pope.'

So off I went on the bus to Castel Gandolfo, marvelling at the beauty of the hills behind Rome, hills and lakes that were already half-familiar to me because they were favourite places painted by our eighteenth-century compatriot, Richard Wilson.[2] It's true that Wilson made pictures of the hills of Wales as though they were mountains in Italy, but it's just as true that in Italy he looked for hills similar to those in his own country. My own gaze was not on the hills so much as on the beautiful little town and on the palace at the far end of the main road. In front of the gate a crowd had gathered and soldiers of the Swiss Guard, in their blue and yellow uniforms, were busy turning away ticket-less pilgrims who were milling at the gate.

'You can't go in without a ticket from the Pope's chamberlain,' a soldier said to me.

There was nothing for it but to stand and watch. And I fell into conversation with a young American near by, a girl from somewhere like Iowa, if I remember right, who suddenly said to me, 'Look, I have two entrance-tickets. My friend happens to know the Pope's chamberlain, but she's gone to take a rest because she can't stand the heat. Will you come into the palace with me for company?'

A moment later we were both back at the gate and showing our cards to the soldier, and being given permission to go into the courtyard inside the palace.

Strait was the gate and great the multitude, more than two hundred people, probably, with no room for anyone to kneel. It was the building's backyard, with kitchen and storehouse doors on every side, and a row of dusters washed and hanging on a clothes-line in one corner. The crowd sang heartily while waiting for the Pope. The hymns were in Latin, and the languages a Babel between the hymns. One blessing, besides that of the Pope, was that the yard was in a lovely shade. It was a good thing the other American girl didn't know that. Then at three o'clock, quite unannounced, servants came to open a window a few feet above our heads and draped a bedspread of multi-coloured plush material over the windowsill. A silence fell upon the throng.

It was Pope Pius XII who came to the window and, leaning out a little, started speaking to the crowd, and went on without interruption for an hour and a quarter and in various languages, even in Polish. He spoke quite a lot of German. I was to bring this back to mind years later when Rudolf Hochhuth wrote his play, *The Representative*, in which Pius XII was accused of dishonest compromise with the Nazis before and during the War, to such an extent that he was very far from being Christ's Vicar on Earth. I knew nothing of all that, of course, on this particular afternoon. What I saw was a man of wonderful presence and aristocratic mien, and I was astonished that someone of such frail physique could speak so energetically for an hour and a quarter. The palace was unpretentious enough, and an old man had got up after his afternoon siesta to see and bless us, and there was a curious paradox in the blend of dignity and simplicity without ceremony. The whole thing was a real experience, and I felt that I had received a blessing, as well as being lucky.

About two years or more after that, Pius XII was in his grave, and as a stop-gap, let's say, an old, old man was elected Pope, John XXIII, but a Pope who was to live long enough to confound the world and the Church. At the time of his election, I was an undergraduate who happened to be studying the terrible predicaments in the history of the Church during the fourteenth and fifteenth centuries, with the popes and anti-popes all excommunicating one another.

One of these anti-popes had been a professional soldier by the name of Baldassare Cossa, who called himself John XXIII. I can recall my History teacher (now Sir John Hale) remarking, 'The world holds its breath. Of all the names to choose! John XXIII!'. It was everyone's opinion that his reign would last for about a year. But it wasn't to be so, and during his papacy the Vatican Council was held, the first since 1870, a council for the modernization of the Church.

The next time I was in Rome the wheel was beginning to turn, creakily and querulously. Once again I was a pilgrim staying at the convent and this time I asked the mother superior in good time for an invitation-ticket from the Vatican's chamberlain.

'There's not so much demand for tickets these days,' she said. 'Just about anyone can get into Castel Gandolfo now. Everything has changed there. You'll see.'

Instead of the confined and unceremonious backyard, there was a hanger big enough to hold a Boeing 737, a wide expanse of glass and concrete, and it was there that the pilgrims in their thousands awaited the Pope. The whole atmosphere of the place was like an airport concourse, slick and American, and as contemporary as a glass pavilion representing some country or other at an international fair. Despite the shock, we went in and stood near a group of handsome Spanish ladies, a sobriety of black mantillas and large hair-combs. On catching sight of the Pope the crowd began applauding and cheering, and the Spanish ladies nearly deafened me with their shouts of '*España por el Papa!*', just like the fans of a pop-singer. As the Pope made his way towards us, the cheering grew louder, and we saw first of all the soldiers, ranged according to rank and dressed in their special uniforms, then servants waving huge fans made from ostrich feathers, and lastly the Pope himself, being carried on a palanquin that resembled an open sedan chair, clad in scarlet velvet and white ermine, the nearest you ever did see to Father Christmas, except that the throne and the ostrich feathers were like something out of a film about Cleopatra by Cecil B. de Mille. From his throne the Pope smiled endearingly and in a friendly, grandfatherly sort of way, more like Jack XXIII than John XXIII.

The old man was put to sit on his throne on a stage at the far end of the pavilion, and the atmosphere there resembled that on the afternoon of the Crown or Chair ceremonies at the National Eisteddfod.[3] The old man spoke warmly in his own dialect — he came from a district not far from Venice — and laughed when a man in the crowd boldly interrupted him in a thick, unintelligible dialect, and replied just as mischievously and demotically, and everyone burst out laughing. After a few minutes there was a call for silence and a solemn blessing was given. Then he was borne out on his throne, as imperial and as Cleopatra-like as before. I recall some Englishman telling me once that he couldn't understand how the Archdruid was able to tease the audience so light-heartedly during the most solemn moments of the Eisteddfod's ceremonies. That Englishman would have been at a loss in the Vatican. Nor would Castel Gandolfo have been to his taste, either. But it was indeed difficult to believe that this man, Pope John XXIII, was the very man who would turn the Church inside out in his bid to modernize it. In the eyes of this crowd he was an ordinary man of the people, a sort of grandpa or uncle to them all. And yet, all about him there was the pomp and circumstance of a Caesar, much grander than anything I had witnessed about the late Pius XII, a man who was much more of an aristocrat. And to compound the confusion, the ceremony took place in a pavilion that had been built to make pilgrimage into a business — big business.

I didn't have an opportunity of going to Rome again for years after that, and the next time I was there it was Easter time and not summer. For that reason the Pope wasn't at Castel Gandolfo; it wouldn't have been proper for him to leave the city at Easter. It was Flowering Sunday, and the churches of Rome were dark and unadorned and as candleless as any Nonconformist chapel. I followed the huge crowd into St. Peter's without knowing that the Pope himself would be there that Sunday morning. There's always some service or other going on there, but I was unaware that this was the main Mass of the day. It was difficult to make out what was happening, or who was leading the service, because the chatter from the congregation all around me was so unheeding. It was strange to look up at the marble expanses of Michelangelo, and then down upon hundreds of ordinary mortals waving sprigs of palm made out of green plastic, that acid-green you see in the plastic parsley which decorates the marble slabs of butchers at home in Wales. I grew tired of the base jabbering in the throng all about me, and in order to see better what was going on near the altar and under the canopy of the *baldacchino* in the middle part of the church, I pushed my way forward. Suddenly the crowd parted and I saw the Pope. It was Paul VI who was leading the service. I could hear his voice and see his face behind a forest of aluminum microphones, astonishingly like President Reagan's behind similar microphones at a press-conference in the White House. On either side of the Pope there were rows of little boys in their everyday clothes, jacket-less and tie-less, and these lads were reading the texts and offering up the prayers. Above their heads was the *baldacchino* erected by Bernini, above that the dome and the words *Super Hanc Petram*, but the language of the Mass that day was Italian. Everything was as open and as comprehensible and as unclerical as any Welsh Protestant might have wished it to be.

The Pope himself delivered a long apologue, clear and unaffected, a sermon addressed to the young people of Italy, the sort of thing he might have given if he had been invited to preach, say, at the half-centenary jubilee of the Urdd[4] in Wales. It wasn't an expository sermon of the true kind, but something that my grandfather's generation, or my parents' if it comes to that, would have called a sermonette. It brought to mind the story about the Archdeacon in Swansea who, one Sunday morning, on meeting Mr Leeke, a Baptist minister in the town, explained to Mr Leeke that Church people no longer expected a long sermon, preferring little more than a sort of sermonette, at which Mr Leeke turned to his friend and said, 'I must warn you of one thing, Archdeacon — sermonettes make Christianettes'.

There's a contemporary French novel about the Vatican and the Popes by Roger Peyrefitte. I don't know whether it's been translated into English, but even if it has, I wouldn't urge anyone to go to the trouble of reading it, it's so bad. But I remember one sentence in the novel where a cardinal is trying to explain the services of the Church in Rome to some priest or other, and he says that a man must go to England, to the Catholic cathedral in Westminster, in order to witness services that are immaculate in their ceremonial. Their honed perfection springs from the fact that the Catholics there have to compete with the church-goers at Westminster Abbey. I therefore wonder whether the Italians take their services seriously. It's difficult to say. How often have we seen the words *allegro con brio* at the beginning of a sheet of music. Fun and games, *allegro con brio*, is an exact description of the light-heartedness to be had so often in the ceremonies of the Church of Rome in Italy. And that's what we had in St. Peter's on Flowering Sunday.

At the end of the Mass the Pope was borne out and into the palace, exactly as John XXIII had been on my first visit to Castel Gandolfo. It was amusing to hear the crowd clapping and shouting after him as though they were at Ninian Park[5]. This was an example of the 'Modern Enthusiasm' that old Theophilus Evans[6] used to condemn so roundly. Perhaps the Methodist Fathers would have been better pleased. I can recall preachers, from my younger days, going into the *hwyl*[7] but I'm not old enough by a long way to recall whole congregations getting into it. It was strange to witness the phenomenon in Rome.

Such a Mass was a strange experience for a Welshman, and I do believe it would have been just as puzzling to a chapel-goer as to a Churchman. We find it difficult to cope with a combination of the demotic and the imperial, the sublime and the vulgar. Yes, I dare to use the word 'vulgar'. For if the rows of microphones were modernistic, then the green plastic palms were vulgar. Yet the two were interwoven and as one. We have grown so accustomed to dignified services, and to liturgical sobriety, with everyone dressed in their Sunday best. The Italian combination of the imperial and the demotic may be glimpsed on the stage of the National Eisteddfod, to be sure, but is not to be seen in our religious worship. Is this accounted for by the fact that we are all under the influence of the most ritualistic church in Europe, the Church of England? I remember my parents saying that they used to be astonished, while on holiday in Ireland in the mid-1930s and calling at village churches, to see the congregation at Mass in their everyday clothes, with dung sticking to their boots and straw on their coats.

How old is this paradoxical combination in the Church of Rome? The attempt to bring the altar down into the midst of the church and to replace Latin with the vernaculars suggests that it's a recent tendency. And yet, in the old baroque churches of Spain and Italy from say the seventeenth century, you can see the same bizarre combination of pomp and princely splendour side by side with the raw emotion of an illiterate peasantry, and that's what explains the curious blend in these churches of majestic architecture on the one hand and, on the other, decorations like those on a hoop-la stall. Isn't it the ethos of a culture that is at one and the same time aristocratic *and* of the people which is to be seen in these churches, while in our own churches and chapels what we have is the ethos of a culture that is middle-class and bourgeois?

Of course, my three visits to Rome were all different. Pius XII was aristocratic and old-fashioned, the absolute head of an institution that was intransigent, dauntless in the face of its enemies, looking back to the infallibility of the previous century. John XXIII was transforming the Church and forcing it to face up to the problems of the contemporary world. And yet it was he, not Pius XII, who was being carried in with the pomp of Caesar. A windowsill in the backyard was good enough for Pius XII; he didn't have to worry about the media, the blasted media. I believe the elements of the admixture were the same during all three visits.

Back in the 'sixties, people used to marvel at my saying that I had seen the Pope and were even more astonished to hear that I had received his blessing on my birthday. Today things have changed completely, and Pope John Paul II goes everywhere, and has even been to Wales. Millions all over the world have seen him in the flesh and received his blessing — some of them on their birthdays, no doubt. But one thing remains certain in my mind: Pius XII wouldn't have liked the Popemobile.

Taliesin (61, Mawrth 1988)

On Memory

Gruffudd Parry

Peculiar things, remembering and forgetting. There's something comic about a schoolboy's face as he struggles to remember an answer to a question, his forehead creasing, his brows heavily knitted, and a faraway, pained expression in his eyes. Some also have the knack of pleating their mouths in order to emphasize the impression of a special mental effort. And you have to smile because you already know that the lad hasn't the slightest idea of what the answer is. Indeed, it's the surest of all signs that he doesn't know. Behind it all there lies a vacuum. There was nothing there to remember in the first place. And there's something very sad, too, about the face of an old person whose memory is failing; time has creased the forehead, old age made the brows heavy, and there's a look of bewildered innocence in the eyes. It's sad because you know full well that what's being sought is there somewhere, but that for the moment it's beyond recall. The experience of many years' living lies behind the eyes' innocence and the worries of a lifetime are all jumbled up with the memory. But those are two extremes.

It's probably one of the first signs that a man's beginning to fail when he starts recalling things. Almost unawares there will come a flash of memory like a phantom from among the spirits of things that happened long ago. Perhaps growing old means that these spirits put on flesh and become substantial things, until a man's interest in the passing of time has been changed and he looks back and lives with his memories instead of looking ahead and living with his dreams. At least at first, they are insubstantial things, that no one would dare to speak about except to himself. Not that there's anything wrong with them, but they are too childish and too inconsequent for anyone to be able to open a conversation by saying, 'I remember . . .' Who could ever start a conversation in that way, and then go on to talk about the time he came home from Llŷn one summer on the train from Pwllheli, a little chap in short trousers and a sailor-suit? A train was of great interest in those days, and particularly so the thin chain that dangled from something like a bottle's neck in each compartment. I don't know who it was explained the significance of the red lettering under that chain, but whoever it was, he aroused in me a curiosity that remains unsatisfied to this day. And in that sentence, 'Penalty for improper use,' the word 'penalty' was the only one I understood, and it didn't mean a fine of five pounds. A penalty was something controversial that would happen sometimes while playing football in the field behind the cowsheds. One of the players would suddenly stop as if gripped by cramp and shout 'Penalty!'. Then the other four or five players would come up to him and, in the best traditions of local government, after long deliberation, one side would say, 'All right, you take it, then, but it wasn't really a penalty!'. The ball would be carefully placed in front of the two stones or the two piles of coats that served as goalposts; a clod of turf would be kicked up to hold it, and then three members of the unlucky team would spread themselves as wide as possible in an attempt to block the goal, looking as if they were out to catch a tiger, and two members of the other team watched a third. A kick, and far too often the ball would rise gently and soar through the air high above the three goalies and over the byres, falling neatly in the middle of the pool by the dunghill. There would be further claims that it had gone too high, a short argument, and always the same conclusion; the visiting team picked up their coats and set off home, sulking; and the other side would go into the house to have supper, taking off their boots before going to bed.

Those are memories, trifles of no importance, the only distinction of which is that they are sometimes brought to mind by chance. But they also have their own peculiar character, and by now their sadness and their joy, their happiness and misery, and sometimes there is to some of them a strange sense of discomfort which, at the time, they didn't have. Indeed, there was nothing at all to them at the time of their occurrence. It's in coming back that they reveal their true characteristics.

There was the time I went up to the waterworks. It's a concrete construction set into the side of the mountain, and the building of it was an important chapter in the history of our village. One definite rule about the works was that children were to go nowhere near it. The building had grown bigger with each passing day, and soon it was finished, a big square concrete box. We were allowed to go on to the mountainside to look at it from a distance, but as far as I know, nobody ever disobeyed the warning: Trespassers will be Prosecuted. By Order. We didn't have the faintest idea who this Order was who had put his name in bold letters under that impudent sign. The general opinion was that he was a policeman, though none had the least idea why he was called Order. But then, there was no understanding the workings of grown-up people's minds. They had the tiresome habit of detecting sin in the most harmless things. But to return to the waterworks. Having come down from the mountain one evening, I was loitering out of curiosity at the top of the small path that led from the road to the gate at the side of the waterworks. I walked gingerly up the path and tried to look in through the cracks in the door that had been put there by the workmen to block the entrance until the following day. But I couldn't see anything. So I set off home, intending to make a greater effort next day by asking one of the men to let me in for a minute. But like many another dream of tomorrow, that too turned out to be a disappointment. The stonemason was pleasant enough — he was a fine, kind man, and what wonder? He had been inside the works for weeks on end. But the barrier that had been placed across the entrance the night before had now been removed, and a big iron door with a lock on it had been put in its place, and it was heart-rending to hear the stonemason say with a laugh, 'Well, my lad, why didn't you come yesterday? You would have been allowed in and been welcome, but it's half-full of water this morning.' The waterworks had been completed and the golden opportunity to inspect it had slipped by without anyone giving it a thought. And even if it had been possible, at some later date, to see the waterworks, it would never have been the same again. And to this day I feel uneasy whenever I look down on it from the mountainside.

This feeling of uneasiness is part of every change, somehow or other. There's an old, undeniable certainty about things past, and nothing can be done about it other than to accept it and rest content. Sometimes a number of things happen all together under certain circumstances, and no thought is given to them at the time. But when they turn up again as part of a man's memories, he realizes that they could very well have been different. Clouds in the sky between five and six o'clock in the morning, obscuring the sun. The whole thing was supposed to last for a few minutes but the clouds intervened, and in the end turned into mist and then drizzle. And that was one chance in a lifetime of seeing an eclipse of the sun. Smelling the scent of may after a shower of rain in Spring-time, and knowing full well that those scents had their own special associations, but being unable to recall what they were. Regretting, in vain, that so little notice was taken of the may's scents at the time. Hearing the sound of far-off singing coming from somewhere over the mountain after chapel one Sunday evening in summer, but nothing to back up the memory; only a faint recollection of its happening and then ceasing. Something similar to 'the memory, the memory of old' that awakened the wind's sound in the sedges in the heart of the Poet of Summer[1]. Remembering suddenly, and with no particular reason, the taste of speckled bread in the Sunday School[2] tea-party, and someone saying that it was excellent, with plenty of spices in it. Remembering how the sand at the seaside felt warm under foot, but when? Or with whom? No, nothing of it will come back. Only some unconnected, scattered moments with their own particular atmosphere and associations.

But perhaps it's all imagination and fancy, anyhow, and what's needed to put the memory in order and things in their proper place is the psychologist's technique. It may be so, but without these memories life would somehow be a lot emptier. The remnants of things, that's what they are, probably, but they bring with them no responsibility, no pain, no difficulty. And there's neither rule nor season to them. They come at their own whim and in their own time they go away. And they aren't really personal things, either. Their associations may be personal, perhaps, but their substance is a part of every man's inheritance, and every generation's. It was about them that Waldo Williams[3] was thinking when he talked about 'the old forgotten things of humankind', and perhaps they were in the mind of Keats when he imagined, on looking at that Greek vase, a life so petrified and earthbound that its aspirations remain unchanged and for ever young. But that, too, was disheartening in the end. For aspirations aren't so interesting when it's certain that they will never be fulfilled.

Perhaps these faint memories weaving through one another are the best background for life, after all, like the small waves of the sea moving across the waters in moonlight. No more than some turbulence within defined boundaries, and the boundaries themselves gradually shifting. And even if things could be changed, it would hardly be worth trying, since the memories are also part of the future. Every year, in times long past, a fall of snow was eagerly anticipated, and every night we looked hopefully to the north to see whether in the grey darkness there was any sign that snow might be on its way. Yet though some nights the sky looked promising, the snow was very reluctant to fall in real earnest. It would threaten a large, soft flake or two, and then turn into rain or cease altogether, but our hope wasn't one bit diminished for all that. And at last our hopes were fulfilled. It had been extremely cold that morning, and a few flakes had fallen from a dark grey sky, but this time it didn't let up and it didn't turn to rain either. By playtime at eleven o'clock a slight breeze had arisen, and by one o'clock it was high time to be on our way home. The snow lashed in from the east, until there were drifts on the roads and the hedges were lost from sight, and no school for a fortnight. That storm fulfilled the hopes of years, and perhaps it's because they were so completely realized that a man, almost in spite of himself, will still look hopefully into a dark grey sky towards the end of January and the beginning of February. And anyway, it's much easier to think on winter's cold in August, however poor that month turns out to be, because there's only one kind of snow at summer's end, and that's the snow of yesteryear.

No, things might as well be left as they are from now on, a ragged hotch-potch of yesterday, today, and tomorrow. There's a pattern to the weave somewhere, no doubt, although it's hard to make out while the stuff is on the loom and the weaver's fingers busy hurtling the shuttle back and forth. It will be easier to see the pattern when the material is a bit longer. But then perhaps the material itself is merely a part of some greater pattern. On its own it's only something very, very small, like one of those hundreds of pieces in a ragmat.

Mân Sôn (Gwasg Dwyfor, 1989)

Uncle John's Boots

Bernard Evans

There's a black sheep or two in every family, about whom no one speaks without a shake of the head and a lowering of the eyes. Uncle John is one such. I can remember him at home in my grandmother's house among the rest of my father's brothers, a collier just like them. And then he disappeared.

He was there, and then he wasn't, as some chap[1] from North

Wales once said. And as I was so young at the time, I forgot all about him. I was aware that there was someone missing between Wil and Alf among the flock of men, my father's brothers, who used to roost in my grandmother's house, but it was very hard to fill in that gap with the round face, with its long tapering moustache, that had gone for ever from the noisy, argumentative hearth of Angorfa. I would hear the name mentioned from time to time, and my grandmother's eyes would cloud over now and again when we two were sitting either side of the fire. A sigh would come from the depth of her bosom, far down under her canvas apron, and she would say, 'Where's our Shoni by now, I wonder?'. Then, whenever there was commotion in the house, some great disaster like Mam's forgetting to put currants in Father's rice-pudding, which caused one of those family rows that blow up like a hurricane and subside as suddenly as a summer storm, his name would crop up again like a phoenix from the flames. 'I don't know why you can't remember something simple like black currants,' Father would say. 'But there we are, you can't depend on the Nant-y-gros memory when there's something else on their minds.'

Now Mam was one of the Nant-y-gros family and to say something against them was as sure to cause strife as to doubt the veracity of the Doctrine of Atonement in the monthly meetings of the Methodists. Mam's brother, Lewis, had gone to a miners' conference at Porthcawl one year in order to raise some issue like pay for working in water, and he'd met some girl and taken her to the fair. When the time came for the matter to be put before the delegates, Lewis was on the dodgems with nothing further from his mind than water in heading or coal-face. It hadn't entered his mind until he was on the ghost train. But in the village nobody forgot it, and the name of Nant-y-gros has ever since been maligned. The only answer Mam could give to something like that was, 'Well, at least Lewis came back, which your Shoni never did.' And it would be Mam who had won yet another skirmish.

Despite what she said, Father's brother John did come back, and more than once. But I'm talking about the first time. By then I was starting to face some of life's trials and having to work for my exams. Father's brothers had all been married one by one, as tends to happen. Only Wil and Bert were left at home, and so there was more room and more peace for me to do my homework at Angorfa than there was in our house. So there we were, my grandmother and I, all on our own, she having forty winks in the armchair and I reading *War and Peace* instead of learning French verbs, when suddenly the door opened. I didn't recognize him at all, nor he me if it came to that. My grandmother got up in fright, as if she were seeing an apparition. 'Shoni, Shoni, my love!' she cried, and started to drown in tears on the very spot.

I had a good chance to look at him properly while my grandmother was preparing food. I'm sure that the Prodigal Son didn't enjoy more of a feast than the one Uncle John was given. But all I could do was stare at him in astonishment. He was wearing a dark-blue coat and a light-yellow tie exactly like the ones painters wear in the pictures entitled '*La Vie Bohème*'. His tie was more of a cravat than a tie, and exactly the same colour as his coat. The trousers had a small light check all over and they were tight around his legs, and there was a pair of boots on his feet that were a real marvel.

'What are you staring at?', he asked. It was impossible to answer. 'Is it these clothes taking your eye?' I nodded. 'A bit more colourful than the black suit and white collar your father wears of a Sunday, eh?'

'But the boots!' I exclaimed.

'Yes, these boots have made me a small fortune,' he replied, and inserted his finger between the edge of the boot and his ankle, and then tugged. The material stretched and snapped back on his ankle with a clack. 'Elastic!', he said by way of explanation, before settling down to his meal. I didn't have a chance to ask how elastic-sided boots could make someone a fortune, but I was given a small part of that fortune before he got up to go and disappeared back to his mysterious life.

The following Saturday afternoon Mam had gone into town and there was no one save Father and me in the house. I wasn't sure whether I should risk it or not; I didn't know how Father would react to being questioned about the skeleton that lurked in the family's darkest, deepest cupboard. But indeed, the old Puritanical Socialist was glad of the opportunity to boast about what had happened to the black sheep.

John had turned out to be different from the other brothers, a dreamer rather than a man of action, a romantic not a realist. He had been a quite good worker but used to spend his money on clothes, and rubbish like that, in preference to translations of *Das Kapital* or such precious tomes as *The Struggle of the Proletariat*. One of his fancies had been the boots with elastic sides. One Friday, instead of attending the evening class on 'The Worker's Role in the Overthrow of Capitalist Society', John and some of his frivolous friends had gone to the circus. There he had fallen head-over-heels in love. In those days it was disastrous so much as to think about one of the town girls, but John had gone off the rails completely: he had taken a shine to one of the circus girls. He had been entranced by a girl on the trapeze. Seeing her flying back and forth far above the heads of the crowd had seduced him utterly.

Every man with an ounce of romance in him is sure to have been enchanted at some time or other by Greta Garbo, Rita Hayworth, Marilyn Monroe, or Raquel Welch, but the majority are sensible enough to realize that they are in love with a reflection on the screen. But not John. He had gone off to follow the circus.

Every night he had gone as far as Cydweli, and then to Llanelli for a whole week, just to stare admiringly at the object of his infatuation — to sit and stare for a whole week. After that he went even further afield, to Swansea and even Neath. By the time he reached Swansea he had to decide whether to try and have a word with her or else to give himself a permanent crick in the neck. He had decided to have a word. By the end of the week the pair were dining out on faggots and peas in a small café near Swansea Market. By the Wednesday night performance at Neath, John and his sweetheart were sure that neither could live without the other, and after the last show on Saturday night it was high time the young man had a word with the girl's father.

Now in a small circus everyone is related to everyone else. The father is the ring-master, the mother helps with the horses, while the sons are weightlifters or throw themselves around the ring. Asking for Isabel's hand in marriage, for that was her name, was like asking to remove a cog from a car's motor. If Isabel were to marry John a part of the circus would be lost and the whole caboodle would grind to a halt, like a car with a plug or two missing.

All Father's family are quite small of stature, and John was no exception. But obviously it's not in inches that love is measured. Because what John did after hearing all this was to offer to join the circus. It was as if someone living in Surbiton and working in the Stock Exchange had offered to move to Trebanos and work underground. He wouldn't last a fortnight. John was capable of doing little more than helping to put up and take down the marquee, and that was only thanks to two weeks at the Urdd camp. That was the long and short of what he was able to offer the circus, and the response from Isabel's family to the suitor's request had been, as was only to have been expected — the finger and thumb pointed downwards as definitely as any Roman Emperor's after a performance that was anything less than satisfactory.

John knew nothing about looking after animals. He was a collier, not a haulier. He could cut coal, but he wasn't any good at lifting weights. He had been working underground, not up in the air on a tight-wire. Isabel and family looked at one another and shook their heads.

A less determined man, someone in whose head love had not consumed the little grey matter and turned it into coke, would have given up on the spot. But John was a lover of the true sort. 'I'll give the trapeze a try,' he said in a faint voice. Some of the brothers burst out laughing, and shrugged their shoulders a bit as if to say, 'On your head be it'. Then up they went, preparing to throw the little collier high above the open ring. Fear is terrifying, but love is greater than fear, or at least that's what I've heard people say.

Up the rope-ladder went John, although his knees had turned to water, and his ears had filled and were deafening him with the pounding of his blood. He shut his eyes as he was hurled from one pair of hands to another, while the two brothers were enjoying the excitement and terror which they could feel in the hands that clutched theirs. To finish the little collier off once and for all, they decided to give the limp John one more turn, letting the others grab him by his heels as he flew past. Everything worked perfectly, except for one small thing — those feet and heels were still inside the elastic-sided boots. John had stayed inside his boots until the swing slowed down and then took his leave of them, and fell. The fall was not intentional, nor graceful, nor comely in any way, but it was definite enough, and he landed neatly in the net above the ring, leaving his boots in the hands of one of the brothers.

'So that was why he didn't come back — because he'd failed to join the circus?', I said to Father after he had finished his story.

'Good heavens, how did I beget such a stupid child! No, that's why John is still in the circus, and why he's married to that Isabel,' he said.

And whether you believe me or not, if you ever go to the circus at Blackpool and see a little man with a pointed moustache climbing over the ring-side and demanding to have a go on the trapeze, then you'll have seen Uncle John, Father's brother. He's the one who gets hurled helplessly from one pair of hands to the next high above the ring, and he it is who falls out of his boots, to the immense astonishment and terror of the crowd every night of the week and twice on Saturdays and Sundays.

It's not surprising that he thought so much of those elastic-sided boots. They must have been worth a couple of hundred pounds a week to him.

Taliesin (66, Mawrth, 1989)

The Fur Coat

Gareth Alban Davies

'There were six or seven fur coats in Bethesda,' my father once remarked, while referring to more prosperous years in the Chapel's history, back in the 'thirties. But perhaps I'm mistaken as I try to recall the voice that made that statement. It would have been more in keeping with my mother's viewpoint, for she was more sensitive than he to the gradations in society and the lines drawn between one class and another. But there was no doubt about the facts: they were confirmed by my own childhood memory. Indeed, those coats were part of life's wonder.

Seated in our pew, with the waves of organ-music swelling the eddies of heat that swirled down the aisle, I was well placed to see the coats as they came into Chapel. On winter nights they would be pulled tight around the body, but of a Spring evening they billowed free, a fit adornment for their owners rather than a necessary garment. I wasn't well enough acquainted with the world of nature to be able to say where these various pelts had come from, but it would be an irreverence to suggest that they had once belonged to cat or rabbit, since it was so obvious to the eye that they had adorned the backs of exotic creatures in the far corners of the earth — the rare Siberian fox, or Persian lamb, or the musquash about which I knew nothing save the fragrance of its name.

But who were the owners of these luxurious furs? A Marxist analysis would lead inexorably to the conclusion that they were the wives and daughters of the exploiting classes, and in the Valleys during the 'thirties there was no doubt as to who *they* were — the owners and managers of the coalmines. It must be admitted that several of these were to be found among Bethesda's members, and that one or two had been elected to office in the Chapel. Let it not be forgotten, either, that a fur coat adorned the back and shoulders of the wife of the Ocean Coal Company's[1] general manager. ('Ocean, thou mighty monster,' was the mischievous suggestion for the solo in one of the musical competitions at the Treorci Eisteddfod of 1928!). And to that fine, dark coat there was, moreover, a sheen very different from those others seen here and there in the congregation: sable has a sedate, unshowy quality which suits a woman who is well aware that she's wealthy, and that everybody else knows it too. There remains in my memory a picture of a beautiful woman, of well-bred deportment and manners, with the night's blackness closing like death around the whiteness of her flesh.

At the other extreme from this capitalist coat there was quite a different one, which at first beggars Marxist definition. It belonged to the wife of a collier and was made from sealskin. The family must have sacrificed quite a bit to have been able to afford such an expensive garment. The coat might even have been described as defiant, since it demonstrated that an ordinary collier could, with effort, rise to the same level as his masters. The plain truth is that this particular collier didn't rise at all, and perhaps the coat merely made up for his failure to realize a dream that had become reality only in the case of some of his fellows: after all, the manager of the Ocean had risen from the same community as he himself had.

One of my contemporaries at Bethesda remembers the sealskin coat well, for it had belonged to his grandmother. She used to keep it strictly for Sunday services. During the week it would be hung in state in the darkness of the wardrobe, with camphor balls placed in the pockets to keep out the moths. When Sunday came round once more it would be taken out, and in its pockets would be a plentiful supply of mints, so that its owner could keep her grandchildren quiet during the sermon. Not surprisingly, some of the camphor's scent would stick to the mints, leaving in the boy's memory a Proustian stimulus that has remained frustrated ever since, for it's almost impossible in these prosaic days to hit upon the precise aromatic combination that would awaken the memory from its deep slumber.

Those two examples were to be found at either extreme of the phenomenon — in between there were coat-owners who were much more typical, mostly schoolteachers in their thirties and early forties, indeed, so many, now that I come to count them carefully, that I doubt the statistical accuracy of my parents in noting only six or seven. Among those wearers of fur there was a pit-manager's daughter, and a local schoolmaster's wife who was so small that she looked just like a feathery wren. But speaking generally, the rest were the womenfolk of ordinary colliers.

The fur coat itself set those teachers apart, but there was something else, too: they were unmarried. The most obvious explanation of this fact was that the Glamorgan Education Authority, during the years of the Depression, used to refuse permission for a woman to remain in her post as a teacher once she had married. In the cruel economic circumstances prevailing in those days it was very difficult to leave your job because a whole family might be dependent on your salary. In some instances there was another explanation for this maiden state, of which I as a child was completely unaware. Among those teachers there were some who were old enough to have experienced what it was like to be a young woman during the years of the Great War. It had been a part of the sadness of their lives to see their sweethearts going off patriotically to Death's great harvest in the trenches in France, from where many never returned. This experience had left a scar on the soul of some of these women, a scar unhealed by the passing of the years, and people would sometimes be heard to comment that a 'tragedy' had occurred in the life of this one or that.

But how do we explain that the majority were the daughters of colliers? First of all, a passion for education was widespread, often arising from aspirations that were quite materialistic. It offered boys a chance to escape from poverty and from the dangers of the pit, and for girls there lay hope of another wage with which to supplement the family's slender purse. Such was the craving to give an education to the children that it produced many more schoolteachers than the local society could find employment for. As a consequence, coal and teachers were for many years the main exports of the Valleys. And through the efforts of these young people, in London, and Birmingham, and elsewhere, some other member of the family would have a chance of higher education, and a teacher's certificate, later on.

Despite these losses to the local community, a small proportion remained to leaven it. It was easy enough to recognize them, and not only by the fur coat. That was a sign of their independence, and of the fact that they enjoyed a comparatively prosperous way of life. It must be remembered that the coat was a reward for years of thrift in a period when the ownership of a motor-car was not at all common: that was why the coat was worn by teachers of more mature years, rather than by those on the ladder's lower rungs. The wearers of the coat were an élite within a group that was already an élite in society.

I referred to their independence. That was to be observed in the very way they moved, in their self-confidence, in the *joie de vivre* that seemed to possess them whenever they found themselves in one another's company. Two other things should be noted about them: they had money and spending power at a time when other people had but small means; also, in a society where the male was dominant, and traditionally the family's bread-winner, a woman with money in her pocket, and the right to spend it as she wished, stood apart from the rest. Another characteristic: some of these women used to smoke, doing so openly. But the most striking thing about them was their choice of holidays. In those days, long before people had acquired the habit of going to the Costa Brava — it wasn't until the 'fifties that they began doing that in the Rhondda — few families could afford to go on holiday, even for a few days. In contrast, a few of these teachers used to take their holidays on the continent, or even further afield. I well remember one calling to see us after coming back from North Africa: for my part, I felt as if I'd met someone who had just returned from Annwn[2] itself! I know of another who went on walking tours in the Alps, and of yet others who'd been to Belgium and Germany. Before the decade was out several had joined their Welsh-speaking compatriots on the cruises organized by Urdd Gobaith Cymru[3] on board the *Orduna*, to Norway, Spain and Portugal, and Morocco.

I've already mentioned the prohibition on marriage. This rule was relaxed at the beginning of the second world war, but it was too late for many of these women to think of marrying then: some had grown too fond of their independence, while others found themselves responsible for their parents, who by this time were elderly or infirm. In some instances the courting had gone on for many a long year, without hope of union in 'holy matrimony'. As a result some courtships came to an abrupt end, because one or other had tired of waiting and had met someone else who was readier to go to the altar. It was a sad sight, too, to see 'old' sweethearts wandering the paths of the Bwlch, or setting out on holiday in the company of other unmarried women. It should be added that some women had affairs with married men — which caused delicious scandal locally — and that between some couples there was a lesbian relationship, which was accepted without anyone's attaching much significance to it.

Some teachers flouted the ban by keeping their marriages a secret, in the hope no one would notice. In other cases a man and his prospective wife would move away from the area completely, and find work in one of England's cities. But it was more usual to conform, by marrying and giving up one's job. This created a different category, a rarer one, but one that was quite plain to see. 'Once a teacher, always a teacher,' — so the saying goes. Although these ex-teachers had married and raised a family, they still had the stamp of authority that sticks to anyone who has ever stood before a class of children. And it could be said that a few had managed to retain something of the independent spirit that had been characteristic of them in their years of freedom. They knew, too, from personal experience — and this was in a society that was quite macho in its attitudes — that a wife has the same capabilities as her husband, and the right, to say the least, to some of his privileges. For some of the more old-fashioned colliers the thought of taking a wife who had once been a teacher was something hard to entertain. Many were ready to rag mercilessly any man who did such a thing. One such worked in the Maendy pit, and I remember the regular line of defence the poor chap used to come up with for those who plagued him: 'My wife is an educated woman.' Fair play to him.

That story illustrates the gap between the uneducated majority and the privileged few. In a poor society where education offered a means of escape and the guarantee of a job, it possessed a special mystique. This was clearly to be seen in the home, for the educational process had created an inevitable gap between the privileged and the others. The goddess Education called for visible testimony of the cult by which she was worshipped, and these virgins became willing, well mannered priestesses at her shrine. It may be that some women had encouraged the process, but it's easier to believe that it usually had its origins in their adoring and credulous parents. The fact is there was created sometimes, within the home, a special sanctuary for them. This minority tended to live separately from their family in a room that was set aside for them, a circumstance that was a sign of their higher status and the sacrifice that had been made for their sakes. Even in less extreme cases, a special respect was shown towards a woman who had 'got on in the world'.

There were dangers, to be sure, in such separateness. Snobbery was the most evident thing about it, but sometimes, I imagine, a tension would arise between the teacher and the rest of her family. There was also a quite natural temptation to exploit her advantageous position in the home. The fur coat itself was the expression of this snobbery, this feeling of social superiority. But it was manifested by other means too. For example, one or two used to speak in an unusual way. As a social group, they consciously identified with the Welsh language and its culture, and took pride in them, but in some cases the pride gave rise to a strange phenomenon, namely a tendency to speak a Welsh that was too correct, affected, and almost anglicized! It was as if they needed a bit of Englishnesss to maintain the authority of their Welshness. Given the nature of my relationship with this group of teachers, it was only their Welsh I ever heard, but I understand from other witnesses that one or two spoke an over-rich English, an effective weapon in a society where an English accent was a badge of power.

One aspect of this snobbery was the tendency to make a show of themselves. That probably accounted, at least in part, for one particular incident at a chapel in the Pen-y-graig area. Three fur coats were to be seen there, and their owners — because they wished to make a splash — always tended to arrive late for the service. The minister had become fed up with this performance, for it interfered with the course of things. One evening the three teachers arrived at more or less the same moment, whereupon the voice from the pulpit said sardonically: 'As the three bears have arrived, we can now proceed with the service.'

An unexpected manifestation of this snobbery — and yes, I'm referring here to a wider bourgeois class — was the success enjoyed by a dentist, a German Jew, who had fled his own country at the outbreak of the second world war, and settled as a *rara avis* at the lower end of the Valley. Somehow or other he had become fashionable as a dentist. It was considered to be something of a privilege to go to him, as if this were a sign of your status in society. Indeed, some ladies used to travel the slow miles from the upper reaches of the Rhondda Fawr just to pay him wide-mouthed homage. Naturally, in such circumstances, it was often felt that the appropriate thing was to wear one's best clothes, including of course, the fur coat. But what these wretched women did not realize was that the dentist was an old Socialist, and that he had a unique tariff for his services. He charged according to the clothes you were wearing — a pound, say, for working-trousers, but five pounds for a fur coat! In this just man's surgery the most unwealthy of the exploiting classes paid dearly for their privilege.

I don't want to give the impression that these fur-clad teachers and their less fortunate sisters were all Welsh-speakers. And yet a very high proportion of them were, and it was quite definitely they who were the mainstay of Welsh cultural life in the two Valleys. Without them Urdd Gobaith Cymru wouldn't have taken such firm root, establishing its groups and branches here and there, and creating activity in the schools that was later to express itself in local and regional eisteddfodau, or in folk-singing concerts. Without them the local drama companies would have been short of leading players, and the same could be said of the chapels' drama companies in the 'thirties. It's only fair to note that some of them contributed with the same enthusiasm to those companies performing plays in English. Bearing in mind how barren the cultural life of the Rhondda is nowadays, one can only wonder at the bustle of those far-distant times.

Evening classes also flourished, where these women were just as ready to show their commitment. This continued right up to the beginning of the second world war, and I remember several of them attending the weekly Welsh Literature classes of T.J. Morgan at the Boys' Club in Treorci. In the life of church and chapel their contribution was equally indispensable. In their daily work, too, they kept the spirit of the Welsh language alive within an educational system that scorned it and tried to crush it to death. Later on it would be they, or rather a minority among them, who would fight to establish Welsh

Schools in the two Valleys, and make efforts at producing textbooks for the teaching of the Welsh language in the other schools.

The word today is 'feminism' but *'ffeministiaeth'* didn't even get into the supplement of the first volume (1967) of the University of Wales Dictionary. Is it right to mention the word in the context of this particular élite? Were they a protest movement against the condition of other women in less fortunate circumstances? Were they in some way a sisterhood similar to an order of nuns? In fact, I doubt whether they had any group consciousness. If they did, then they saw themselves as dedicated teachers, or as keen Welsh people, and not as a group of women. As far as I know, they didn't consider their maiden state (assumed or real) as having any value in itself. Rather, as in the case of nuns, it offered them a wider freedom, and the spur to direct their sexual energy towards worthy ends of a different kind.

On the other hand, it was clear that they took particular pleasure in one another's company — the daily train-journeys to and from school, the committee meetings and eisteddfodau in one place or another, and the tendency to go on holiday together. And this last gave them an opportunity of displaying their independence and status, since they usually put up at guest-houses or hotels that were of an appropriate standard. Indeed, the enjoyment of the status which they had earned was obviously important to them. And if we look closely at their contribution as a group, we can see that they placed before the imagination of other women a kind of lifestyle and behavioural possibilities that the rest wouldn't even have dreamed about had it not been for their example. Without any doubt, it was the need for female labour in the arms factories after 1939 which was to create the greatest revolution in the development of Rhondda women. Nevertheless, there was something quite pioneering in the lifestyle of those teachers in the 'thirties, and in many ways the 'broadening of horizons' which came in their wake was a creative, nourishing process, rather than a vulgar one lacking in good taste.

The fur coats continued to keep their owners warm throughout the war years, through the greying of middle age, and the wintry winds of old age. I don't recall ever seeing either blemish or spot on those everlastingly young pelts. They must have taken special care of them, placing them between warm, camphor-smelling sheets at each season's end. By the 'fifties the coat had ceased to be a symbol of defiance: it became, rather, a visible part of nostalgia for better days, for the verve and adventure of youth, for a way of life which had challenged the system.

Some time in the 'sixties it became the custom for students at English universities to wear their mothers' fur coats. Usually they were in tatters, even dirty and foul-smelling — an attempt on their owners' parts, perhaps, to demonstrate that they were in revolt against the bourgeois values of their parents. I myself felt a certain abhorrence for those furs, because they somehow brought into disrepute the forests of Siberia, Africa, the Himalayas, or the Andes. I realize now that my aversion had a deeper and more irrational basis. After all, I had been used to seeing the fur coat as a sign of noble effort. It had somehow been a challenge to the grey poverty of the Depression, a coat-of-arms in revolt against a system that gave victory to others, a bright spark that would turn, in the fullness of time, into the bonfire of the feminist movement. And here was a barbaric pelt on the backs of women who had come to college as a matter of course, rather than by personal effort and family sacrifice! I could feel no respect for such a thing. Twenty years later those furs too have completely disappeared and a generation has grown up which sees the fur coat as nothing more than proof of man's cruelty to animals. I have to confess that there remains in me a sneaking admiration for a garment that was such a part of my boyhood. And I keep in my memory the fragrance of those golden creatures who walked with their heads held high down the aisles of Bethesda. Alas, like the russet-red fox of Williams Parry[4], their fate was to be, and then cease to be, 'like a shooting star'.

Taliesin (75, Hydref, 1991)

An Holy Kiss

Robin Williams

A street pavement isn't the most ideal place to hold a conversation, especially if it's early morning and everyone's in a hurry to get to the shop or bank or office. What happens is that people pass one another with only a curt greeting, more or less echoing each other, like this: 'Hello! — Hello!' 'How are things? — How are things?' 'How are you? — How are you, then?' 'Fine day! — Fine!' 'Rain again! — Yes, rain again!', and so on.

In the morning bustle there's time only for short, polite, throw-away syllables. But at more leisurely moments we have quite deliberate ways of greeting one another. On these occasions it's not people's voices that are brought into play as much as their bodies. What they do then is not to pass flittingly by, but to wait patiently and intently for the act of recognition.

If rubbing noses is the Eskimo's way, in the West our custom is rather more hesitant. We extend the right hand towards the other person, grasp his or her right hand, and give it a light shake. Although quite recently I've observed that, on certain occasions, the left hand also comes in on the act, wrapping itself around the others until there's a bunch of four hands all doing the shaking.

On the mainland of Europe the mode of greeting is even more complicated. When Hetsch, a refugee from Hungary, came to live at Glanrafon when I was minister there, I noticed that gentleman's way of greeting my wife was to bow slightly, kick his left heel with a sharp click against his right, and then kiss the back of her hand.

But even further to the East, things are more dramatic still. There they literally embrace one another, and having kissed the one cheek, it is permissible to kiss the other, and sometimes the first cheek is kissed a second time. In writing to the small cells of churches that he had established, it was quite natural for Paul to end his epistle with the sentence: 'Salute one another with an holy kiss'.

During the 'eighties, half-a-dozen of us went to Turkey to film the story of the Seven Churches of Asia that the Book of Revelations talks about. Our plane landed in Izmir, and there to meet us was a Turk by the name of Mehmet Akargün. Having put our baggage safely to one side for a moment, the six visitors extended their right hands in the cold manner of the West, and each in turn shook hands with the foreigner.

After all the filming-gear had been inspected by the customs officers under the gaze of armed soldiers, Mehmet led us out to a small bus. Over the next fortnight that little chassis was to hold all the equipment, a good twenty boxes, and unwieldy odds-and-ends of various shapes and sizes. That bus was also to transport us and our personal luggage, not forgetting Mehmet and a member of the police-force who had been ordered to accompany us everywhere, as required by the Turkish Government.

The name of the minibus driver was Dinsher Hazirol, a thin young man with shiny black hair, eyes like two embers, and a most charming smile. As Mehmet introduced us each in turn to his partner, we reached out at arm's length towards Dinsher Hazirol, shaking his right hand formally. Unfortunately, none of us was able to speak Turkish. It's true that Mehmet had quite a good grasp of English, but Dinsher couldn't speak one syllable of that language.

Nevertheless, there are some strange virtues in the complex stuff of human nature. Despite the lack of a common language, there was some innate sympathy that insisted on growing between us strangers — that warmth which is able to turn foreigners into friends. Another magic blessing that helps to break down barriers is that strange mischievousness that we call a sense of humour.

So, having lived in each other's company from morn to night, day in day out, from one week to the next, not to mention travelling hundreds of miles through the great heat, Dinsher and I became firm friends. Whenever we had an hour to spare, I would sit in the seat next to the driver's, and there we would chatter away, he in Turkish and I in Welsh, using face and arms and hands and fingers to try to convey what we wanted to say. And when things went awry, we would scrawl pictures on a piece of paper in a laborious and hilarious attempt to explain the matter under discussion. Then we would both have a bout of laughter as we realized that we had at last understood each other. We laughed even more when we had completely misunderstood things!

Although I've gone into detail elsewhere about the time Dinsher and I changed a flat tyre under the palm trees in the city of Denizli, it's worth mentioning again the Turk's response that hot morning. Having put the lame vehicle back in working order by dint of sweating streams, and having washed our hands clean of grease and dust and oil, Dinsher's way of acknowledging the little help I had rendered him was to put an arm round my shoulder and say, to my great astonishment, 'Ah! Robin Hood!'

After three weeks in each other's company, the last morning came — time for us to be taken to the airport at Izmir. And after I had given him a small gift as a token of my thanks for everything, Dinsher suddenly came up to me, embraced my shoulders tightly, and kissed me first on the one cheek and then on the other.

It was a strangely unexpected experience, but one which showed that the young Turk had accepted me as a friend. And he had demonstrated it with the strong embrace of the East, and not with the limp, arm's-length handshake of the West.

What was painful, however, was the realization that it wasn't so much a greeting that had taken place between Dinsher Hazirol and myself on the morning of our departure, as a farewell. And a farewell for ever. But for as long as I live, I shall never forget that holy kiss on the airfield at Izmir.

Tynnu Llwch (Gwasg Gomer, 1991)

Notes on Authors and Texts

These notes are intended for readers who have only a little knowledge of the history, language, and literature of Wales. Further biographical and bibliographical details will be found in *The Oxford Companion to the Literature of Wales* (ed. Meic Stephens, 1986, 1990); see also the monographs in the *Writers of Wales* series (eds. Meic Stephens and R. Brinley Jones).

Owen Morgan Edwards (1858–1920), one of the pioneers of modern Welsh prose, was born and brought up at Coed-y-pry, a small farmhouse near Llanuwchllyn in Merioneth. Educated at the U.C.W., Aberystwyth, and at Balliol College, Oxford, he was appointed Fellow and Tutor in History at Lincoln College, Oxford, in 1889. Returning to Wales in 1907 as Chief Inspector of Schools, he lived for the rest of his life in his home village. He devoted his immense energies to the fostering of education through the medium of Welsh and, in all his many writings, encouraged the people of Wales to learn about their country's history and literature. His description of the village school, and the infamous practice of the Welsh Not which flourished in many parts of Wales during the latter part of the nineteenth century, is taken from the opening chapter of his autobiography, *Clych Atgof* (1906).

1 Sunday Schools, founded in Wales during the last decade of the eighteenth century, were primarily intended for the religious instruction of the common people. Under the leadership of Thomas Charles (1755-1814), they spread rapidly, especially among the Methodists. Attended by young and old, male and female, the schools were largely responsible for ensuring that Nonconformist congregations became literate in the Welsh language and thus equipped to read the Bible.

2 The first verse of a hymn by Morgan Rhys (1716–74).

3   The Society for Promoting Christian Knowledge was founded in London in 1699. Its aims were the spreading of the Gospel in foreign lands and the establishment of charity schools, where children were taught to read and write. The Society's membership was confined to the Church of England, but some of its publications, including two editions of the Bible, were in the Welsh language.

Eluned Morgan (1870–1938) was the daughter of Lewis Jones (1836–1904), a founder of the Welsh settlement in Patagonia. Educated in Wales, she took charge of a school for girls at Trelew, the town named after her father, and edited the colony's Welsh newspaper. She lived in Wales from about 1903, but in 1918 settled in Patagonia, where she became prominent in Welsh religious and cultural life. Having made her literary début in *Cymru*, the magazine edited by O.M. Edwards, whom she greatly admired, she went on to publish a good deal of journalism and four travel-books.

1   The writer was born on board ship during a voyage to Patagonia; she was given the name Morgan because her parents took it to mean 'sea-born'.

Robert Williams Parry (1884–1956), poet, was born at Tal-y-sarn in Dyffryn Nantlle, Caernarfonshire. He was a teacher at schools in England and Wales until his appointment in 1921 to a lectureship at the U.C.N.W., Bangor, where he had been an undergraduate; he lived thereafter at Bethesda. Although he published only two volumes of poetry, he is among the most celebrated Welsh poets of the twentieth century. His poems are much admired for their lyrical response to nature and their observations on the transitoriness of human life.

1   A line from '*Cywydd y Farn*' by Goronwy Owen (1723–69).

William John Gruffydd (1881–1954), poet, scholar, and critic, was born at Bethel in the parish of Llanddeiniolen, Caernarfonshire, and educated at Jesus College, Oxford, where he came under the influence of O.M. Edwards. In 1906 he was appointed to a lectureship in the Celtic Department of U.C., Cardiff, and became Professor of Welsh there in 1918. From 1922 until 1951 he was editor of the influential magazine *Y Llenor*, in which he wrote trenchantly about Welsh and world affairs. A Nonconformist by conviction, he found all formalized systems of religion and politics uncongenial, and was highly critical of many eminent Welshmen and institutions of his day. The mock-obituary of Lemuel Parry (a type rather than any recognizable individual) is a good example of his scathing style. W.J. Gruffydd was also a notable poet, a respected scholar, and briefly Member of Parliament for the University of Wales.

1 Llanfihangel Mechdeyrn, a fictitious name, translates as the Church of Michael the Overlord (or Tyrant).
2 Matthews Ewenni was the name by which the preacher Edward Matthews (1813–92) was generally known; he was a minister with the Calvinistic Methodists at Ewenni, near Bridgend, Glamorgan. He delighted his congregations by a droll use of the Glamorgan dialect of Welsh and his dramatic pulpit-style.
3 This reference is to the Established Church (the Anglican Church, the Church of England) as distinct from the various Nonconformist denominations.
4 The Church of England was disestablished in Wales in 1920; the Anglican ecclesiastical province created in that year is known as the Church in Wales.
5 Abraham Wood (1699?–1799) was the founder of a large family of Welsh gypsies, many of whom were gifted harp-players; gypsies are known in Welsh as 'teulu Abram Wood' ('Abraham Wood's family').
6 The Gorsedd of Bards of the Isle of Britain, invented by Edward Williams (Iolo Morganwg, 1747–1826) in 1792, admits eminent Welsh people to its orders in recognition of their outstanding contributions to the cultural life of Wales; it is now part of the ceremonies of the National Eisteddfod.
7 Gwalia, a name for Wales, derived partly from Latin, was popular in Victorian times, and is used here for its period flavour.

Thomas Herbert Parry-Williams (1887–1975), poet, essayist, and scholar, was born at Rhyd-ddu, Caernarfonshire, and educated at the U.C.W., Aberystwyth. In 1912, while still a student, he won both the Chair and Crown at the National Eisteddfod, a feat he was to repeat three years later. From 1920 until his retirement in 1952, he was Professor of Welsh at his old College. In both his verse and prose he rejected any attempt to give absolute meaning to life, but was fascinated by its complexity and mystery. He was the first Welsh writer to devote himself to the essay form, publishing more than a hundred during his lifetime, and many writers were to use his essays as models for their own writing. A small selection of his essays has been translated by Meic Stephens under the title *The White Stone* (1987).

1. The Red Cobbler of Rhuddlan, in a Welsh nursery rhyme, goes to drown a cat in a river, but the animal escapes from the sack, and he becomes famous for his incompetence.
2. A quotation from the hymn '*Gras yn Gorchfygu*' by William Williams (Pantycelyn, 1717–91).

John Owen Williams (1892–1973) was a native of Bethesda, a village in the slate-quarrying district of Caernarfonshire. He is remembered chiefly for his collaboration with Jennie Thomas (1898–1979) in the writing of *Llyfr Mawr y Plant*, a book for children, of which four volumes appeared between 1931 and 1975. This book delighted Welsh children at a time when there was a dearth of reading material in the language. J.O. Williams also published a novel and two collections of essays.

Saunders Lewis (1893–1985) is generally considered to be the greatest Welsh writer of the twentieth century. He was born in Wallasey in Cheshire and educated at Liverpool University, where he studied English and French. After active service in the first world war, he joined the staff of the Welsh Department at U.C., Swansea, in 1922, but was dismissed from his post in 1936 after he, and two other leaders of the Welsh Nationalist Party, were found guilty of an act of arson at Penyberth on the Llŷn peninsula. He resumed his career in 1952 on his appointment as Lecturer in Welsh at U.C., Cardiff. Dramatist, novelist, poet, critic, literary historian, and scholar, he excelled at every form he attempted. His work is informed by a passionate love of Wales, seen in the context of European culture and the Roman Catholic faith, to which he was converted in 1932.

1. R.T. Jenkins (1881–1969), the historian and author, one of whose essays appears on pp. 34.
2. The Welsh Nationalist Party, or Plaid Genedlaethol Cymru (now known as Plaid Cymru), was founded in 1925 by a group of intellectuals among whom Saunders Lewis was pre-eminent; he was President of the Party from 1926 to 1939. Saunders Lewis's argument in favour of European unity, expressed here as early as 1930, was central to the Party's philosophy from the beginning and a constant theme in all his writings.

Robert Beynon (1881–1953), a native of Pontyberem, Carmarthenshire, was for forty-two years the Calvinistic Methodist minister at Abercraf. A poet and hymn-writer, he won the Crown at the National Eisteddfod in 1922. He published only one collection of essays, *Dydd Calan* (1931).

Thomas Gwynn Jones (1871–1949), poet, novelist, translator, dramatist, and scholar, was born at Betws-yn-rhos, Denbighshire. He began his career as a journalist but was appointed Lecturer in Welsh at the U.C.W., Aberystwyth, in 1913 and to the Gregynog Chair of Welsh Literature six years later. A prolific writer, he excelled as a poet, in both the traditional metres and in new, experimental styles of his own invention. His major poems employ Celtic legend and classical Welsh diction to portray some of the great issues facing modern Man in an age of materialism and philistinism.

Robert Thomas Jenkins (1881–1969), historian and author, was born in Liverpool but brought up at Bala, Merioneth. Educated at the U.C.W., Aberystwyth, and at Trinity College, Cambridge, he was appointed Lecturer in Welsh History at the U.C.N.W., Bangor, in 1930, and later Professor. He wrote mainly about the history of Wales in the eighteenth and nineteenth centuries; he also published short stories, essays, and a novel in Welsh. The style of all his writings was colloquial, sometimes perambulatory, but always highly readable and informative. It was he who was mainly responsible for editing *The Dictionary of Welsh Biography* (1953).

1 A translation of the title of one of the author's own books, *Yr Apêl at Hanes* (1930).
2 The author was for some years a teacher in Brecon, before moving to Cardiff.
3 Llangeitho is a village in Cardiganshire, known as 'the Mecca of Welsh Methodism' on account of its association with Daniel Rowland (1713–90), the preacher who led the Revival of 1762.
4 The town of Bala in Merioneth became a centre of Methodism after Thomas Charles (1755–1814), the leader of the second generation of Welsh Methodists, settled there in 1783. Charles's Dictionary, *Geiriadur Ysgrythrawl* (4 vols. 1805–1811) presented new learning about the history and geography of the Bible lands, together with informed discussion of Biblical ideas.
5 Llanddewibrefi is a village in Cardiganshire associated with St. David, the patron saint of Wales, who was said to have preached there, the ground miraculously rising so that all could see and hear him.
6 Maesyronnen, Heol Awst, Capel Cildwrn, Salem, Cefncymerau are some of the oldest and most important chapels of Welsh Nonconformity.
7 Ann Griffiths (1776–1805), hymn-writer, was born at Dolwar Fach in the parish of Llanfihangel-yng-Ngwynfa, Montgomeryshire. She was converted to Methodism during a sermon

preached at Llanfihangel in 1796 and joined the Methodist Fellowship at Pontrobert in the following year. She is among the finest of Welsh hymn-writers and many of her hymns are still popular.
8 The National Eisteddfod is proclaimed a year-and-a-day in advance in the district where next it is to be held.
9 The valley of the Rhondda Fawr is in the old parish of Ystradyfodwg.

Iorwerth Cyfeiliog Peate (1901–82), poet and scholar, was born in the parish of Llanbryn-Mair, Montgomeryshire, and educated at the U.C.W., Aberystwyth. He joined the staff of the National Museum of Wales in 1927 and later became the first Curator of the Welsh Folk Museum at St Fagans, near Cardiff. In all his writings he was a champion of the Nonconformist, Radical folk-culture into which he had been born. An uncompromising pacifist, he suffered persecution for his beliefs during the second world war. The essay by which he is represented here describes his experience while visiting the Epynt district of Breconshire shortly before it was taken over by the War Department for the purposes of establishing a military base.

1 The essay's title is a quotation from a verse found in manuscripts of the late medieval period, sometimes wrongly ascribed to the poet Taliesin. The verse refers to the ancient British, the original inhabitants of the island of Britain:

> 'Their lord they shall praise,
> Their language they shall keep,
> Their land they shall lose,
> Except wild Wales.'

2 John Penry (1563–93), Puritan pamphleteer and martyr, was born at Cefnbrith, a house near Llangammarch in Breconshire, on the northern slopes of Epynt. He was executed on suspicion of being the 'Martin Marprelate' who had written a number of tracts attacking the corruption of bishops in the Church of England.
3 William Williams (1717–91), of Pantycelyn, one of the greatest of all Welsh hymn-writers, was born in Carmarthenshire but educated at a Nonconformist Academy near Talgarth in Breconshire, and became an Anglican curate in the same county. On being refused priest's orders in the Church of England on account of his activities with the Methodists, he devoted himself entirely to the Methodist cause.

David Gwenallt Jones (1899–1968), poet, critic, and scholar, was born at Allt-wen, near Pontardawe in the Swansea Valley. During the first world war he was imprisoned on account of his conscientious objection to the war, which he based on Christian pacifism, international Socialism, and Welsh national feeling. He later studied at the U.C.W., Aberystwyth, and became a Lecturer in the Welsh Department there. He was eventually reconciled to a religious position within the Calvinistic Methodist Church, but never ceased arguing for social justice. He won the Chair at the National Eisteddfod in 1926 and 1931. Many of his poems, which were published in five volumes during his lifetime, deal with the industrial communities of south Wales.

1 Sunday School, see note on p. 217.
2 Keir Hardie (1856–1915), miners' leader and founder of the Independent Labour Party, was a Scotsman who was elected Member of Parliament for Merthyr Tydfil in 1900 — the first Socialist to be returned to Parliament as member for a constituency in Wales.
3 'There will be many wonders', a hymn written by Richard and Joseph Williams of Liverpool.

Ffransis George Payne (1900–92), folk-historian, was born and brought up at Kington, on the border between Radnorshire and Herefordshire. Educated at the U.C., Cardiff, he joined the staff of the National Museum of Wales in 1936 and became Head of the Department of Material Culture at the Welsh Folk Museum in 1962. He wrote on the county of Radnor in the *Crwydro Cymru* series (2 vols., 1966, 1968) and a selection of his essays was published under the title *Cwysau* in 1980.

1 Llundain Fach (lit. Little London), a township near Llangeitho in Cardiganshire; the name seems to have no particular significance and may be only a corruption of some other.
2 Sarah Siddons (1755–1831), actress, was born at the Shoulder of Mutton inn in Brecon, the daughter of the strolling players Roger Kemble and Sarah Ward.
3 The Revd. Joseph Jenkins (1743–1819), Baptist minister of Wrexham, was well-known for his tirades against all sorts of worldly pleasures.
4 A quotation from a poem by Robert ap Gwilym Ddu (Robert Williams, 1766–1850).

Jac Lewis Williams (1918–77), scholar and author, was born at Aberarth, Cardiganshire, and educated at the U.C.W., Aberystwyth.

From 1945 to 1956 he was a Lecturer at Trinity College, Carmarthen, and was appointed Professor of Education at Aberystwyth in 1960. A prolific writer for the periodical press, mostly on the subject of bilingual education, he was a staunch supporter of the Welsh Schools Movement and a champion of the federal structure of the University of Wales. He also published a number of short stories and essays.

1   A phrase from the poem '*Y Llwynog*' ('The Fox') by R. Williams Parry (1884–1956).
2   Sunday School, see note on page 217.
3   'Behold the day is dawning yonder,' the first line of a hymn by John Thomas (1730–1803) of Rhaeadr.
4   A verse from a hymn by Benjamin Francis (1734–99).

Edward Morgan Humphreys (1882–1955), journalist and novelist, was born in Dyffryn Ardudwy, Merioneth. He joined the staff of the weekly newspaper *Y Genedl Gymreig* in 1905 and was appointed editor three years later; he also wrote for other papers, including the *Liverpool Daily Post* and the *Manchester Guardian*. For further details about the painting of Salem by Curnow Vosper (1866–1942) see Tal Williams, *Salem: Painting and Chapel* (1991).

1   *Yr Herald Cymraeg* (lit. 'The Welsh Herald'), a weekly newspaper established in Caernarfon in 1855.

Thomas John Morgan (1907–86), scholar and essayist, was born at Glais in the Swansea Valley, and educated at U.C., Swansea. He began his academic career as a Lecturer in the Department of Welsh at U.C., Cardiff, and became Registrar of the University of Wales in 1951, but returned to Swansea as Professor of Welsh ten years later. His most important work of scholarship was a study of the mutation system in Welsh. The essay was the literary form which most attracted him and in it he displayed his wit and wide interests. He also wrote literary criticism and, with W.J. Gruffydd, was editor of the magazine *Y Llenor*.

1   Prys Morgan, one of the author's sons, has confirmed that the family outing was to the town of Pontypridd.
2   Branwen, daughter of Llyr, in the Second Branch of the Mabinogion, is married to Matholwch, King of Ireland. When war breaks out between the Welsh and the Irish, she is put to work in the kitchen of the Irish court, but manages to send a message to Wales by means of a tame starling.
3   Iolo Goch, Guto'r Glyn, and Tudur Aled, were three poets of the medieval period, renowned for their praise-poetry addressed to patrons.

4 Llew Llaw Gyffes is the hero of the Fourth Branch of the Mabinogion. Gronw Pebr attempts to kill him with a spear but he escapes in the form of an eagle.
5 One of the major forms of Welsh prosody. The most popular type consists of rhyming couplets, each line of seven syllables, written in *cynghanedd*, with the accent falling alternately on the last and penultimate lines.
6 An ancient and intricate system of sound-chiming within a line of verse, involving the serial repetition of consonants in precise order. Over the centuries a great deal of Welsh poetry has been written according to the rules of *cynghanedd*.
7 Goronwy Owen (1723–69), poet, a native of Anglesey. His great ambition was to write an epic poem in Welsh on Miltonic lines. His letters, published in various journals, were widely accepted as canons of literary criticism.

David John Williams (1885–1970, prose-writer, was born at Rhydcymerau in Carmarthenshire, the countryside and inhabitants of which he described with great affection in his autobiography and short stories. After working in the coalmines of the Rhondda, he was educated at the U.C.W., Aberystwyth, and at Jesus College, Oxford, where he read English. He was a teacher of English at the Grammar School in Fishguard for many years. Among the first members of Plaid Cymru, in 1936 he took part with Saunders Lewis and Lewis Valentine in the symbolic act of burning a bombing-school at Penyberth on the Llŷn peninsula, for which he spent nine months in Wormwood Scrubs — 'one of his majesty's palaces'. His volume of autobiography, *Hen Dy Fferm* (1953), was translated by Waldo Williams as *The Old Farmhouse* (1961).

1 Gwalia, see note on page 219.
2 Prosser Rhys (1901–45), poet, editor, and publisher.
3 Gwynfor Evans (born 1912) was, from 1945 until 1981, President of Plaid Cymru; he became the Party's first Member of Parliament when he was elected to represent Carmarthenshire in 1966. One of the Party's aims in 1953 was Dominion Status for Wales within the British Commonwealth.
4 *Y Faner*, a national weekly newspaper, edited in 1953 by Gwilym R. Jones; Saunders Lewis contributed a regular column entitled '*Cwrs y Byd*'.

Edward Tegla Davies (1880–1967), prose-writer, was born at Llandegla-yn-ial, Denbighshire, a quarryman's son, and later became a minister with the Wesleyan Methodists. He published several collections of essays, books for children, and a novel, *Gŵr Pen y Bryn* (1923), translated as *The Master of Penybryn* (1975).

1   Bishop William Morgan (1545–1604), translator of the Bible into Welsh.

Harri Gwynn (1913–85), poet and essayist, was born in London but brought up at Penrhyndeudraeth in Merioneth. He worked as a teacher, civil servant, journalist, and broadcaster, and also as a farmer in Eifionydd. He published two volumes of verse and a collection of essays, *Y Fuwch a'i Chynffon* (1954, reprinted 1993). Eirwen Gwynn is Harri Gwynn's widow.

Ifor Williams (1881–1965), scholar, was born at Tregarth, near Bethesda, Caernarfonshire, and educated at the U.C.N.W., Bangor, where he later became Professor of Welsh. He was a popular broadcaster and many of his radio talks, including the one by which he is represented here, were published. A selection of his most important scholarly articles was edited by Rachel Bromwich in the volume *The Beginnings of Early Welsh Poetry* (1972).

1   Carnedd Llywelyn is a mountain to the south-east of Bethesda (alt. 1,062 m.); Carnedd Dafydd (alt. 1,044 m.) stands near by.
2   Goronwy Owen (1723–69), poet, see note on page 225.
3   John Thomas Jôb (1867–1938), poet, was at one time a minister with the Calvinistic Methodists at Bethesda.

Islwyn Ffowc Elis (born 1924), novelist and essayist, was born in Wrexham, Denbighshire, but brought up as a farmer's son in Dyffryn Ceiriog. Educated at the U.C.N.W., Bangor, he became a minister with the Calvinistic Methodists, but later worked for the BBC and the Welsh Books Council; at the time of his retirement he was Lecturer in Welsh at St. David's U.C., Lampeter. His novels, especially those about the Lleifior family, won a new popularity for the Welsh novel, particularly among young people.

1   The Gododdin were a British tribe whose disastrous assault on Catraeth (Catterick in modern Yorkshire) about the year 600 was the subject of an heroic poem attributed to Aneirin.
2   Cadwallon, King of Gwynedd in the seventh century; Rhodri, King of Gwynedd and Powys in the ninth century; Gruffudd ap Llywelyn, King of Wales for a brief period after 1055; Llywelyn ap Gruffudd, known as the Last Prince, ruled over Gwynedd in the thirteenth century, but was killed by English troops in 1282.
3   Offa's Dyke is an earthwork which runs, with interruptions, from the river Wye near Monmouth to Prestatyn; it was prob-

ably built by Offa, King of Mercia, as a boundary between his territory and that of the Welsh, in the eighth century.
4   William Morgan (1545–1604), translator of the Bible into Welsh; Williams Pantycelyn (William Williams, 1717–91), hymn-writer see note on p.222; O.M. Edwards (1858–1920), see note on page 217.
5   Gwales, the island of Grassholm, off the coast of Pembrokeshire. In the Mabinogion the seven who return from the fighting in Ireland spend eighty years on the island, without ageing or any recollection of their former sorrows, until they are obliged to leave when one of their number opens a door looking on to Cornwall.
6   The Mabinogion, a collection of medieval tales generally considered to be the most outstanding masterpiece of Welsh prose.

Robert Gerallt Jones (born 1934), poet, novelist, and critic. Born and brought up on the Llŷn peninsula in Caernarfonshire, the son of an Anglican clergyman, he was educated at public schools in England and later read English at the U.C.N.W., Bangor. He has been an English teacher, a Lecturer in Education, Principal of a college in Jamaica, Warden of Llandovery College, a tutor in the Extra-Mural Department at the U.C.W., Aberystwyth, and Warden of Gregynog, the University of Wales centre in Powys. One of the most prolific of contemporary Welsh writers, he has published verse, novels, and literary criticism on a wide variety of subjects, and he won the Prose Medal at the National Eisteddfod with a novel in 1977.

1   *Yr Herald Cymraeg* and *Y Cymro* are weekly newspapers.

Ifan Gruffydd (1896–1971), prose-writer, was born at Llangristiolus in Anglesey, where he lived for most of his life. He was a farm-labourer and caretaker employed by the local council, but came to literary prominence with the publication of his two volumes of autobiography, *Gwr o Baradwys* (1963) and *Tân yn y Siambar* (1966), both of which are masterly portraits of country life in Anglesey between 1900 and 1930.

Gomer Morgan Roberts (1904–93), historian and prose-writer, was born at Llandybie, Carmarthenshire, and became a coal-miner at the age of thirteen. He was educated at the Theological College in Aberystwyth and entered the Calvinistic Methodist ministry in 1930. A prolific writer, especially on hymnology and the history of his denomination, he published two collections of essays and a volume on upland Glamorgan in the *Crwydro Cymru* series.

1. Ivor Emmanuel, a popular singer and entertainer, perhaps best-known for his part as the Welsh soldier in the film *Rorke's Drift* who rouses his comrades with a rendering of 'Men of Harlech'.
2. The Calvinistic Methodist or Presbyterian Church of Wales, is called the Old Connexion because it was the first to break away from the Church of England (in 1811).
3. John James Williams (1869–1954), poet and short story writer, wrote mainly about the industrial districts of Glamorgan, especially Ynysybwl where he once worked as a collier.
4. Pantycelyn, see note on page 222.
5. Peter Hughes Griffiths (1871–1937), minister and author, was minister of Charing Cross Chapel in London from 1902 until the end of his life.
6. The second verse of a hymn by William Williams (Pantycelyn, 1717–91).
7. Aneurin Bevan (1897–1960), Labour politician, Member of Parliament for Ebbw Vale from 1929 to 1960.
8. A quotation from the poem '*Maes Bosworth*' by Eben Fardd (Ebenezer Thomas, 1802–63).
9. Siencyn Penhydd was the nickname of Jenkin Thomas (1746–1807), Methodist exhorter, a native of Margam, who was notorious on account of his unkempt appearance and unusual preaching style.

Kate Roberts (1891–1985), novelist and short-story writer, was born at Rhosgadfan, a slate-quarrying village near Caernarfon. Educated at the U.C.N.W., Bangor, she became a teacher of Welsh at schools in Ystalyfera and Aberdare. From 1935 to 1956 she was the publisher of the weekly newspaper *Y Faner*. She is generally considered to be the most distinguished Welsh novelist of the twentieth century and a masterly exponent of Welsh prose-style. Many of her stories are about the district of her youth but in her later work she explored the problems of old age and the loneliness of urban living. A selection of her writing has been translated by Joseph P. Clancy under the title *The World of Kate Roberts* (1991).

1. Margiad Evans, the pen-name of the novelist Peggy Eileen Whistler (1909–58); the quotation is from her book *A Ray of Darkness* (1952).
2. The Black Book of Carmarthen is one of the most important collections of medieval Welsh manuscripts.
3. William Llŷn (1534/5–80), poet.

Dafydd Rowlands (born 1931), poet, essayist, and novelist, was born at Pontardawe, Glamorgan, where he still lives, and educated at U.C., Swansea. A former teacher and Lecturer in Welsh at Trinity College, Carmarthen, he won the Crown at the National Eisteddfod in 1969 and 1972, and the Prose Medal with his collection of essays, *Ysgrifau yr Hanner Bardd* in 1972.

1 David Lloyd George (1863–1945), politician and statesman, was Prime Minister of Great Britain from 1916 to 1922.
2 Sunday School, see note on page 217.
3 A verse from the poem '*Y Rhai sydd Ynom*' by Gwilym R. Jones (1903–93).

John Griffith Williams (1915–87), prose-writer, was born at Llangwnadl in Caernarfonshire. He left school at the age of fifteen to work as a carpenter, and later became a teacher of woodwork. His second volume of autobiography, *Maes Mihangel* (1974), ends during the second world war, during which he was imprisoned for his refusal on Nationalist grounds to be conscripted. He also published a novel about Owain Glyndwr and a study of the *Rubaiyat* of Omar Khayyam.

1 The author was first incarcerated at Walton Prison, Liverpool, and later at Strangeways in Manchester.
2 Sir Thomas Artemus Jones (1871–1943), a Denbighshire man, and a county court judge. As Chairman of the North Wales Conscientious Objectors' Tribunal from 1939 to 1941, he became identified with the view that objection to military conscription was permissible only when couched in religious terms.
3 Ben Owen (1896–1960) was a Congregational minister at Llanberis who supported conscientious objectors in their stand against military conscription.
4 J.E. Jones (1905–70) was for many years Secretary of Plaid Cymru; the Three Men of Penyberth were the Nationalist leaders who set fire to part of an RAF bombing-school on the Llŷn peninsula in 1936, namely Saunders Lewis (1893–1985), D.J. Williams (1885–1970), and Lewis Valentine (1893–1986); Jack Dan was J.E. Daniel (1902–62), eminent Nationalist thinker; Wil Berry (1914–82) was an active member of Plaid Cymru at Llanrwst; Fred Jarman was A.O.H. Jarman (born 1911), later Professor of Welsh at U.C., Cardiff; Trefor Morgan (1914–70), a prominent Nationalist; Owain Glyndwr (c. 1354–c.1416), national hero; the two Llywelyns, Llywelyn ap Iorwerth (Llywelyn Fawr, 1173–1240) and Llywelyn ap Gruffudd (The Last Prince, c. 1225–1282).

5   Epynt, a Welsh-speaking farming district in north Breconshire, cleared of its people to make a British military base during the second world war; see the essay by Iorwerth C. Peate.

Robert Tudur Jones (born 1921), church historian and prose-writer, was born at Llanystumdwy in Caernarfonshire, but brought up at Rhyl in Flintshire; he was educated at the Universities of Wales, Oxford, and Strasbourg. He was a Congregational minister at Aberystwyth before becoming Professor of Church History and later Principal of Bala-Bangor Theological College. Besides many works of scholarship in both Welsh and English, he has published some of his occasional writings under the title *Darganfod Harmoni* (1982).

1   Llywelyn ap Iorwerth (1173–1240), also known as Llywelyn Fawr (the Great), was the greatest of all the rulers of medieval Wales. In 1205 he married Joan (1195–1237), known in Welsh as Siwan, the daughter of King John of England.
2   Thomas and Richard Bulkeley, members of the family which owned substantial lands in Anglesey and north-west Wales from the middle of the fifteenth century.

Alun Llywelyn-Williams (1913–88), poet and prose-writer, was born in Cardiff and educated at the U.C. there. He saw active service with the Royal Welsh Fusiliers during the second world war. Appointed Director of Extra-Mural Studies at the U.C.N.W., Bangor, in 1948, he held a personal chair at that College until his retirement. His three volumes of verse won him a reputation as an accomplished poet with a scholarly, humane, and cultured view of the world. He is represented here by an extract from a volume of autobiography, *Gwanwyn yn y Ddinas* (1975).

1   Urdd Gobaith Cymru, known in English as the Welsh League of Youth, was founded by Sir Ifan ab Owen Edwards in 1922.
2   Medraud, Bedwyr, King Marc, and Trystan, heroes of Arthurian romance.
3   A quotation from an *englyn* by Dewi Wyn o Eifion (David Owen, 1784–1841), to the Menai Bridge.
4   Cantre'r Gwaelod (lit. 'The Lower Hundred'), in Welsh folklore, was said to have been a drowned kingdom under what is today Cardigan Bay.

Urien Wiliam (born 1929), novelist and playwright, was born in Swansea and educated at the U.C. there. He was Senior Lecturer in Welsh at Barry College of Education (later the Polytechnic of Wales) until his retirement in 1981. He has won the Drama Medal at the

National Eisteddfod on two occasions, and he also written for television.

1 Llandrindod won its reputation as a spa town in the nineteenth century: people went there to drink water in the Pump Room in the belief that it had medicinal properties.
2 Urdd Gobaith Cymru, see note on p. 230.

Glyn Mills Ashton (1910–91), prose-writer, was born in Barry, Glamorgan, and educated at the U.C., Cardiff, where he later became Curator of the Salesbury Library. He was the author of several humorous novels, written under the pseudonym Wil Cwch Angau, as well as works of scholarship.

1 Chartism was a mass-movement in favour of social and political reform in the mid-nineteenth century. In Wales it reached its climax in 1839 with an insurrection, when about 20,000 workers marched on the town of Newport in Monmouthshire.
2 Richard Mills (1809–44), musician, had a son of the same name (1840–1903) who carried on the family's musical tradition.
3 Charles Ashton (1848–99), bibliophile, was put to work in the lead-mines of Dylife at the age of twelve. He later became a policeman, but towards the end of his life suffered from mental illness.
4 Dewi Wyn o Eifion, the bardic name of David Owen (1784–1841).
5 Radyr is a northern suburb of Cardiff, just a few miles from Barry.
6 A quotation from '*Y Gorwel*', an *englyn* by Dewi Emrys (David Emrys James, 1881–1952), on the subject of the horizon.
7 Daniel Rowland (1713–90), see note on page 221.
8 An *englyn* is a traditional form in Welsh prosody, a poem with four lines and alliteration.
9 The last line of '*Cymru*', a sonnet by D. Gwenallt Jones (1899–1968).

Gwilym Richard Jones (1903–93), poet and journalist, was born at Tal-y-sarn in Caernarfonshire. He was editor of the newspaper *Y Faner* from 1945 until his retirement in 1977. As well as poetry, he wrote two novels about the effects of poverty and the first world war on the quarrying communities of Dyffryn Nantlle, and he won the Chair, Crown, and Prose Medal at the National Eisteddfod.

Dyfnallt Morgan (1917–94), prose-writer, critic, and translator, was born at Dowlais, Merthyr Tydfil, Glamorgan. He was a forestry worker, hospital orderly, and BBC producer before becoming a Lecturer in the Department of Extra-Mural Studies at the U.C.N.W., Bangor. He published poetry, critical studies of Gwenallt Jones, T.H. Parry-Williams, and Waldo Williams, wrote plays for radio, and translated many *libretti* into Welsh.

1   A reference to the line '*Ti wyddost beth dywed fy nghalon*' ('You know what my heart says'), from the song by John Ceiriog Hughes (1832–87).
2   Griffith John (1831–1912), Welsh missionary to China.
3   Urdd, see note on page 230.
4   A quotation from the poem '*Y Dilyw, 1939*' ('The Deluge, 1939') by Saunders Lewis (1893–1985).

R. Emyr Jones (born 1923), poet and prose-writer, was born at Tregarth in Caernarfonshire, the son of a quarryman. He saw active service during the second world war and later worked for the Young Farmers' Clubs in Merionethshire. He has published three novels and selections of his essays and radio talks.

1   Tommy Farr (1913–86), boxer, of Tonypandy, British and Commonwealth champion, who lost narrowly on points to Joe Louis in the World Heavyweight Boxing Championship in New York in August 1937.

Selyf Roberts (1912–95), novelist and short-story writer, was born at Corwen in Merioneth, and followed a career in banking. He won the Prose Medal at the National Eisteddfod in 1955 for a collection of essays. He published a number of novels and two collections of stories, and translated Lewis Carroll's *Alice's Adventures in Wonderland* into Welsh.

Eirwen Gwynn (born 1916), was born in Liverpool, but was taken to live in Anglesey when she was twelve. Educated at the U.C.N.W., Bangor, where she read Physics, she married Harri Gwynn in 1942 and they worked in Government departments in London. Returning to Wales in 1950, they took up farming in Eifionydd. She was a lecturer with the Workers' Education Association until her retirement in 1979. Most of her eight books deal with scientific and philosophical subjects.

1   George M Ll. Davies (1880–1949), advocate of peace.
2   J. R Jones (1911–70), philosopher.
3   Gwilym O. Roberts (1919–86), minister and psychiatrist.

David Tecwyn Lloyd (1914–92), essayist and critic, was born at

Glanyrafon, near Corwen in Merioneth. Educated at the U.C.N.W., Bangor, he was employed by the Workers' Education Association, as a Lecturer at Coleg Harlech, and as deputy editor of the newspaper *Y Cymro* from 1956 to 1961. He then joined the staff of the Extra-Mural Department at the U.C.W., Aberystwyth, where he remained until his retirement. His essays have an idiosyncratic sense of humour, a wide-ranging curiosity, and a passionate love of Welsh rural culture.

1 The poet D. Gwenallt Jones (1899–1968) whose essay appears on pp. 46; he wrote a biography of the humourist Idwal Jones (1895–1937) which was published in 1958.
2 The former home of Michael D. Jones (1822–98), patriot and Principal of the Independent College at Bala.
3 Pantycelyn, the hymn-writer William Williams (1717–91), see the note on page 222.

Hafina Clwyd (born 1936), journalist and prose-writer, was born at Gwyddelwern, near Corwen in Merioneth, and educated at the Normal Collage, Bangor. From 1957 until 1979 she was a teacher in London and a prominent member of the London Welsh Association; she later became editor of the weekly magazine, *Y Faner*.

1 Noson lawen (lit. 'a merry night'), an evening of traditional entertainment including songs, recitation, and story-telling.
2 Urdd Gobaith Cymru, see note on p.230.
3 The Honourable Society of Cymmrodorion, a cultural and patriotic society founded in 1751 among Welsh people living in London, and still in existence.
4 'And after battle . . .', a quotation from '*Y Gododdin*', a poem attributed to Aneirin (fl. late 6th cent.); the line ends, 'there was silence.'

Rhydwen Williams (1916-97), poet and novelist, was born at Pentre in the Rhondda Valley. He became a Baptist minister and later worked in television. A prolific writer, he won the Crown at the National Eisteddfod in 1946 and 1964, and was the author of a trilogy of novels set in the industrial valleys of south Wales.

1 Johnny Onions, the name by which Breton onion-sellers are known in south Wales.
2 *Rhodd Mam*, a catechism for children in use among the Calvinistic Methodists.
3 Rhys Lewis is the eponymous hero of a novel by Daniel Owen (1836–95).

4 Hywel Gwynfryn, a popular radio and television personality.
5 Côr Mawr Treorci, one of the most famous male voice choirs of the Rhondda.

John Gruffydd Jones (1932), poet and prose-writer. Born near Pwllheli in Caernarfonshire, and educated at the Manchester Technical College, he is a chemist by profession. He won the Prose Medal at the National Eisteddfod in 1981 with a collection of essays, *Cysgodion ar y Pared*, the Drama Medal in 1986, and the Crown in 1987.

1 At the National Eisteddfod, the principal cultural event held in the Welsh language, the main prizes are for poetry, prose, and drama. The adjudications, and other matters, are discussed in the Literary Pavilion on the Eisteddfod field.

Gwilym Tudur (born 1940), prose-writer, was born at Chwilog in Caernarfonshire and educated at the U.C.W., Aberystwyth. He worked in television and as Organizer for Undeb Cymru Fydd, a cultural movement, before opening a Welsh bookshop, known as Siop y Pethe, in Aberystwyth in 1968. He has been a leading member of the Welsh Language Society.

1 Gorsedd of Bards, see note on page 219.
2 Waldo Williams (1904–71), poet; after the sudden death of his wife in 1943, scarcely a year after their marriage, he left Wales to find work in England.

William Owen (born 1935), prose-writer and dramatist, was born at Garreglefn in Anglesey. Educated at the U.C.N.W., Bangor, he was for many years Head of Religious Education at Ysgol Eifionydd, Porthmadog. Among his numerous publications are books for children, plays, and essays.

1 Bardsey, known in Welsh as Ynys Enlli, an island off the tip of the Llŷn peninsula, now a bird-sanctuary; it is said that twenty thousand saints are buried there.
2 Urdd Gobaith Cymru, see note on page 230.

Gareth Miles (born 1938), short-story writer and playwright, was born in Caernarfon and educated at the U.C.N.W., Bangor. Formerly a teacher and official of a teachers' union, he has been a freelance writer since 1982. He was co-author of the manifesto of the revived Welsh Republican Movement, but later joined the Welsh Communist Party.

1 Hywel ap Dafydd, Chris Rees, and Emrys Roberts are among

members of Plaid Cymru who, for Nationalist reasons, refused to be conscripted.

Ronald Stuart Thomas (born 1913), poet. He was born in Cardiff and brought up at Holyhead in Anglesey. Educated at the U.C.N.W., Bangor, and at St. Michael's College, Llandaf, where he received his theological training, he was a clergyman with the Church in Wales until his retirement. He is undoubtedly the greatest of all living Welsh poets writing in English. A selection of his prose was published in 1983 and his *Collected Poems* appeared in 1993. He is represented here by an address delivered at the National Eisteddfod in 1983.

1 Goronwy Owen (1723–69), poet, see note on p. 225.
2 The Welsh Language Society, founded in 1963, campaigns for a greater recognition of Welsh in the public life of Wales, often by challenging the law and confronting officialdom.

Bryan Martin Davies (born 1933), poet. Born at Brynaman in Carmarthenshire and educated at the U.C.W., Aberystwyth, he was a teacher of Welsh at Yale Sixth Form College in Clwyd until his retirement in 1985. He won the Crown at the National Eisteddfod in 1970 and 1971, and has published several volumes of poetry and a translation into Welsh of Dylan Thomas's story *A Child's Christmas in Wales*.

1 The Poet of Summer is a reference to R. Williams Parry (1884–1956), whose poem *Yr Haf* ('The Summer') was awarded the Chair at the National Eisteddfod in 1910.
2 Gwenallt, the poet D. Gwenallt Jones (1899–1968).
3 Pwyll, Pryderi, Efnisien, and Lleu are characters in the Mabinogion.
4 Daniel Owen (1836–95) and T. Rowland Hughes (1903–49), novelists.

John Roberts Williams (born 1914), journalist and broadcaster, was born at Llangybi in Caernarfonshire and educated at the U.C.N.W., Bangor. He was for many years editor of the weekly newspaper *Y Cymro* but in 1962 he joined the BBC, becoming Head of its North Wales Department in 1970. He has published several volumes of short stories and radio talks, one of which is included here.

Eigra Lewis Roberts (born 1939), short-story writer and novelist, was born at Blaenau Ffestiniog in Merioneth and educated at the U.C.N.W., Bangor. Formerly a teacher, she has won a reputation as one of the most distinguished of Welsh writers with a number of novels and collections of stories. Some of her radio talks, from which one has been selected for publication here, appeared under the title *Seren Wib* in 1986.

1 A *gymanfa ganu* is a singing-festival, usually held in a chapel.

Prys Morgan (born 1937), writer and historian, was born in Cardiff and is one of T. J Morgan's sons. Educated at St. John's College, Oxford, he has been a Lecturer in the History Department of U.C., Swansea, since 1964. He has published several novels and a good deal of historical scholarship; with his father, he is co-author of *Welsh Surnames* (1985). The 'three heads' in the title of his essay is a pun referring to the Calvinist sermon, which always had three heads of discussion.

1 Thomas Charles (1755–1814), Methodist leader, see the note on p.221; Lewis Edwards (1808–87), essayist and theologian.
2 Richard Wilson (1713–82), landscape painter, born at Penegoes, near Machynlleth in Montgomeryshire.
3 The National Eisteddfod is the principal cultural festival of the Welsh people, at which the Chair and Crown ceremonies are among the main events.
4 Urdd Gobaith Cymru, see note on p.230.
5 Ninian Park is the stadium of Cardiff City Football Club.
6 Theophilus Evans (1693–1767), historian.
7 The *hwyl* is an incantatory effect favoured by some Welsh preachers.

Gruffudd Parry (born 1916), prose-writer, was born at Carmel in Caernarfonshire; the distinguished scholar Thomas Parry (1904–85) was his brother. Educated at the U.C.N.W., Bangor, where he read English, he was for thirty-seven years a teacher at Botwnnog Grammar School. Among his publications is a much-admired volume on Llŷn and Eifionydd in the *Crwydro Cymru* series (1960), and several volumes of short stories and essays, in which he demonstrates a mastery of Welsh prose-style. Some of the writing in his book *Mân Sôn* (1989) was done for radio.

1 Poet of Summer, namely R. Williams Parry (1884–1956), see the note on p. 235.
2 Sunday School, see note on p. 217.
3 Waldo Williams (1904–71), poet.

Bernard Evans (1926–91), prose-writer, was born at Carway in the coal-mining area of Carmarthenshire. Educated at U C., Cardiff, he taught Welsh at Aberdare and in Whitchurch, Cardiff, before joining the staff of BBC Wales in 1970. He worked in the Education Department, making radio and television programmes for schools. Among his publications were children's books, studies in local history, and short stories, notably *Glaw Tyfiant* (1990).

1 The 'chap from North Wales' was the poet R. Williams Parry (1884–1956), and the reference is to his poem 'Y Llwynog' ('The Fox').

Gareth Alban Davies (born 1926), poet and prose-writer, was born at Ton Pentre in the Rhondda Valley. He worked as a Bevin Boy in the coal industry between 1944 and 1947. Educated at the Queen's College, Oxford, he was appointed to the Chair of Spanish at Leeds University in 1975; on his retirement he settled in Cardiganshire. He has published several volumes of poetry, travel-diaries, translations, and essays, as well as literary criticism.

1 The Ocean Company, formed in 1887, extracted coal from the Parc and Maendy pits in the Rhondda and were owned by David Davies (1818–90) of Llandinam.
2 Annwn, the Celtic Otherworld.
3 Urdd Gobaith Cymru, see note on page 230.
4 the poet R. Williams Parry (1884–1956), author of the oft-quoted poem 'Y Llwynog' ('The Fox').

Robin Williams (born 1923), essayist and travel-writer, was born at Penycaerau in Caernarfonshire. Educated at the U.C.N.W., Bangor, and the Theological Colleges at Aberystwyth and Bangor, he has been a Presbyterian minister and freelance broadcaster.

Meic Stephens, born at Trefforest, near Pontypridd, Glamorgan, in 1938, learned Welsh as an adult and has made it the language of his home. He founded the magazine *Poetry Wales* in 1965 and is the editor of *The Oxford Illustrated Guide to Great Britain and Ireland* (1992). Among the books he has translated are the memoirs of Gwynfor Evans, *For the Sake of Wales* (Welsh Academic Press, 1996), from the French *The Basques* (Welsh Academic Press, 1997), and Saunders Lewis's novel, *Monica* (Seren, 1997). New editions of his *Cydymaith i Lenyddiaeth Cymru/Companion to the Literature of Wales* will be published by the University of Wales Press in 1997 and 1998. Since 1994 Meic Stephens has taught courses in Journalism, Modern Fiction and Welsh Writing in English at the University of Glamorgan.

Acknowledgements

Grateful acknowledgement is made to the publishers of the following books in which some of these translations first appeared: *The White Stone* (Gomer Press, 1987), *A Book of Wales* (J. M Dent, 1987), and *A Rhondda Anthology* (Seren Books, 1993); and for the same reason to the editors of the magazines *Planet, The New Welsh Review,* and *Books in Wales*, and of *The Western Mail*.

The translator thanks the contributors, or the executors of their estates, for permission to translate their work into English and publish it here. Most of the translations were approved by the authors of the original essays, or by their executors. He also wishes to put on record his appreciation of the advice he was given by six friends in the task of selection and translation: Bobi Jones, Alan Llwyd, the late Rhys Tudur, the late Glyn Jones, Don Dale-Jones, and M. Wynn Thomas. For any infelicities which may remain the translator alone is responsible.

The Welsh Academic Press is grateful to the publishers whose names appear at the foot of the essays for permission to reprint copyright material in English translation. The press has made every effort to contact the holders of copyright and would be glad if any oversights were drawn to its attention.